War in the Twentieth Century

Recent Titles in
Praeger Studies in Diplomacy and Strategic Thought

Alternative to Appeasement: Sir Robert Vansittart and Alliance Diplomacy, 1934–1937
Michael L. Roi

British and American Naval Power: Politics and Policy, 1900–1936
Phillips Payson O'Brien

Defending the Free World: John F. Kennedy, Lyndon Johnson, and the Vietnam War, 1961–1965
Orrin Schwab

Paths Not Taken: Speculations on American Foreign Policy and Diplomatic History, Interests, Ideals, and Power
Jonathan M. Neilson, editor

From Confrontation to Cooperation: The Takeover of the National People's (East German) Army by the Bundeswehr
Frederick Zilian, Jr.

Double-Edged Sword: Nuclear Diplomacy in Unequal Conflicts, the United States and China, 1950–1958
Appu K. Soman

The Evolution of Special Forces in Counter-Terrorism: The British and American Experiences
J. Paul de B. Taillon

Incidents and International Relations: People, Power, and Personalities
Gregory C. Kennedy and Keith Neilson, editors

Witness to Revolution: The Russian Revolution Diary and Letters of J. Butler Wright
William Thomas Allison

Command and Cohesion: The Citizen Soldier and Minor Tactics in the British Army, 1870–1918
M.A. Ramsay

Hijacking and Hostages: Government Responses to Terrorism
J. Paul de B. Taillon

Money for Ireland: Finance, Diplomacy, Politics, and the First Dáil Éireann Loans, 1919–1936
Francis M. Carroll, editor

War in the Twentieth Century

Reflections at Century's End

Edited by Michael A. Hennessy
and B.J.C. McKercher

Praeger Studies in Diplomacy and Strategic Thought

PRAEGER

Westport, Connecticut
London

Library of Congress Cataloging-in-Publication Data

War in the twentieth century : reflections at century's end / edited by Michael A. Hennessy and B.J.C. McKercher.
    p. cm—(Praeger studies in diplomacy and strategic thought, ISSN 1076–1543)
    Includes bibliographical references and index.
    ISBN 0–275–97709–9 (alk. paper)
    1. Military art and science—History—20th century. 2. Military history, Modern—20th century. I. Hennessy, Michael A. II. McKercher, B.J.C., 1950– III. Series.
U42.W379   2003
355.02'0904—dc21   2003046334

British Library Cataloguing in Publication Data is available.

Copyright © 2003 by Michael A. Hennessy and B.J.C. McKercher

All rights reserved. No portion of this book may be reproduced, by any process or technique, without the express written consent of the publisher.

Library of Congress Catalog Card Number: 2003046334
ISBN: 0–275–97709–9
ISBN: 1076–1543

First published in 2003

Praeger Publishers, 88 Post Road West, Westport, CT 06881
An imprint of Greenwood Publishing Group, Inc.
www.praeger.com

Printed in the United States of America

The paper used in this book complies with the Permanent Paper Standard issued by the National Information Standards Organization (Z39.48–1984).

10 9 8 7 6 5 4 3 2 1

Contents

Introduction   1
Michael A. Hennessy and B.J.C. McKercher

1. War in the Twentieth Century   19
   Donald Cameron Watt

2. Disarmament, Arms Control, and Arms Reduction   45
   Erik Goldstein

3. The Economic Foundations of the Cold War Alliance
   Systems, 1945 to 1953   65
   Lawrence R. Aronsen

4. Containment, "Disease," and Cold War Culture   97
   Geoffrey S. Smith

5. Presidential Decision Making and the National Security
   Council in Four Crises, 1950–1990   129
   Gary R. Hess

6. Peacekeeping: Canada's Inevitable Role   145
   Norman Hillmer

7. Three Degrees of Separation: The Evolving Convergence of
   Human Rights Law, Humanitarian Law, and Refugee Law   167
   Donna E. Arzt

8. A View from Above: Watersheds in the Evolution of War
   and Military Institutions during the Twentieth Century   197
   John A. Lynn

   Selected Bibliography   217
   Index   229

Introduction

Michael A. Hennessy and B.J.C. McKercher

> The nature of modern war is not a simple matter. It is subject to numerous modifications according to the character of the contending parties and the various theatres of war.... The fundamental principles of war certainly remain the same, wherever it is waged; but special conditions cause in each case special methods of employment of the fighting forces, and these latter, again, will frequently differ.
>
> Von Bernhardi, 1914[1]

A certain irony emerges when looking at war in the twentieth century. While the principles of war were immutable, the ways and means of conducting armed conflict, plus the nature and scope of military operations, took new paths. Thus, on one hand, the ability to undertake warfare underwent profound change in those one hundred years because of technological advances, the development of completely new weapons and doctrine, and changing public attitudes toward armed conflict. Yet, on the other, the reasons why wars were fought did not change: Great and small powers did not shirk from employing their national armories to defend or extend their perceived national interests; and what in the twentieth century were called "national liberation movements," which in the nineteenth were categorized as "native unrest," used armed force in the attempt to overthrow colonial regimes. Similarly, the broad strategic principles that underlay warfare and have been adumbrated by military philosophers and theorists like Clausewitz, Jomini, and others remained intact.[2] How could essentials like "the culminating point of the offensive," "friction," the "fog of war," and so on, alter? But in the twentieth century, along with evolving legal dicta relating to armed conflict and neutrality and the advent of modern concepts like collective security, the tactical and operational elements of warfare changed, conditioned by those new weapons, advances in technology, and delivery systems.[3]

Beyond these purely military considerations lay changing attitudes toward the use of armed force. In the West, especially, with the emergence of mass democracy tied to modern communications and an enquiring press, disparate sections of informed and uninformed public opinion can at times galvanize into widespread support for or against employing military power. There had been no major war in Europe for one hundred years after 1815. Yet, in July–August 1914 the rush to arms by the citizenry of the European powers and the British dominions showed the widest popular support for a conflict that was supposed to be over by Christmas.[4] At the other extreme, in the late 1960s and early 1970s, was the rise of powerful domestic opposition in the United States to American involvement in the war in Vietnam.[5] Within the realm of twentieth-century public attitudes toward war, there have been efforts by governments and private national and international special interest groups to disarm, codify rules of combat and laws of war, and offer alternatives to battle to settle disputes. Such efforts began even before 1914 with the Hague conferences; they continued thereafter in multilateral governmental organizations like the League of Nations and the United Nations and in mass national and international lobby groups like the Women's International League for Peace and Freedom, the British Campaign for Nuclear Disarmament, Green Peace, and others.[6]

In this context, General Friedrich von Bernhardi's early-twentieth-century pronouncements on the nature of "modern war" had a prophetic quality. While admittedly one of a number of similar books written at that time,[7] Bernhardi's *How Germany Makes War* is especially useful in explaining the complexities of armed struggle as it began its twentieth-century evolution. Part of ongoing work that he was undertaking to explain how new weapons had changed the battlefield, he argued that the next war would be a "total" war: "I think the law of self-preservation ought to have dictated to us an increase of our defensive forces by all means available, so as to throw into the scale at the decisive moment the full strength of our 60,000,000 populace."[8] Writing before the 1914 July Crisis, his analysis of how Wilhelmine Germany should approach war making actually constituted a tract to instill in both the German government and the reading public an acceptance that armed force would be needed to defeat the empire's enemies in an inevitable conflict:

Introduction 3

I believe in the German people; I believe that a great future is in store for it; and that it has to accomplish a high calling in the development of mankind. But it can only put this task to good account if it exerts its military strength to the utmost, and if its policy, while placing its aims high and not afraid of dangerous paths, remains conscious of the truth that, as in war, so also in political intercourse of States, the will and action alone can achieve great things, and that in all human affairs the poet holds good: "Action was the beginning of everything."[9]

Although the original was published in Germany in 1913, its English translation appeared in Britain shortly before the outbreak of the "Great War." As the anonymous British editors observed in their preface:

The book is an attempt to show how war can be successfully conducted with the enormous masses of men now thrown into a conflict between nations, the armies of millions that put the whole fighting power of a people into the battleline.[10]

Thus, as much as this work dealt with strategy, operations, and some tactics, it also had a propagandistic value in proselytizing to a domestic audience the sacrifices they would need to make to attain victory; and for Germany's adversaries it created an awareness of the potential German threat.

It has been argued that war has always been a struggle of societies.[11] This observation is true. But in a major way, warfare in the twentieth century came to be distinguished by the mobilization of entire societies—for providing fighting forces in the air and on sea and land; and just as important, by supporting those forces through the production of agricultural and industrial commodities, through manning industry, through transforming scientific advances into military applications, and through ensuring sound finance. Bernhardi and others saw the future clearly, although he did not quite anticipate the lengthy and bloody fighting that marked the First World War. And what was true between 1914 and 1918 was doubly so for the global struggle that occurred between July 1937, when Japanese forces invaded China south of the Great Wall, and the spring-summer of 1945, when fascist Italy, Nazi Germany, and militarist Japan were finally forced into unconditional surrender. In the second half of the twentieth century, as Donald Cameron Watt eloquently shows in Chapter 1, "war" in the legal sense has never again occurred. But all of the armed struggles from 1945 to 1989 suffused by the Cold War—in Korea, Southeast Asia, the Middle East, and Africa—still required the support of entire societies. So, too, did the American-led coalition response to the Iraqi invasion of Kuwait in 1990–1991. This situation was completely unlike that of the nineteenth century and earlier, when armies in the field and navies at sea fought one another with little regard for what might be termed "public" support. Absolute monarchs like Peter the Great and Louis XV, dictatorial potentates like Napoleon Bonaparte, and entrenched oligarchies like those that dominated Georgian and Victorian Britain made war policy, levied taxes, raised armies and navies, and, generally ignoring their peoples' concerns, engaged in what Otto von Bismarck characterized as "the politics of Great Powers carried on by force of arms."[12]

Total war resulted from the improved technologies that allowed millions of soldiers, sailors, and for the first time, airmen to confront one another between 1914 and 1918. These technologies were designed originally to permit a war of movement and mobility, of envelopment and annihilation.[13] The Europeans looked to the German wars of unification for lessons learned—interestingly, none seemed seriously to look at those lessons that devolved from the American Civil War. Within two months of the outbreak of the war, principally on the western front, the conflict had transformed into one of stasis and immobility. To break the enemy, each side found itself forced to build up forces to achieve victory. Land forces expanded, naval forces were employed to enervate the enemy's economic sinews, and new weapons like gas, the tank, and the airplane were developed. None of this would have been possible without the total mobilization of the respective home fronts. And as the collapse of governments in Berlin, London, Paris, and St Petersburg showed after the devastating battles of 1916, domestic political cohesion could not be taken for granted.

The same issues distinguish both what became preparing for and conducting military operations during the Second World War—the development of strategy; the design and production of particular weapons to achieve those strategic objectives; the development of air, land, and sea tactics and operational skills based on those weapons; and the forging of total domestic support and labor to achieve victory.[14] And given the need to impress potential adversaries of national potency through new mediums of propaganda—the better to achieve foreign policy victories by the threat rather than the use of armed strength—the careers of Adolf Hitler and Benito Mussolini provide brutal testimony to this increasingly important element of twentieth-century war making.[15] None of this is to suggest that dictators have a monopoly on such endeavors. The British prime minister in the late 1930s, Neville Chamberlain, thought that his foreign policy—what he called the double policy of rearmament and better relations with the dictators (that is, appeasement)—could deter Axis aggression; he used the public platform to make his case.[16] The same can be said of other interwar democratic leaders like Edouard Daladier and Franklin Roosevelt. The public in most pre-1939 states had legitimate worries about the possibility of another war on a 1914–1918 scale. Casualties would certainly be high; the financial burdens via taxation would be immense; and the potential havoc that could be wreaked by aerial bombardment meant that the battlefield would not be restricted to where opposing armed forces confronted one another.[17]

But the Second World War—the war started by Adolf Hitler, abetted by fascist Italy and militaristic Japan—proved to be more calamitous than anyone before 1939 could have imagined. While the principles of war remained unchanged, new weapons, new doctrine, and expanded military operations in Europe, the Mediterranean and North Africa, South, Southeast, and East Asia, and the south and western Pacific Ocean helped produce a struggle of truly global proportions.[18] Distinguished by the use of armor supported by tactical airpower, the land war in eastern and western Europe and North Africa after 1940 remained one of movement and mobility.[19] In every theater of operations, air war centering on strategic bombing saw the front lines of the struggle taken deep into each belligerent's homeland.[20] Indeed, by 1944–1945, the introduction of revolutionary aerial weapons—the German "V" rockets unleashed against Britain; the American-controlled "atomic bomb" used against a weakening Japan—meant that the nature and scope of air operations were taking new and extremely lethal paths. The war at sea, chiefly in the north Atlantic and the southern and western Pacific oceans, was increasingly conditioned by submarine operations directed against merchantmen and enemy warships. Improved technology played a major role in finding submarines and destroying them.[21] Respecting battle fleets, there was no major surface sea battle between combined Anglo-American naval forces and their German and Italian counterparts in the Atlantic or Mediterranean—a function of weak German and Italian surface fleets.[22] In the Pacific, however, the U.S. Navy won decisive battles against the Imperial Japanese Navy in May–June 1942 at the Coral Sea and Midway that ended Japan's expansion and inaugurated its armed forces' slow retreat to the home islands. Victory in these battles occurred not because American capital ships sunk Japanese ones in a naval Armageddon; victory came via superior American airpower that, based on aircraft carriers, decimated the Japanese carrier fleet.[23] Just as had occurred with the air war, a new path in naval operations had opened. Importantly, for the first time in modern history, Second World War military planners directed attacks against large civilian targets; and given the vagaries of air and land combat, with battle fronts that sometimes extended a thousand miles, noncombatant death and injury and the destruction of property saw civilian casualties far exceed those in the belligerent armed forces. Here resides a hallmark of twentieth-century war.

The Second World War was also a total war in which each side employed propaganda—sometimes the blackest propaganda—to dehumanize the enemy and exhort the home front to work harder to win the war. Echoing what had happened between 1914 and 1918, belligerent governments portrayed the struggle as a cultural clash. Franklin Roosevelt and

Winston Churchill made a great play that the Americans and the British fought for the preservation of the English-speaking world and its great legacy, universal democratic ideals.[24] The Japanese supposedly looked to end "white" imperial dominion over East Asia and build a "Greater East Asia Co-Prosperity Sphere" under the rubric "Asia for the Asians."[25] Soviet Russian leaders not only admonished their people to fight for "Mother Russia," they were intent on replacing the old regimes in Europe with a Marxist-Leninist utopia.[26] In Germany, Hitler railed against the external enemies of "Aryan" culture, "international Jewry," that supposedly animated the governments of German adversaries.[27] Then in the darkest twist, his henchmen embarked on a program of racial genocide against the Jewish people in both Germany and the states the German armed forces conquered between 1940 and 1945. Six million Jews and several million other non-Aryan "undesirables" like Gypsies perished in Nazi death camps.[28] Of course, German barbarism was not unique. The Japanese treatment of prisoners and their military occupation of southern China, typified by the "Rape of Nanking" in November 1937, had an equally malevolent cachet.[29] And on the Allied side, Soviet Russian actions in the eastern European territories liberated by the Red Army were as bloody—and as supposedly culturally purifying—as anything the Nazis did.[30]

The Second World War proved a true watershed. Again, as Donald Watt shows in his chapter, "war" in the legal sense did not occur again. This does not mean that armed conflict disappeared after 1945. It did not. But what it does mean is that cognizant of the tremendous political, social, and economic cost of the Second World War, plus the new ways and means of conducting military operations that emerged from that struggle and were subsequently improved, a war of 1939–1945 proportions had to be avoided. Of course, the distinguishing feature of international politics in the second half of the twentieth century was the Cold War between the United States and its allies, on one hand, and Soviet Russia and its satellites, on the other.[31] Devolving from a variety of strategic, political, and economic reasons, the victorious Allied alliance that came out of the Second World War broke down immediately after peace was restored.[32] For nearly one-half of the twentieth century thereafter, until the collapse of the Soviet Russian eastern European empire in 1989 and the disappearance of Soviet Russia in 1991, the two superpowers avoided fighting one another directly. Working with their allies, they constructed deterrent alliances like the North Atlantic Treaty Organization (NATO) and the Warsaw Pact.[33] They sometimes assisted proxies in doing their fighting for them—say, the American-supported Nicaraguan "contras" in the 1980s or the Soviet-backed North Koreans in the early 1950s.[34] And when one superpower actually became embroiled in armed conflict—the Americans in Southeast Asia from 1964 to 1973 and the

Introduction

Soviet Russians in Afghanistan in the 1980s—the other would support its enemy's enemy.[35]

But direct superpower confrontation during the Cold War had other dimensions directly linked to the kind of "total" wars fought between 1914 and 1918 and 1939 and 1945. Each side made plans for war—especially nuclear war—to be fought with, at first, long-range bombers and, by the late 1950s, intercontinental ballistic missiles. They worked to improve their armed forces to defend their narrow national interests and keep the enemy at bay. They devised strategy and doctrine to give their improved weapons every advantage in an armed struggle. They utilized propaganda of increasing sophistication to try to demonstrate to their own people, to their supporters abroad, and when possible, to the domestic population of the adversary that their particular political, economic, and social system—their culture—remained vastly superior.[36] Economic vitality was but one, albeit major, strand of the great struggle that remained short of open warfare for forty-five years. In Chapter 3 Lawrence Aronsen explores the economic dimension of these respective Cold War power blocs. Each waged their ideological struggle with a combination of military and social-economic forces. Each tried to win the contest of systems by demonstrating the superiority of theirs. This latter point is important when considering war in the twentieth century. Moreover, a Cold War culture did emerge by the 1950s, especially in the United States and among its Western partners.[37] One organ of the emergent "national security state" was the U.S. National Security Council (NSC). In Chapter 5 Gary Hess explores the diverse role and function of the NSC under four administrations. Each president came to employ his NSC differently; none proved captive to it.

A different form of diversity is examined as Geoffrey Smith shows in Chapter 4 that American culture lacked homogeneity; and its diversity proved to be problematical for all American governments after about 1960 when important and articulate sections of American society came to see their own country as the aggressor in the Cold War because of the government's decision to participate in the Vietnam War.[38] The same kind of situation occurred within the Soviet bloc. The Sino-Soviet split in the 1960s meant that monolithic communism did not exist. More important, the subject peoples in the Soviet eastern European empire—most spectacularly, Hungary in 1956, Czechoslovakia in 1968, Poland in 1979–1980[39]—did not share the Russian view of the world. As nation–states in their own right, they were exploited by Moscow.

The Cold War was a total war. But while Cold War governments and their sympathizers in the legislatures, in the print and broadcast media, and in academia believed in the need for the total mobilization of the state to meet a real threat,[40] total support was never there. Apart from the expected domestic critics of foreign and defense policy in any state, there had existed since before the First World War private international organizations whose purpose was to force governments to disarm and rely on arbitration mechanisms to preserve peace and security. Such organizations gained in strength after 1918, and they held the creation of the League of Nations to be the linchpin of a new international order that would ensure disarmament and guarantee the justiciable settlement of all disputes.[41] With support of the Great Powers, the League sought to achieve these two goals; it was even making headway on disarmament when Hitler came to power in Germany in January 1933. Wanting potent armed forces to underwrite his foreign policy, Hitler took Germany out of the League and the League-inspired World Disarmament Conference. The international organization never recovered; and those who supported its lofty ideals had to wait until after the Second World War and the creation of the United Nations to renew their labors.

In these circumstances, plus the advent of the Cold War and the eruption of "hot" wars in various parts of the globe after 1945, an important dimension of twentieth-century warfare has centered on those individuals and private special interest groups that looked to control war by international agreement expressed through organizations like the United Nations and ancillary bodies like the World Court, the International War Crimes Tribunal, and more. Read with Erik Goldstein's chapter on disarmament (Chapter 2), Donna Arzt's examination in Chapter 7 of the evolving legal pronouncements concerning war and war criminality underscores the fact that the twentieth century has been a period when significant efforts have been made to blunt the sabers of all the powers. In this sense, those who would seek to restrain the ability to make war could be considered to be adherents to Bernhardi because they, too, believe that "will and action alone can achieve great things." Where Bernhardi counseled his countrymen to make every effort to win a "total" war for Germany, peace advocates throughout the century have, in the words of one of them, reckoned, "We are preparing for our own destruction so long as we spend money on armaments."[42] Yet peace advocates and those who seek to restrain warfare by legal means have faced a dilemma. While they have had some success in the West, with its liberal-democratic traditions and openness to criticism, they have no influence with militaristic dictatorships stretching from Adolf Hitler's Germany to Saddam Hussein's Iraq. They have even less with terrorist groups—an increasingly violent twentieth-century expression of guerrilla warfare—like the Irish Republican Army, the Cyprian EOKA (Ethniki Orgánosis Kipriakoú Agónos), or the Islamic fundamentalist Al Qaeda.[43] Powers great and small have to defend themselves from any attack; peace advocacy tended to suffer as a result.

It transpired that as the twentieth century progressed, the groups and individuals that fall under the rubric of "peace advocacy" have divided over the legal right of states to conduct warfare.[44] There were always groups and individuals who consistently argued for the complete dismantling of all armed forces.[45] Although they have had some appeal at particular moments such as immediately after the First World War and during the basing in western Europe of American cruise missiles in the 1980s, total disarmament has generally been seen as impractical and dangerous utopianism. On the other hand, large numbers of men and women who saw danger in the unilateral buildup and use of armed force by individual powers have been supporters of the multilateral use of counterveiling military power to resolve crises. Between the two world wars, the development of League of Nations "collective security" seemed to offer the means to ensure international peace and security.[46] Such hopes died during the Italian conquest of Abyssinia in 1935–1936. After 1945, the advent of the concept of UN "peacekeeping" brought a new wrinkle to the employment of military power to ensure international stability.[47] Norman Hillmer's commentary in Chapter 6 on the Canadian role in the genesis and development of this particular use of military force is helpful in understanding how "international" opinion has come increasingly in the second half of the twentieth century to rely on collective means to ensure peace. The measured use of armed forces to undertake limited warfare in the name of some supranational organization—and thus of ensuring the legal conduct of warfare to right some criminal wrong—expanded as the century ended: chiefly, in the Arabian Gulf, Bosnia, and Yugoslavia.[48] This is not to say that such operations, especially peacekeeping ones, have always been successful. They have not, as the 1967 Arab-Israeli war and the 1990s genocide in Rwanda show.[49] And there is an element of self-interest in mounting peacekeeping operations by some states because it gives gravitas to an otherwise limited foreign policy.[50] But for the Western powers, at least, and for large sections of their public opinion who support securing international peace and security by multilateral effort, armed intervention mandated by the UN Security Council or military operations sanctioned by NATO and other organizations is at least controlled warfare in defense of a legal norm.

But a gray area exists respecting this notion of using legally based coalitions to fight wars. The 1991 Gulf War demonstrated that even the United States, the acknowledged hegemon in the world, found it best to make war in alliance with other powers against expansionist Iraq. With support from the United Nations, it was politically expedient in that for propaganda purposes in the Middle East and elsewhere the American government could claim widespread backing for punishing Iraq for its short-lived conquest of Kuwait.[51] Perhaps more important, military support from French, British, Canadian, and other allied armed forces meant fewer American casualties and a larger number of troops, airplanes, and warships brought into the fighting.[52] That the Iraqi leader was especially odious and brutal—apart from the fact the United States had earlier supported his regime in a war against Iran—only helped each member of the American-led coalition ensure widespread domestic support for fighting in the deserts of Kuwait and Iraq.[53] And that the strategic objectives of the struggle—ensuring a balance of power in the region and safeguarding Western supplies of petroleum[54]—were camouflaged to a degree by the moral and legal arguments for intervention was a double benefit in ensuring public support for the war. Bernhardi's argument that "will and action alone can achieve great things" had not lost its strength eighty years after he committed it to paper.

Thus, the irony of looking at warfare over the past one hundred years. The first half of the twentieth century was dominated by the fact that two "world wars" were fought in a legal and, what might best be termed, a classical manner with declarations of war, ambassadors being handed their passports, and so on. Other wars—little wars in comparison—also occurred: civil war in China, Great Power imperial conquests like the Italian attack on Ethiopia, and small powers like the Balkan states pummeling each other for bits of disputed territory. However, because "the war to end all wars" had been fought between 1914 and 1918, and because of its cost in blood and treasure, the 1920s and 1930s in the West witnessed the advent of strong peace advocacy among public opinion generally; this advocacy helped create the League of Nations as the tangible political expression of the desire to control and eliminate war. Yet, after 1937, because Hitler, Mussolini, and Japanese militarists saw war as a legitimate instrument of national policy, the Second World War broke out. More terrible in its human, political, and material cost than the Great War, and the catalyst for the production of new and even more baneful weapons, the 1939–1945 war proved a watershed in the twentieth century. While the principles of war were unchanging, the powers realized that another world war would be disastrous.

Such recognition did not mean that war planning, doctrine development, and weapons advancement ceased. The almost half century of Cold War attested to the notion that in many political and military quarters war was not an impossibility. Cultural notions surrounding armed struggle might have changed because of the Cold War, but the important issue of culture did not abate. Still, there was a certain restraint between the superpowers, as they never directly confronted one another militarily after 1945. They might support proxies; they might aid the enemy of their enemy; they might build counterveiling alliances and emplace thousands of intercontinental ballistic missiles. But there was forbearance. This forbearance was underscored by the advent of Western peace advocates after 1945 who looked to make systemic change to control war. Understanding that war could not be eliminated and that armies, navies, and air forces were not about to disappear, their demand to give legal sanction to justifiable military actions helped push the nature and scope of military operations along new paths. Police operations, limited war, and peacekeeping were directions these operations took, directions that amenable governments were willing to take.

Hence, while the principles of warfare did not change in those one hundred years—principles like achieving victory over an enemy—the way in which they were to be upheld did. So too did the nature of Western armed forces. In Chapter 8, John Lynn elaborates on the technical and professional transformations of Western armed forces through the century. As Lynn illustrates, the measure of a modern army has changed from mass conscript armies that typified those on the western front in 1916 to the technically sophisticated, long-service professional armed forces that undertook the UN-sanctioned intervention into Kosovo. This and the other lessons learned looking back at war from the vantage of century's end demonstrate that "warfare" in framework, limits, and practice is still evolving at the dawn of the new century.

NOTES

1. Friedrich von Bernhardi, *How Germany Makes War* (London, 1914), 3. The original was published in 1913: Friedrich von Bernhardi, *Deutschland und der nachste krieg* (Stuttgart, Berlin, 1913).

2. C. von Clausewitz, *Vom Kriege. Hinterlassenes Werk des Generals Carl von Clausewitz Sechzehnte Auflage. Vollständige Ausgabe im Urtext mit historisch-kritischer Würdigung von Dr. Werner Hahlweg, Dozent an der Universität Münster* (Bonn, 1952). Cf. C. Bassford, *Clausewitz in English: The Reception of Clausewitz in Britain and America, 1815–1945* (New York, 1994); A. Gat, "Clausewitz's Final Notes," *Militargeschichtliche Mitteilungen*, 1 (1989), 45–50; N.H. Gibbs, "Clausewitz on the Moral Forces in War," *Naval War College Review*, 25 (1975), 15–22; M.I. Handel, ed., *Clausewitz and Modern Strategy* (London, 1986). Of course, debate on the verities of the philosophy exists, for instance, that between the supporters of Clausewitz and those of Antoine Henri Jomini; cf. C. Bassford, "Jomini and Clausewitz: Their Interaction" (paper presented at the 23rd Meeting of the Consortium on Revolutionary Europe, Georgia State University, February 26, 1993); J.D. Hittle, "Introduction," in J.D. Hittle, ed., *Summary of the Art of War: A Condensed Version* (Harrisburg, PA, 1987).

3. Cf. P. Bracken, "Future Directions for the Army," in P. Bracken, ed., *Whither the RMA: Two Perspectives on Tomorrow's Army* (Carlisle Barracks, PA, 1994); J. English, "The Operational Art: Developments in the Theories of War," in B.J.C. McKercher and M.A. Hennessy, eds., *The Operational Art: Developments in the Theories of War* (Westport, CT, 1996), 7–28; J.A. Lynn, "The History of Logistics and Supplying War," in J.A. Lynn, ed., *Feeding Mars: Logistics in Western Warfare from the Middle Ages to the Present* (Boulder, CO, 1993); J.N. Rosenau, "Armed Force and Armed Forces in a Turbulent World," in J. Burk, ed., *The*

Military in New Times: Adapting Armed Forces in a Turbulent World (Boulder, CO, 1994).

4. See M. Eksteins, *Rites of Spring: The Great War and the Birth of the Modern Age* (Boston, 1989). Then H. Herwig, *The First World War. Germany and Austria-Hungary, 1914–1918* (London, New York, 1997), 33–37; J.C. Jauffret, *Parlement, gouvernement, commandement: L'armée de métier sous la 3è république, 1871–1914*, vol. 2 (Chateau de Vincennes, 1987); J.M. Osborne, *The Voluntary Recruiting Movement in Britain, 1914–1916* (Ann Arbor, MI, 1987); H. Strachan, *The First World War*, vol. 1: *To Arms* (Oxford, 2001), 103–62.

5. See K.J. Turner, *Lyndon Johnson's Dual War: Vietnam and the Press* (Chicago, 1985). Then cf. B. Andrews, *Public Constraint and American Policy in Vietnam* (Beverly Hills, CA, 1976); C.C. Moskos, Jr., ed., *Public Opinion and the Military Establishment* (Beverly Hills, CA, 1971); B. Stora, *Imaginaires de guerre: Algérie, Viêt-Nam, en France et aux États-Unis* (Paris, 1997); B. Van De Mark, *Into the Quagmire: Lyndon Johnson and the Escalation of the Vietnam War* (New York, 1991).

6. Cf. M. Ceadl, *Pacifism in Britain, 1914–1945* (New York, 1987); G. Delcoigne and G. Rubinstein, *Non-prolifération des armes nucléaires et systèmes de contrôle* (Bruxelles, 1970); M. Gorbachev, *Pour un monde sans armes nucléaires: Receuil de discours et d'allocutions du Secrétaire général du C.C. du P.C.U.S. sur les problèmes du désarmement nucléaire: Janvier 1986–janvier 1987* (Moscow, 1987); N. Ingram, *The Politics of Dissent: Pacifism in France, 1919–1939* (Oxford, 1991); D. Kreiger and F.K. Kelly, eds., *Waging Peace in the Nuclear Age: Ideas for Action* (Santa Barbara, CA, 1988); C. Pollock, "Feminist Pacifist Ideas, the International Congress of Women and the Foundation of the League of Nations," in League of Nations Archives, *The League of Nations 1920–1946* (New York, Geneva, 1996), 17–21.

7. For instance, W.E. Cairnes, *The Coming Waterloo* (Westminster, 1901); E.L.V. Cordonnier, *The Japanese in Manchuria, 1904*, C.F. Atkinson, trans., 2 vol. (London, 1912–1914); H. von Kiesling, *The Battle of Encounter*, General Staff, War Office, London trans., (London, 1913); A. Millerand, *Pour la défense nationale: Une année au Ministère de la guerre (14 janvier 1912–12 janvier 1913* (Paris, 1913); A.W.A. Pollock, *Lord Roastem's Campaign in North-eastern France* (London, 1911); Ubique [F.G. Guggisberg], *Modern Warfare, or How Our Soldiers Fight* (London, 1903); S. Wilkinson, *Britain at Bay*, 2nd ed. (London, 1910). Cf. I.F. Clarke, *Voices Prophesying War, 1763–1984* (London, 1966).

8. Bernhardi, *Germany Makes War*, xiii. His other books include *Cavalry in Future Wars*, C.S. Goldman, trans., 2nd ed. (London, 1906); *Vom heutigen kriege*, 2 vols. (Berlin, 1912), published in English as *On War of To-day*, Karl von Donat, trans. (London, 1912–1913).

9. Bernhardi, *Germany Makes War*, 248.

10. Ibid., v.

11. M.E. Howard, *The Franco-Prussian War: The German Invasion of France, 1870–1871* (London, 1961).

12. Quoted in W. Carr, *The Origins of the Wars of German Unification* (London, New York, 1991), 59.

13. Cf. A. Bucholz, *Moltke, Schlieffen, and Prussian War Planning* (New York, 1991); W. Foerster, *Graf Schlieffen und der weltkrieg* (Berlin, 1925); P.M. Kennedy, ed., *The War Plans of the Great Powers 1880–1914* (Boston, 1985); M.A. Ramsay, *Command and Cohesion: The Citizen Soldier and Minor Tactics in the British Army,*

1870–1918 (Westport, CT, 2002), 113–43; R.M. Ripperger, "The Development of the French Artillery for the Offensive, 1890–1914," *Journal of Military History*, 59 (1995), 599–618; G. Ritter, *The Schlieffen Plan: Critique of a Myth* (London, 1958); Strachan, *To Arms*, 1–102; J.L. Snyder, *Defending the Offensive: Biases in French, German, and Russian War Planning, 1870–1914* (Ann Arbor, MI, 1984); Stephen Van Evera, "The Cult of the Offensive and the Origins of the First World War," in Steven Miller, ed., *Military Strategy and the Origins of the First World War* (Princeton, NJ, 1985).

14. Cf. R. Citino, *The Evolution of Blitzkrieg Tactics: Germany Defends Itself against Poland, 1918–1933* (New York, 1987); H. Dutailly, *Les problèmes de l'Armée de Terre française, 1935–1939* (Paris, 1980); M. Geyer, *Aufrüstung oder Sicherheit: Die Reichswehr in der Krise der Machtpolitik, 1924–1936* (Wiesbaden, 1980); J.T. Hendrix, "The Interwar Army and Mechanization: The American Approach," *Journal of Strategic Studies*, 16 (1993), 75–108; R.J. Jarymowicz, "Jedi Knights in the Kremlin: The Soviet Military in the 1930s and the Genesis of Deep Battle," in B.J.C. McKercher and R. Legault, eds., *Military Planning and the Origins of the Second World War* (Westport, CT, 2001); T. Kataoka, *Waiting for a "Pearl Harbor": Japan Debates Defense* (Stanford, CA, 1980); M. Knox, *Mussolini Unleashed, 1939–41: Politics and Strategy in Fascist Italy's Last War* (New York, 1982); R.H. Larson, *The British Army and the Theory of Armoured Warfare, 1914–1940* (Newark, DE, 1984); R.J. Overy, "Air Power and the Origins of Deterrence Theory before 1939," *Journal of Strategic Studies*, 15 (1992), 73–101; H.F. Scott and W.F. Scott, *Soviet Military Doctrine: Continuity, Formulation, and Dissemination* (Boulder, CO, 1988); P. Wetzlar, *Hirohito and War: Imperial Tradition and Military Decision Making in Prewar Japan* (Honolulu, HI, 1998).

15. On Hitler, see A. Bullock, "Hitler and the Origins of the Second World War," *Proceedings of the British Academy*, 53 (1967); M. Funks, *Sanctioned und Kannonen: Hitler, Mussolini und der internationale Abessinienkonflikt, 1934–36* (Düsseldorf, 1970); D. Cameron Watt, *How War Came: The Immediate Origins of the Second World War, 1938–1939* (New York, 1989); G. Weinberg, *The Foreign Policy of Hitler's Germany*, 2 vols. (Chicago, 1970–1980). On Mussolini, see H.J. Burgwyn, *Il revisionismo fascista: La sfida di Mussolini all grande potenze nei Balcani e sul Danubio, 1925–1933* (Milan, 1979); R. De Felice, *Mussolini il duce: lo Stato totalitario, 1936–40* (Turin, 1981); M. Knox, *Mussolini Unleashed, 1939–41: Politics and Strategy in Fascist Italy's Last War* (New York, 1982).

16. Quoted in I. Colvin, *The Chamberlain Cabinet: How Meetings in 10 Downing Street, 1937–1939, Led to the Second World War—Told for the First Time from the Cabinet Papers* (New York, 1971), 46. Cf. D.J. Dilks, " 'We Must Hope for the Best and Prepare for the Worst': The Prime Minister, the Cabinet and Hitler's Germany, 1937–1939," *Proceedings of the British Academy*, 73 (1987), 309–52; R.A.C. Parker, *Chamberlain and Appeasement: British Policy and the Coming of the Second World War* (London, 1993).

17. See M. Ceadl, *Pacifism in Britain 1914–1945: The Defining of a Faith* (London, 1980). Then cf. D. Birn, *The League of Nations Union, 1918–1945* (London, 1981); M. Ceadl, *The Origins of War Prevention: The British Peace Movement and International Relations, 1730–1854* (Oxford, New York, 1996); C. Lynch, *Beyond Appeasement: Interpreting Interwar Peace Movements in World Politics* (Ithaca, NY, 1999); J.D.B. Miller, *Norman Angell and the Futility of War: Peace and the Public Mind*

(Houndmills, UK, 1986). For contemporary views, cf. N. Angell, "Man Can Abolish War," *Spectator*, 150 (1933), 207–8; P.J. [Noel-] Baker, "Menace of Armaments," *Nation*, 35 (1924), 613–14; R. Cecil, "Case for Disarmament," *Nation*, 45 (1929), 99–100; A.J. Enock, *The Problem of Armaments* (London, 1923).

18. G.L. Weinberg, *A World at Arms: A Global History of World War II* (Cambridge, UK, 1994); H.P. Willmott, *The Great Crusade: A New Complete History of the Second World War* (New York, 1990).

19. See C. D'Este, *Decision in Normandy* (New York, 1994); G. Forty, *Road to Berlin: The Allied Drive in Normandy* (London, 1999); A. Horne, *To Lose a Battle: France 1940* (London, 1969); P. Warner, *The Battle of France: 10 May–22 June 1940* (London, New York, 1990); J. Erickson, *Stalin's War with Germany*, 2 vols. (London, 1975, 1983); D.M. Glantz and J.M. Houser, *When Titans Clashed: How the Red Army Stopped Hitler* (Lawrence, KS, 1995); R.D. Muller, *Hitler's War in the East, 1941–1945: A Critical Reassessment* (Oxford, 1995).

20. See C.C. Crane, *Bombs, Cities, Civilians: American Airpower Strategy in World War II* (Lawrence, KS, 1993); A.J. Levine, *The Strategic Bombing of Germany, 1940–1945* (New York, 1992); J. von Lang, *Krieg der Bomber: Dokumentation einer deutschen Katastrophe* (Berlin, 1986); C.K. Webster and N. Frankland, *The Strategic Air Offensive against Germany: 1939–1945* (London, 1961).

21. See G. Hessler, *The U-Boat War in the Atlantic, 1939–45* (London, 1989); A Niestlé, *German U-Boat Losses during World War II: Details of Destruction* (Annapolis, MD, 1998); C.H. Waddington, *O.R. in World War II: Operational Research against the U-Boat* (London, 1973).

22. See P. Kemp, *Key to Victory: The Triumph of British Sea Power in World War II* (Boston, 1957); S.W. Roskill, *The War at Sea, 1939–1945*, 3 vols. (London, 1954–1961).

23. See G. Bischof, ed., *The Pacific War Revisited* (Baton Rouge, LA, 1999); R.B. Frank, *Downfall: The End of the Japanese Empire* (New York, 1999); R.W. Spector, *Eagle against the Sun: The American War with Japan* (New York, 1985); H.P. Willmott, *The Barrier and the Javelin: Japanese and Allied Pacific Strategies, February to June 1942* (Annapolis, MD, 1983).

24. T. Hoopes, *FDR and the Creation of the U.N.* (New Haven, CT, 1997); K. Sainsbury, *Churchill and Roosevelt at War: The War They Fought and the Peace They Hoped to Make* (London, 1994); T.A. Wilson, *The First Summit: Roosevelt and Churchill at Placentia Bay, 1941*, rev. ed. (Lawrence, KS, 1991). Cf. British Library of Information at New York, *Speech by Winston Churchill to the Pilgrims, January 9, 1941* (New York, 1941).

25. P. Duus, "Imperialism without Colonies: The Vision of a Greater East Asia Co-Prosperity Sphere," *Diplomacy and Statecraft*, 7 (1996), 55–71; J.C. Lebra, ed., *Japan's Greater East Asia Co-Prosperity Sphere in World War II: Selected Readings and Documents* (Kuala Lampur, London, 1975).

26. M. Perrie, *The Cult of Ivan the Terrible in Stalin's Russia* (Basingstoke, 2001). Cf. V.M. Molotov et al., *The German Attack on the USSR: Speeches* (London, 1941).

27. For instance, C.-E. Bärsch, *Die politische Religion des Nationalsozialismus: Die religiöse Dimension der NS-Ideologie in den Schriften von Dieter Eckhart, Joseph Goebbels, Alfred Rosenberg, und Adolph Hitler* (Munich, 1998); W. Donner, *Propaganda und Film im "Dritten Reich"* (Berlin, 1995); D. Welch, *The Third Reich: Politics and Propaganda* (London, New York, 1993).

28. See M. Gilbert, *Never Again: A History of the Holocaust* (London, 2000); Y. Lozowick, *Hitler's Bureaucrats: The Nazi Security Police and the Banality of Evil* (New York, 2002); K. Pätzold, *Tagesordnung, Judenmord: Die Wannsee-Konferenz am 20 Januar 1942: Eine Dokumentation zur Organisation der "Endlosung"* (Berlin, 1992); R. Rhodes, *Masters of Death: The SS-Einsatzgruppen and the Invention of the Holocaust* (New York, 2002). Also see O. Bartov, *The Eastern Front, 1941–45: German Troops and the Barbarisation of Warfare*, 2nd ed. (New York, 2001).

29. Cf. F.N. Davies, *The Man behind the Bridge: Colonel Toosey and the River Kwai* (London, 1990); R.S. La Forte, R.E. Marcello, and R.L. Himmel, eds., *With Only the Will to Live: Accounts of Americans in Japanese Prison Camps, 1941–1945* (Wilmington, DE, 1994); and T. Brook, ed., *Documents on the Rape of Nanking* (Ann Arbor, 1999); I. Chang, *The Rape of Nanking: The Forgotten Holocaust of World War II* (New York, 1997).

30. A.M. De Zayas, *A Terrible Revenge: The "Ethnic Cleansing" of East European Germans, 1944–1950* (New York, 1994); S. Mikolajczyk, *The Rape of Poland: Pattern of Soviet Aggression* (Westport, CT, 1972); M.A. Paul, *Kat'yn: The Untold Story of Stalin's Polish Massacre* (Toronto, New York, 1991).

31. F. Harbutt, *The Cold War Era* (Malden, MA, 2001); R.C. Grogan, *Natural Enemies: The United States and the Soviet Union in the Cold War, 1917–1991* (Lanham, MD, 2001); G. Roberts, *The Soviet Union in World Politics: Co-existence, Revolution, and Cold War 1945–1991* (New York, 1999).

32. See M. Hogan, *A Cross of Iron: Harry S. Truman and the Origins of the National Security State, 1945–1954* (Cambridge, UK, 1998); S. Lucas, *Freedom's War: The United States Crusade against the Soviet Union, 1945–1956* (Manchester, 1999); V. Mastny, *The Cold War and Soviet Insecurity: The Stalin Years* (New York, 1996); W.R. Smyser, *From Yalta to Berlin: The Cold War Struggle over Germany* (New York, 1999).

33. On NATO, see D. Haglund, *Alliance within the Alliance? Franco-German Military Cooperation and the European Pillar of Defence* (Boulder, CO, 1991); L. Kaplan, *The Long Entanglement: NATO's First Fifty Years* (Westport, CT, 1999); K. Ruane, *The Rise and Fall of the European Defence Community: Anglo-American Relations and the Crisis of European Defence* (Basingstoke, 2000); M. Smith, *NATO Enlargement during the Cold War: Strategy and System in the Western Alliance* (Basingstoke, 2000). On the Warsaw Pact, see G. Holden, *The Warsaw Pact: Soviet Security and Bloc Politics* (Oxford, 1989); C.D. Jones, *Soviet Influence in Eastern Europe: Political Autonomy and the Warsaw Pact* (Brooklyn, NY, 1981); W.J. Lewis, *The Warsaw Pact: Arms, Doctrine, Strategy* (New York, 1982); G. Zieger, *Der Warschauer Pakt* (Hannover, 1974).

34. On Nicaragua, see R. Kagan, *A Twilight Struggle: American Power and Nicaragua, 1977–1990* (New York, 1996); H. Sklar, *Washington's War on Nicaragua* (Toronto, 1988); T.W. Walker, ed., *Revolution and Counterrevolution in Nicaragua* (Boulder, CO, 1991). On North Korea, see D.A. Mayers, *Cracking the Monolith: US Policy against the Sino-Soviet Alliance, 1949–1955* (Baton Rouge, LA, 1986); R.R. Simmons, *The Strained Alliance: Peking, Pyongyang, Moscow, and the Politics of the Korean War* (New York, 1975).

35. On Southeast Asia, see W.J. Duiker, *U.S. Containment Policy and the Conflict in Indochina* (Stanford, CA, 1994); G.C. Herring, *America's Longest War: The United States and Vietnam, 1950–1975*, 2nd ed. (Philadelphia, 1986); A.F. Krepinevich, *The*

Army and Vietnam (Baltimore, MD, 1986); J. Prados, *The Blood Road: The Ho Chi Minh Trail and the Vietnam War* (New York, 1998); Michael A. Hennessy, *Strategy in Vietnam: The Marines and Revolutionary War in I Corps, 1965–1972* (Westport, CT, 1997). On Afghanistan, see F. Grare, *Le Pakistan face au conflit afghan (1979–1986): Au tournant de guerre froid* (Paris, 1997); H. Hubel, *Das Ende des Kalten Kriegs im Orient: Die USA, die Sowjetunion und die Konflicte in Afghanistan am Golf und im Nahen Osten, 1979–1991* (Munich, 1995); Russian Federation General'nyi.shtab, *The Soviet-Afghan War: How a Superpower Fought and Lost*, L.W. Grau and M.A. Gress, trans. and eds. (Lawrence, KS, 2002).

36. For the Anglo-Americans, cf. U. Bar-Noi, "Anglo-Soviet Relations during Churchill's Peacetime Administration, 1951–1955: Cold War Politics, Propaganda, Trade, and Détente" (Ph.D. diss., University of London, 2000); B. Gary, *The Nervous Liberals: Propaganda Anxieties from World War I to the Cold War* (New York, 1999); W.L. Hixson, *Parting the Curtain: Propaganda, Culture, and the Cold War, 1945–1961* (Basingstoke, 1997); S.J. Perry-Giles, *The Rhetorical Presidency, Propaganda, and the Cold War, 1945–1955* (Westport, CT, 2002). For the Soviet Union, cf. G. Bailey, *The Perception Mongers: Reflections on Soviet Propaganda* (London, 1990); L. Bittmann, *The New Image Makers: Soviet Propaganda and Disinformation Today* (Washington, DC, London, 1988); B. Hazun, *Soviet Propaganda: A Case Study of the Middle East Conflict* (New York, 1976).

37. Cf. K. Cuordileone, *Politics in an Age of Anxiety: Masculinity, the Vital Canter, and American Political Culture in the Cold War, 1949–1963* (New York, London, 2001); R. Saull, *Rethinking Theory and History in the Cold War: The State, Military Power, and Social Revolution* (Portland, OR, 2001). But such developments were not unique to the Cold War period; for instance, see D. Petzina, *Geschichte und Identität*, vol. 2: *Deutschland und Japan im 2. Weltkrieg* (Bochum, 1994).

38. Turner's *Lyndon Johnson's Dual War* provides a structure. Cf. L. Berman, *No Peace, No Honor: Nixon, Kissinger, and Betrayal in Vietnam* (New York, 2001); S. Brown and L. Ackland, eds., *Why Are We Still in Vietnam* (New York, 1970); L.C. Gardner and T. Gittingen, eds., *Vietnam: The Early Decisions* (Austin, TX, 1997); R.R. Tomes, *Apocalypse Then: American Intellectuals and the Vietnam War, 1954–1975* (New York, 1998).

39. On Hungary, see J.M. Bak and L.H. Letyers, eds., *The Hungarian Revolution of 1956: Reform, Revolution, Repression, 1953–1963* (Harlow, 1996); F. Fejtö, *Budapest, l'insurrection: La première révolution anti-totalitaire* (Brussels, 1990). On Czechoslovakia, see K. Dawisha, *The Kremlin and the Prague Spring* (Berkeley, CA, 1984); K. Williams, *The Prague Spring and Its Aftermath: Czechoslovakian Politics, 1968–1970* (Cambridge, UK, 1997). On Poland, see L. Goodwyn, *Breaking the Barrier: The Rise of Solidarity in Poland* (New York, 1991); M.D. Kennedy, *Professionals, Power, and Solidarity in Poland: A Critical Sociology of a Soviet-Type Society* (Cambridge, UK, 1990). Then cf. G. Ekient, *The State against Society: Political Crises and Their Aftermath in East Central Europe* (Princeton, NJ, 1996).

40. The best example of an influential journalist is the American Walter Lippmann who popularized the term *Cold War*. See his *U.S. Foreign Policy: Shield of the Republic* (Boston, 1943); and *The Cold War: A Study in U.S. Foreign Policy* (London, 1947). Two influential immigrant academics to the United States, one German and one Polish, are also exemplary. Cf. H.A. Kissinger, *Nuclear Weapons and Foreign Policy* (New York, 1957); idem, *Problems of National Security: A Book*

of Readings (New York, 1965); Z. Brzezinski, *Ideology and Power in Soviet Politics* (London, 1962); idem, *The Soviet Bloc: Unity and Conflict* (Cambridge, MA, 1967). Kissinger served first, as national security adviser and then as secretary of state between 1969 and 1976; Brzezinski served as national security adviser from 1976 to 1981.

41. See Birn, *League of Nations Union*; Viscount Cecil of Chelwood, *A Great Experiment* (London, 1941).

42. A. Ponsonby, "Disarmament by Example," *International Affairs*, 7 (1928), 231.

43. For the Northern Irish example, see M.C. Maguire, *The Vision of Peace: Faith and Hope in Northern Ireland* (Maryknoll, NY, 1999); C. McKeown, *The Passion of Peace* (Belfast, 1984); R. Needham, *Battling for Peace* (Belfast, 1998).

44. For a succinct exposition, see Å. Hammarskjöld, "The Permanent Court of International Justice and Its Place in International Relations," *International Affairs*, 9 (1930), 467–97; idem, "The Permanent Court of International Justice and the Development of International Law," *International Affairs*, 14 (1935), 797–817. Then cf. M. Pomerance, *The United States and the World Court as a "Supreme Court of the Nations": Dreams, Illusions, and Disillusions* (The Hague, 1996); N. Singh, *The Role and Record of the International Court of Justice, 1945–1988* (Dordrecht, Netherlands, 1989).

45. Two British examples are P.J. Noel Baker, "Disarmament," *International Affairs*, 13 (1934), 3–25; Ponsonby, "Disarmament."

46. Instructive are M. Bourquin, ed., *Collective Security: A Record of the Seventh and Eighth International Studies Conferences, Paris, 1934, London, 1935* (Paris, 1936); E.H. Carr, "The League of Peace and Freedom: An Episode in the Quest for Collective Security," *International Affairs*, 14(1935), 837–44. Baron McNair, *Collective Security: An Inaugural Lecture* (Cambridge, UK, 1936); W.R. Tucker, *The Attitude of the British Labour Party towards European and Collective Security Problems, 1920–1939* (Geneva, 1950).

47. A.B. Fetherston, *Towards a Theory of United Nations Peacekeeping* (Basingstoke, 1994). Then see A. James, *Keeping the Peace in Cyprus* (New York, 2001); S.M. Hill and S.P. Malik, *Peacekeeping and the United Nations* (Aldershot, 1996); N. Macqueen, *The United Nations since 1945: Peacekeeping and the Cold War* (London, New York, 1999); R.C. Thakur and A. Schnabel, eds., *Peacekeeping Operations: Ad hoc Missions, Permanent Engagement* (Tokyo, New York, 2001).

48. The Persian Gulf War is handled in the next paragraph. On Bosnia and Yugoslavia, see X. Bougarel, *Bosnie: Anatomie d'un conflit* (Paris, 1995); M. Ignatieff, *Virtual War: Kosovo and Beyond* (New York, 2000); M. Rose, *Fighting for Peace* (London, 1999); UN Department of Public Information, *The United Nations and the Situation in the Former Yugoslavia* (New York, 1993). Then cf. M. Littmann [Committee for Peace in the Balkans], *Neither Legal Nor Moral: How NATO's War against Yugoslavia Breached International Law* (n.p., 2000).

49. For the Rwandan example, see M.N. Barnett, *Eyewitness to Genocide: The United Nations and Rwanda* (Ithaca, NY, 2002); E. Kabagema, *Carnage d'un nation: Génocide et massacres au Rwanda 1994* (Paris, 2002).

50. Cf. N. Hillmer, "Peacekeeping: Canadian Invention, Canadian Myth," in J.L. Granatstein and Sune Akerman, eds., *Welfare States in Trouble: Historical Perspectives on Canada and Sweden* (North York, Ontario, 1994), 159–70.

51. For example, M.A. Brown [prepared for the Sub-Committee on Europe and the Middle East of the Committee on Foreign Affairs, House of Representatives], *U.N. Security Council Resolutions on Iraq: Compliance and Implementation* (Washington, DC, 1992); C. Dandeker, "Public Opinion, the Media and the Gulf War," *War and Society*, 22 (1995–1996), 397–402; J. Murphy, "De Jure War in the Gulf: Lex Specialis of Chapter VII Actions Prior to, During and in the Aftermath of the United Nations War against Iraq," *New York International Law Review*, 5.2 (1992), 71–88; P.M. Taylor, *War and the Media: Propaganda and Persuasion in the Gulf War* (Manchester, 1992). Cf. P. Bennis, "False Consensus: George Bush's United Nations," in P. Bennis and M. Moushabeck, eds., *Beyond the Storm: A Gulf Crisis Reader* (New York, 1991), 112–25.

52. Cf. E. Bergot, *Operation Daguet: Les Français dans la guerre du Golfe* (Paris, 1991); M.J. Inacker, *Unter Ausschluss der Öffentlichkeit?: Die Deutschen in der Golfallianz* (Bonn, 1991); M.A. Rice and A.J. Sammes, *Command and Control: Support Systems in the Gulf War: An Account of the Command and Control Information Systems Support to the British Army Contribution to the Gulf War* (London, 1994). Then see F.N. Schubert and T.L. Kraus, eds., *The Whirlwind War: The United States Army in Operations Desert Shield and Desert Storm* (Washington, DC, 1994); U.S. Department of the Navy, *The United States Navy in "Desert Shield" and "Desert Storm"* (Washington, DC, 1991).

53. Not so some vituperative domestic American critics of the war, who argued that the United States' action was criminal. See Ramsay Clark et al., *War Crimes: A Report on United States War Crimes against Iraq* (Washington, DC, 1992).

54. See D.P. Calleo, "The Lessons of the Gulf War for Europe and America," in P. Ludlow, ed., *Europe and North America in the 1990s* (Brussels, 1992), 47–67; L. Freedman, "The Gulf War and the New World Order," *Survival*, 33.3 (1991), 195–209; A. Kubursi and S. Mansur, "Oil and the Gulf War: An 'American Century' or a 'New World Order,'" *Arab Studies Quarterly*, 15.4 (1993), 1–18; S. Spanik, "Der Golfkrieg als Kampf um Macht auf dem Ölmarkt," *Europäische Wehrkunde*, No. 10 (1990), 583–88.

CHAPTER 1

War in the Twentieth Century

Donald Cameron Watt

When asked to discuss some general subject, as it might be, for example, "war in the twentieth century," the unwary historian is apt to go charging in, without ever thinking about the nature of the topic to be discussed, let alone defining it. In actuality the topic presents both conceptual and terminological problems. In strictly accurate terms, there has been no war in the world since the end of the Second World War. The term *war*, used loosely, can, of course, have the broadest of meanings. It is habitually used to cover all forms of conflict, from the Cold War, in which the principal belligerents never used arms against each other, to civil strife. But *war* per se, as the term was conceived in 1900, that is, a state of war, is a term derived from international law and contains within its ambience a whole set of legal and cultural consequences, both for the participants and for all remaining "civilized" states who are "nonbelligerents" or "neutrals," as the terms were understood in the international law.

In international law, war is more than a simple state of not-peace. In relations between states "war" is the equal and opposite state to "peace." A state of war has to be declared formally to exist between named states; the formal declaration of war is usually preceded by an ultimatum. It can be ended or interrupted so far as the actual pursuance of hostilities is concerned by a cease-fire or an armistice incorporating a cease-fire. But so far as international law is concerned, this only moves relations between the participants into a state of not-war, as defined by the terms of the armistice, until either the belligerents sign a treaty of peace between them, the armistice is denounced, or, as with U.S. participation in the First World War once the Senate had failed to ratify the Treaty of Versailles, it is ended by a unilateral declaration by the belligerent in question.

Apart from the legal state of affairs existing between armistice and peace treaty, international law recognizes three sets of conditions governing relations between states; war, neutrality, and peace, the last being seen as the normal state of relations between "civilized states." So far as the minor belligerents on the side of the Axis powers were concerned, the Second World War was ended by a series of peace treaties signed in 1946–1947. Austria, whose citizens had fought in the armed forces of the Third Reich, but that had ceased to exist as a state after the recognition of its annexation in March 1938 to Germany, remained under military occupation until the signature of the State Treaty of 1955. The state of war between the victorious Allies, on the one hand, and the two rival successor states to the Third Reich was ended as part of the Helsinki Agreements of 1975 on Peace and Security in Europe. In the Far East, war between Japan and the United States and its non-Soviet allies was brought to an end by the Peace Treaty of 1951. No Treaty of Peace was ever negotiated between Japan and the Soviet Union to end the hostilities that only began in August 1945, days before the Japanese declaration of surrender. With the breakup of the Soviet Union, one can safely say that no treaty of peace ever will be signed.

In the international system of international law that originated in eighteenth-century Europe, that was consolidated in the three Hague Conferences of 1900–1907, and that was universalized, at least in theory, by the Covenant of the League of Nations, a legal state of war could only exist between states that were recognized as equal members of the system and were signatories to the relevant treaties. The system never governed relations between European colonialist states and their "uncivilized" neighbors (although it was employed from time to time, largely to satisfy domestic opinion)—in Africa, in the Gulf, and on the North-West Frontier of India, for example. Hitler expressly forbade his army commanders to apply those of its provisions that governed the treatment of prisoners of war to any Soviet citizens, giving as his ground that the war that opened with the German attack on the Soviet Union was a war of destruction (*Vernichtungskrieg*) between rival ideologies (*Weltanschauungen*) between whom no agreement could exist. Such a division of the world into "civilized" and "barbarian" states was paralleled by the medieval systems of Islamic international law, which divided the world into the Abode of Peace, the *Dar ul-islam*, and the Abode of War of Chaos, the *Dar ul-Harb*. Between these two there could at best be limited periods of nonhostility based on treaty. A twentieth-century equivalent was provided by the practice of the Soviet Union, whose international lawyers followed their ruler/theorists in regarding relations between the capitalist-imperialist states and the socialist system as one of war and devised the Non-Aggression Treaty, a legal device of which only one example existed before 1917, to regulate relations with their immediate neighbors. The traditional European system regarded war as an exceptional state requiring regulation both by treaty and by customary law. The Islamic and Soviet systems reversed this concept. Soviet practice did, however, accept that treaties, both general and particular, could be entered into with capitalist states, on specific issues, and tried desperately after the German attack on the Soviets had begun to obtain German agreement to the application of the Geneva convention of 1929 on the treatment of prisoners of war to their serving soldiers—in vain.[1]

War and neutrality, armistice and afterwar, and peace. These were the three possible states of relations between states. In this sense there have been no wars since 1945, as there have been no formal declarations of war. There have been ultimata that led to fighting, as with the 1956 Anglo-French ultimata to Israel and Egypt, demanding their withdrawal from the banks of the Suez Canal, in 1982 over the Argentinian occupation of the Falkland Islands, or in 1991 over the Iraqi occupation of Kuwait. But there have been no formal declarations of war, with all their consequent implications for the belligerents. Indeed, in the case of the Falklands, I well remember a briefing of selected academics after the close of hostilities given by the Ministry of Defence, at which the head of the Foreign and Commonwealth Office legal advisers, a Mr. Darwin, watched like an angry eagle about to swoop on any foolish soldier, sailor, or airman, let alone civilian member of the ministry, who might say anything that implied that a state of war had existed between the Argentine and Britain. There were in fact no attacks by either side on the metropolitan territory of the other (though the Special Air Service [SAS], a disavowable force, is alleged to have considered an action against the Argentinian mainland),[2] there was no action against the maritime trade of either belligerent by the naval force of the other, and there was only limited interference with the citizens of each state who were discovered by the outbreak of hostilities to be placed in the territory of the other.

The year 1945 also saw the only use of nuclear weapons in conflict in this century. As such, it marked the end of the concept and practice of total war, although it took a little time for that to sink in. The Soviet development of their own atomic and thermonuclear weapons and delivery systems made a nonsense of any planning for the total mobilization of the resources of the state once war had broken out. The first half of the century had seen two so-called world wars in which the principal European powers had developed the theory and practice of planned total mobilization of their economies for war, so that the entire population, male and female between the ages of twelve and seventy, was enlisted in some way to contribute to the provision of supplies for the war, if not for the fighting itself. In this sense, the 1914–1918 war was only a trial run for the Second World War.

This can be seen most clearly in the case of Britain where, between the wars, guided both by the experience of a generation of civil servants who held office from one war to the next, the machinery of government for the waging of war was coordinated and refined while there was still time. September 1938 provided a trial run for the testing of this machinery, at which all the chaos and unresolved issues of mobilization could be ironed out—so well that by the declaration of war on Germany on September 3, 1939, the children were evacuated from the big cities, the population was provided with free gas masks, and air raid shelters from the single-family back-garden size to the deep tube shelters were ready to see the people of London and the other large conurbations through the Blitz. More than one diary of the time records the complaints of those in charge of these measures that they had nothing to do![3]

The central idea behind this careful organization, ever since the original Committee of Imperial Defense had been set up in 1904, not as a subcommittee of the cabinet but as a committee to advise the prime minister, was to make the prime minister, through the Cabinet Office, the overall minister for the waging of war and effective commander in chief of the armed forces. War was to be waged not by a single superministry of defense with a superminister but by the whole machinery of government, as coordinated by the Cabinet Office under the prime minister. From the experience of 1940–1945, when Winston Churchill acted both as prime minister and as minister of defense, with the machinery of the chiefs of staff responsible directly to himself, the reformers both within the bureaucracy and within the Labour government of 1945–1946 created a single Ministry of Defense to which the three service ministries, War, Admiralty, and Air, were nominally subordinate. But the minister of defense was simply an organizational deputy to the prime minister, as Albert Alexander was for Prime Minister Attlee and Field Marshal Lord Alexander was for Churchill in the great man's last ministry, from 1951 to 1955. Thereafter, it became clear that a war in the long term, like those of the first half of the century, was fantasy. Nuclear war would be a short and nasty episode fought with the forces available at its outbreak. There would be no time to mobilize the full resources of the nation for war, if war was to begin with an all-out nuclear exchange. Organization was needed—but of a very different kind.

THE PSYCHOLOGICAL LEGACY OF THE TWO WORLD WARS

So far as the bulk of writing on war in this century is concerned, the experience of the two world wars dominated thinking for at least three quarters of the century. Both wars exhibited ideological as well as national-imperial agendas. Analysis is complicated by the limited and disputed recognition by various schools of analysis of the concept that the antagonists in both wars, especially Germany, the United States, and the Soviet Union, were states in which nationalism and ideology were so interlocked at the governmental level and in the perceptions of an indeterminate but substantial section of their leading elites that patriotic values were expressed in ideological terms, and vice versa. Less attention has been paid to those smaller bilateral wars that occurred before 1914 and between the wars such as the Russo-Japanese war of 1904–1905, the Balkan Wars of 1912–1913, the colonial wars in the Moroccan Rif and of Italy against Ethiopia, the Chaco war in South America, the Saudi war against and capture of the Hejaz, and the various pieces of British "imperial policing" as against the "mad Mahdi" in Somalia and the rebellious tribesmen in Iraq and on the North-West Frontier of India. The civil wars in Ireland from 1919 to 1924, the civil wars in China, and the conflicts following on the extension of Kuomintang rule into northern China and Manchuria have also to be included. There is also substantial disagreement between national historiographies as to when the Second World War can be said to have begun, from the Chinese date of July 7, 1937, to that once favored by the catalogers of the Library of Congress, that is, December 7, 1941.

THE CRIMINALIZATION OF "AGGRESSIVE" WAR

This process can be seen as covering three stages, or possibly even four, if one includes some desultory and unsuccessful discussion at the three Hague conferences before 1914. The first is the abortive attempt to extradite the Kaiser from his refuge in the Netherlands to stand trial on charges of responsibility for the outbreak of the First World War, which was thwarted by the Dutch refusal to extradite him to the victorious Allies. This did not prevent the inclusion in the terms of the Treaty of Versailles of clauses in which Germany was forced to admit its "guilt" for the outbreak of the war; nor did it prevent in the Covenant of the League of Nations, an integral part of the treaty, the inclusion of the Anglo-Saxon legal concept of the "hue and cry," by which all members of the League were bound to join in any proposals by the Council of the League for action against declared aggressors. This approach was held to have been strengthened by the so-called Kellogg-Briand Pact of 1928 "outlawing" war as an instrument of national policy, the aforesaid strengthening lying mainly in the fact that, unlike the Covenant of the League of Nations, the United States was a signatory to the Pact but not to the Treaty of Versailles incorporating the Covenant of the League of Nations.

The final stage came with the London convention of 1945 on which the charges leveled at Nuremberg against the "major war criminals" on the German side and at Tokyo against those Japanese statesmen regarded as their equivalents from the Japanese leadership (but not the emperor) were based.[4] The charges included new crimes "against Humanity"; but the most novel were charges I and II, of "conspiracy to commit aggressive war" in general and against specific named states in particular. Two international tribunals were set up, one with four member states at Nuremberg and one of ten at Tokyo, foreshadowing the courts now meeting at The Hague and in central Africa. It should be noted, however, that since the Nuremberg and Tokyo tribunals were wound up, no individual or state has been arraigned on charges analogous to counts I and II of the postwar indictments, although there have been cases since that date—the Anglo-French "collusion" in October 1956 and the Iraqi invasion of Kuwait in 1991 being only two—where there would seem to have been evidence enough for a prima facie case to have been made.

MODELS FOR THE ESCALATION OF CONFLICT AND THE SPREAD OF WAR

Debate over the prevention and limitation of conflict and the prevention of its escalation have swung between what might loosely be described as the 1914 and 1939 models.[5] Explanations for the process by which a conflict between Austro-Hungary and Serbia over the assassination, by a Bosnian with Serbian conspiratorial backing, of the heir to the Hapsburg throne developed into a conflict involving France, the Czarist Empire, Belgium, and the British Empire and Dominions focus of necessity on the structure of existing alliances, the military timetables of mobilization, the uncertainty over the functioning of the Anglo-French and Anglo-Russian Ententes, the failure of the civil power in the three empires (Russia, Germany, and Austro-Hungary) to control their military coequals in the policy structures of their states, and the influence of successive arms races—the assumption being that none of the belligerents, with the possible exception of the clandestine Black Hand organization in Serbia, had been actually working to bring about war. British historian Sir Llewellyn Woodward spent a considerable amount of time and energy, after the German records had fallen into Allied hands in 1945, trying to find an Imperial equivalent to the conference of November 5, 1937, between Hitler and his war leaders, at which the Fuehrer announced his plans for war, so convinced was Woodward that Germany had planned for and helped to initiate the war of 1914 in the way in which Hitler had provoked the outbreak of the Second World War; but Woodward failed to find one.

The evidence produced for the trial of the major war criminals at Nuremberg in 1946 and that produced at Tokyo the following year showed that the Second World War both in Europe and in the Far East by the Japanese attack on the United States and on British and Dutch colonial possessions in Southeast Asia was the result of planned and intended aggression, though under rather different circumstances. The main features of the decision-making process both in Germany and in Japan were the prior destruction or silencing of all alternative sources of power and influence from which a challenge to the dominant ideology might have been launched and the discovery of points of time, such as the various conferences at which Hitler announced to his military and diplomatic advisers his intention of attacking his next targets, and the Imperial conferences of 1940 and 1941 at which the rival Japanese army and navy leaderships and the dominating Treasury and Foreign Office ministers arrived at the decision to challenge American economic pressure by the use of military force rather than yielding to it and won Imperial assent for their actions. Much of the early American and British reactions to Stalin's attempts to exploit the Soviet position in 1945 stemmed from the conviction that Stalin, if anything, enjoyed greater control over the Soviet state than Hitler had over Nazi Germany and had long ago destroyed the possibility of institutional resistance to his policies. Stalin, however, was not the gambler that Hitler was; nor was his empire as desperate for vital raw materials as was Japan in 1941. The idea that the Soviet Union, instead of entertaining an ideology that made war between itself and its capitalist enemies a matter of historical inevitability, saw aggression as a goal to be actively pursued while the West was divided took a long time to die in certain Western circles. But it did not survive the overthrow of Khruschev. It was middle-ranking powers of the second division, like Iraq under Saddam Hussein, that seemed to offer the closest parallels to Hitler's actions.

THE INTERSERVICE DEBATE OVER WAR-WINNING STRATEGIES

From 1919 onward the control of war and the waging of war have been bedevilled by doctrinal disagreements within the major Anglo-Saxon powers between the three separate armed services, army, navy, and air force. Does victory or conquest come by invasion and occupation by armies, by blockade and the interdiction of resources and trade, or by the destruction of cities and industry from the air? The choice of strategies had serious implications for the division of the total defense budget in the period between the wars, when all governments were under pressure to reduce their expenditures on defense; the debate was made much worse in those countries where the establishment of separate air forces was accompanied by claims that the conventional armed forces, whether armies or navies, had been made obsolete by the rise of air power and that only the technologically backward, Luddites in uniform, so to speak, stood in the way of the new manner of winning wars.

Theorists of air power, whether they were would-be Clausewitzes like the Italian general Douhet or obsessive heads of air forces like British Air Marshal Lord Trenchard, preached the doctrine even where the existing technology was grossly inadequate, or even deteriorating as in Britain, and in circumstances, such as a war against Japan in the Pacific, where it was entirely irrelevant. Trenchard even maintained that airfields could be defended against attack by land by arming the aircraft maintenance staffs. In fact, the Royal Air Force (RAF) never dared experiment with bombing sights for fear that they would not match up to the accuracy assumed by air force doctrine, and whereas the RAF in 1919 had bombers capable of reaching Berlin with a reasonable bomb load, it was another fifteen to twenty years before the RAF again had aircraft of such range and capacity. In countries such as Germany, France, or the Soviet Union, where the army dominated strategic thinking and social acceptability, air forces were seen only as an adjunct to land warfare, a combination of long-range reconnaissance and flying artillery.

For Britain seaborne airpower remained an adjunct to the Royal Navy's battle line. When the Fleet Air Arm used its aircraft to cripple the Italian battle fleet in harbor at Taranto, the successful commander apologized to their Lords of the Admiralty for using his aircraft in a manner excluded by current doctrine![6] Only in the United States and Japan did airpower at sea become a force on its own and the aircraft carrier replace the battleship as the capital ship in battle. And only in the United States did the army air force develop a strategic bombing capacity and bomb sights to match. Even there the notion of the Flying Fortress, able to stand off attack by enemy fighter aircraft by sheer gun power, proved enormously costly. The effectiveness of the fighter escorts substituted was limited by range until 1944, as the disastrous raid on the Ploesti oil fields in 1943 was to demonstrate.

The cost to the total defense budget of this internecine conflict over strategic choice between the three armed services was to continue to manifest itself after 1945, enhanced by the development of a fourth arm—that provided by the development of intercontinental long-range missiles. In the United States in the 1950s each of the three armed services developed its own intercontinental ballistic missile (ICBM) program. Indeed a science fiction writer postulated that when the U.S. space program finally succeeded in putting men on the moon, they would find their presence there contested not by the Soviet armed forces but by the U.S. Navy. By the beginning of the 1960s, efforts to control this competition led in both Britain and the United States to radical reform of the whole structure of defense policymaking and to a nearly disastrous crisis in the Anglo-American alliances: the U.S. Air Force's strategic missile Skybolt, which the British understood they had been promised, was canceled as one system too many, and the State Department and the Pentagon refused British delivery of the U.S. Navy's submarine-launched Polaris missile except as part of an integrated European deterrent under American command. The competition continued, an arms race between the United States and the Soviet Union in the field of delivery and antimissile systems, until the threat of a foolproof U.S. system, known by the phrase "Star Wars," broke the nerve of the Soviet command establishment. Britain shared in the American seaborne capacity, first with Polaris and then with Trident, mounting their own warheads on the American delivery systems. France and China, unwilling to commit themselves to their ideological partners, found themselves constrained to delay much of their general technological and industrial investment and development by the need to concentrate their scarce resources of nuclear scientists and engineers on the development of their own delivery systems.

THE ARMAGEDDON MODEL OF WAR

The breakup of the anti-Hitler coalition on Germany's defeat was probably inevitable given the initial Soviet support for Germany and Stalin's conviction that socialism and capitalism could not coexist save on the basis of conflict of some kind. But the permanent confrontation of Soviet conventional military power and that of western and southern Europe under American command in central Europe resulted directly from two of Stalin's actions—(1) the stationing of Red Army troops in eastern Europe as an alternative to the overrapid demobilization of their men under arms by the United States and (2) the failure to restrain the ambitions of his North Korean satellite to win control of the whole Korean peninsula in 1950. Nervousness among the west European states had led to the conclusion of the Brussels Five Power Treaty in March 1948 and the conclusion the following February of the North Atlantic Treaty involving the United States and Canada. But the first meeting of the North Atlantic Treaty Organization's (NATO) Military Committee thereafter had revealed to America's Allies in Europe that they could expect no American aid on the ground, for the very simple reason that America had run its armed forces down so far that there were no extra divisions to add to the bits and pieces that were all that was left of the six U.S. armies that had ended the war in Europe. The outbreak of the Korean conflict led the Americans to offer four infantry divisions to buttress the strength of the main European front, but only until the West Germans produced a twelve-division army to take their place. The Europeans managed to delay the rearmament of West Germany until 1955; but they made sure that there would be no U.S. withdrawal by ensuring that all the most senior commands were filled by Americans, even, to Churchill's horror, those of the naval fronts in the North Atlantic and the Mediterranean.[7]

The confrontation of American and Soviet-led coalitions had three aspects: the nuclear (to be dealt with later), the geographic, and the strategic. The commanders and staff officers of NATO and the Warsaw Pact cut their teeth as young officers in the regular set-piece battles of the years 1943–1945, regular set-piece battles between enormous numbers of men, guns, and vehicles, fought with hundreds of guns, increasingly heavily gunned and armored tanks, and tactical air forces, over fronts hundreds of kilometers wide. The senior American and Soviet commanders of the 1960s and 1970s had been the junior officers of 1944–1945. The battles they envisaged, should hostilities ensue, would be large-scale, fast-moving, calling for ever heavier guns and tanks, fought over the plains of central Europe, rolling, as they do, north and south of the Carpathians, ending up against the Alps in the south but in the north running uninterruptedly, save for rivers, from the Urals to the North Sea. The American experience in Vietnam and the Soviet in Afghanistan were to demonstrate that the two largest and most powerful armies in the world were unable to cope with terrain and weaponry that did not match with the heavily industrialized, high-technology and high-cost wars that were the only kind they knew how to fight. The result was denial and deception at the higher levels of command and the collapse of morale among the ranks. Diplomatically, NATO provided a visible shield behind which Europe's economies could recover and embark on an era of economic growth that has still to end. Much the same happened in Japan and with the U.S. allies in South-east Asia. Militarily however, the manner in which both sides seemed to prepare for war was imitated and executed in the Middle East, the Indian subcontinent, and the Korean peninsula. It also ate up much of the enormous manpower reserves of China. It was, essentially, modern rather than postmodern, highly expensive, and only suitable to a limited range of terrain.

THE DISAPPEARANCE OF WAR AT SEA

The First World War had seen the failure of German sea power to break Britain's geographical stranglehold on the European exits to the Atlantic, at Scapa Flow at the northern exits from the North Sea, at the Dover Straits, Gibraltar, and the Suez, and the defeat of the subsequent

German attempt to destroy Britain's overseas supply routes by unrestricted submarine warfare. In the 1930s the German navy was planning for a new-style guerre de course, which would have used heavy ships to disperse and distract enemy convoy escorts and submarines to destroy the slow and scattered merchant ships sailing under their protection. Hitler's miscalculation over British and French support for Poland landed the Reichsmarine, to Admiral Raeder's fury and despair, in war with Britain, four to six years too soon. But the sea war in the winter of 1939–1940 and the fate of the Russian convoy PQ.17 in 1942 showed how dangerous such a threat would have been. The subsequent course of the war at sea against Germany brought Britain victory, though at very great cost to its merchant marine. It took the Luftwaffe's domination of the Mediterranean in the summer of 1941, rather than the Reichsmarine, to demonstrate quite how vulnerable the British position at sea could be, a lesson emphasized by the disaster that overtook the British fleet in Southeast Asian waters at the hands of the Japanese naval air forces in the early months of 1942. It was the U.S. Navy using submarines against Japanese seaborne communications and aircraft carriers as the new capital ships that broke the last challenge to the Anglo-American command of the world's oceans.

GEO-POLITICAL CONSEQUENCES

The victory of the dominant sea powers in the Second World War was absolute. From 1945, the prophetic views of Sir Halford Mackinder, the Edwardian geopolitician, came true.[8] The "Eurasian world-island" had been encircled by the Anglo-American thalassocracies, frustrating Chinese attempts to claw back Taiwan, fighting Chinese and North Korean attempts to a standstill in the Korean conflict, ended to this day by an armistice but no peace, leaving Britain free to develop an amphibious or, strictly speaking, triphibious capacity to intervene off the coasts of Arabia, East Africa, and Borneo in the 1960s and against the Argentinian occupation of the Falkland Islands in 1982, while the development of the submarine-based ICBM extended the powers of thalassocracies to intervene against land-borne targets from the ten miles inland of the Second World War battleships to the thousands of miles into the rear of the world-island attainable by the submarine-borne missiles Polaris and Trident.

The result is best illustrated by the statement of a Royal Navy spokesman, introducing a new documentary series for British television screens in the year 2000, under the title *Navy in Action*: "The hostage storyline has been chosen to reflect the Navy's modern role in peacekeeping and 'defence Diplomacy.' . . . The Navy doesn't really fight wars any more . . . this shows the kind of action today's sailors really face."

The U.S. Navy is having painfully to learn again how to use its ships and the U.S. Marines in the kind of "police actions" it used to carry out so regularly in the Caribbean and Central American areas in the 1920s. Its fixation on the one big battle theory of sea power, as much the dominant doctrine in the U.S. Navy as its equivalent in the U.S. Army (and one held for much longer), is proving the same obstacle to rethinking its new mission or developing a new doctrine—it is characteristic of American strategic argument that the issues are formulated in so theological a form. In the meantime, numbered U.S. fleets are patrolling the sea frontiers of the world-island.

"MODERN" AND "POSTMODERN" CONFLICTS SINCE 1945

The hundred or more armed conflicts that have taken place since 1945 make most sense if they are divided into two categories, "modern" and "postmodern" wars, omitting for a moment the case of the war that has not happened, the Third World War. Modern wars are fought, as the two world wars were fought, on the battlefield between forces armed with so-called conventional arms. Total engagement of the economy and manpower of the belligerent states has in fact been the exception rather than the rule, though most of the belligerents have based their armed forces on conscription in time of peace, at least of the relevant male age groups. These modern wars have been fought since 1945 with "conventional" weaponry. They have been fought between regional powers with professional command and staff officers, using the most technologically advanced nonnuclear weapons, acquired in part as military aid, in part from purchase on the world arms markets, enabling the arms industries of the major arms-producing countries, especially those of the United States, the Soviet Union, Britain, France, and China, to maintain a level of output that made their own acquisition of such weaponry economic and generating a degree of almost cutthroat competition between respective national arms industries, which has now been succeeded by a good deal of transnational cooperation. Failure to secure foreign orders could make the prototype of a new weapon uneconomic and force its abandonment, a fate that overtook several of the British-developed aircraft and nonnuclear missiles in the 1960s.

The weapons developed by the major arms-producing powers and marketed to the regional powers demanded so high a rate of consumption of ammunition that wars between regional powers tended to be interrupted in a matter of weeks by the belligerents' need to approach their suppliers for fresh supplies. Suppliers were able to use this need as a means of pressure to bring the contestants to the negotiating table—that is, if they were unwilling to allow the conflict to continue. A classic case of this can be seen in the Soviet mediation in the Indo-Pakistani conflict of 1966 over the Rann of Kutsch. Observation of this led the then shah of Iran to diversify his sources of arms so that he would never find his country dependant upon any other single power for permission to continue with a conflict into which it had entered. In Egypt's case the serious losses of tanks, guns, and aircraft in its three conflicts with Israel in 1956, 1967, and 1973 led to so astronomical a growth in Egypt's debt to the Soviet Union as to inspire a rapprochement with Israel and a switch to the United States as a supplier of arms. There are only two cases of "modern" wars since 1945 that do not fit this pattern, the Korean conflict of 1950–1954 and the final stages of the French involvement in Indo-China and the defeat at Dien Bien Phu. In both cases, one of the belligerents controlled or had access to the controller of nuclear weapons. In both, they were *not* used.

POSTMODERN CONFLICTS

The distinctive mark of the postmodern conflict is the absence of large-scale weapons and the unchallenged command of the air by one participant in the conflict. After experience of an early form of this approach to warfare in Indo-China, French military theorists coined the term *la guerre revolutionnaire* and praised the work of the Vietnamese military commander and writer General Giap. (It should, however, be noticed that as soon as the leaders of the North Vietnamese armed forces felt they could cope with more orthodox warfare, they abandoned Giap's doctrines for conventional battles with conventional weaponry, both in 1954 in the siege of Dien Bien Phu and, after the withdrawal of U.S. forces, against the South Vietnamese army in the last stages of that conflict.)

Later Anglo-Saxon theorists invented the broader terms *brushfire wars*[9] and *low-intensity conflicts*. Neither term is entirely adequate; neither covers those in which assault on the civil population, either by large-scale massacre and "ethnic cleansing" or by the selective targeting of local leadership,[10] has been an important weapon of one or more of the participants. Britain has found itself involved in a substantial number of such conflicts, the nature of which involves the use of small units under decentralized command.[11] The result can be seen in the fact that in only one year since 1945 have British forces not been engaged somewhere in the world in active service and suffering casualties and that in no case since *the war* has a British general found himself in command of anything larger than an army corps. The average command strength of British forces in action in any individual conflict has been that of an augmented division. In this experience the British army has benefited from a military tradition rich in examples of small-scale conflicts but poor in the record of large-scale conflict at the army level, an area in which successful British generalship is the exception rather than the rule and has usually taken a lengthy war to uncover the necessary talent. The early history of the Napoleonic wars, not to say the two world wars of the twentieth century, is redolent with the lost reputations of the military commanders under whom British forces have entered the conflicts.

Postmodern wars, it should be emphasized, may be low-intensive wars. They are by no means necessarily low-technology wars, save in one respect, the command of the air, and in the use of the more sophisticated forms of gathering intelligence. Against the use of electronic intelligence gathering, satellite imaging, and infrared sensing, the targets of such measures have often excelled in more traditional forms of Human Intelligence (HUMINT) gathering. And the command of the air and the use of gunships and airlift capacity have been contested by the use of handheld ground-to-air missiles.

WARS OF DECOLONIZATION

The postmodern conflicts in the first subcategory occurred as part of the processes of decolonization, as with the Netherlands in Indonesia in 1946–1948, the French in Madagascar, Indo-China, Tunisia, Morocco, and Algeria, and the British in Palestine, Kenya, Malaya, Cyprus, East Africa, Aden, Kuwait in 1962, Oman, and (militarily rather than politically) Northern Ireland. On the one side in such conflicts are nationalist guerrillas aiming at the obstruction and reduction of military power and morale among both the armed forces and the civilian population of their adversaries and at making the continuation of conflict too expensive for the metropolitan power to wish to continue; on the other side is a military power acting in a police role, intent on disarming the military wing of the nationalist movement, disabling or neutralizing its leadership, and eroding the civilian support in whose name the nationalist forces claim to be acting and without which they could not operate. In its most potent form the conflict centers on who should be the inheritors of colonial power, a battle that the British won in Kenya and Malaya in the 1950s, using ordinary conscripts, and in Borneo in the 1960s, using professionals, and lost in Aden, where the ultimate victors concentrated not on causing a British withdrawal (that had been decided on already and publicly announced) but on identifying and assassinating those who were leading the most prominent nationalist faction in the hope of taking power once the British withdrew. British successes gave the lie to the school of thought that held guerrilla victory to be inevitable in all cases, showing that conditions of local solidarity and a methodology of combat that was adapted to the peculiarities of the local terrain could defeat and demoralize their militant opponents, provided the will to resist was present among both the colonial power and its local allies.

NEOCOLONIALIST WARS

Ironically, the sweep of decolonization and the emergence of new states with charismatic leaders and party systems shaped by the drive for unity against the colonial power were to be followed in many cases by the new states plunging into foreign ventures every whit as imperialist as the actions of their former opponents. Colonel Nasser's Egypt, having joined in 1960 with Syria and Yemen in the United Arab Republic, alienated the Syrians to the point of secession by the Herrenvolk-like behavior of the Egyptians sent to teach the Syrians how to be good Arabs and plunged headlong into military intervention in Yemen, failing completely to adapt to the terrain and suffering as ignominious and expensive a failure as any colonialist power in history. Egypt was largely bankrupted by the costs of maintaining an army on active service on foreign unfriendly soil.

Sukarno's Indonesia, using low-level intervention (*confrontatsie*) as a form of blackmail, plunged successively into Western New Guinea and Borneo. In the first case, pressure from the Kennedy regime nervous at Sukarno's hints that he might invite Soviet aid forced the Dutch to abandon the native Melanesian nationalist parties they were raising and hand the territory over to the United Nations as a go-between for Indonesia. In the second case, Britain, with vigorous support from both Malaya and Singapore, stood off Indonesian infiltration, with professional forces much more competent in jungle warfare than the urban Indonesian conscripts and officers who opposed them. The Indonesian economy, like the Egyptian, was incapable of sustaining the burden of prolonged hostilities, and the consequent chaos opened the way for an army coup against Sukarno's Indonesian Communist Party supporters and the great man himself.

Iraqi expansionist ambitions, following those of a single Turkish governor in the 1880s, relied on claims that its own artificiality made it the successor to the Ottoman Turkish claims of suzerainity over most of the southern coast of the Gulf, starting with Kuwait but expanding to cover northern Saudi Arabia, Qatar, and at least the westernmost Trucial states. Twice, in 1962 and in 1991, ambitious Iraqi dictators threatened Kuwaiti independence. The second occasion followed a seven-year conflict with Iran, ostensibly over the Shatt al-Arab, a cause of dispute between the two countries ever since the creation of Iraq out of the old Turkish provinces of Baghdad, Basra, and Mosul. This war between Iraq and Iran is the only case of a prolonged "modern war" since 1945, the explanation being the willingness of Western arms suppliers to continue to sell arms to Iraq, whose oil revenues made it creditworthy and who, it was hoped, would contain the revolutionary Islamic fundamentalist xenophobia of the Iranian revolutionary government. The Iranians, in their turn, were sustained by Soviet and Chinese arms in the hope of embarrassing and containing the increasing dominance of the United States in the Middle East.

Military and political miscalculation led the tottering Argentinian military regime in 1982 into attempting to annex the Falkland isles. As with the Indonesians in Borneo, the Argentinian army, with one hundred years of parade-ground glory but not an atom of military experience behind its inexperienced but arrogant officers, and a soldiery consisting of ill-trained conscripts, proved incapable of anything but brave incompetence in the face of British small-force professionalism backed by sea-air mobility. The Argentinian air force, armed with the latest French missiles and fighter aircraft, proved courageous and dangerous. But the danger was diminished by their inability to turn their aircraft around in less than two days and by their inability to add to their very limited armory of Exocet missiles.

CIVIL CONFLICTS

The majority of postmodern conflicts, once those of decolonization and neocolonialism were past, have fallen into the new category of Third World civil wars. These have wracked, and continue to wrack, Africa, Central America, Southeast Asia, the Lebanon, and Sri Lanka and have in the last decade spread to the lands of the former Yugoslavia and the former Soviet Union. To this one should add that both the defeats suffered by the superpowers, in Vietnam and in Afghanistan, came from their intervention into what were basically civil wars in those two countries.

These civil conflicts arise from a variety of conditions. The abandonment of colonial rule without adequate provision for a successor regime, capable of maintaining the civil order that had made the colonial power acceptable, led in many cases to a return of the anarchy that had originally prompted colonialist intervention. A classic case is that of the Congo where the Belgian withdrawal revealed their failure to produce any native educated class or social structure covering more than minute sections of the territory on which a viable government could be based. The processes of decolonization tended to range traditional structures of power, authority, and legitimacy on the side of the retiring colonial power as against the modernizing, Western-trained, and Westernized leaders of the nationalists. They, in turn, by virtue of their acquisition of Western manners and mores, tended to lose touch after independence with the lower strata of the society over which they now presided and to find themselves replaced by military leaders who had succeeded in creating out of the troops under their command pseudotribes of which they were the tribal chieftains, often dressing, or adding to their Western dress, with accoutrements that identified their status as pseudotribal chiefs. Western intervention in Africa had taken place at a time when the epic move of the Bantu warrior tribes out of central Africa southward had broken much of the Africa of the great kingdoms of the medieval period into smaller and more vulnerable statelets. So the pattern of tribal leaders legitimized like medieval European kings by their prowess on the battlefield was and is a familiar one. The military governments created by a succession of coups and pronunciamentos in postcolonial Africa are reminiscent of nineteenth-century politics in Latin America without the social framework that limited these militaristic regimes (save in two appalling exceptions) to enjoying the power they had won rather than exploiting it by going to war.

These military coups produced governments that were dictatorial and failed to command legitimacy in the eyes of any of the inhabitants, save those who shared their tribal identities. Even there, there was plenty of room for factionalism. Outside sub-Saharan Africa, the breakdown of plural or multiracial societies into long-standing civil wars in and after the 1970s could be seen in Lebanon, in Sri Lanka, in the Sudan, in Algeria, and in Yugoslavia after the death of Tito and the collapse of the Soviet Union. In Lebanon, a model of power sharing between the eleven largest political communities, who had lived at peace with each other through the Ottoman and French occupations for a century, broke down because of the pressure of Sunni Arab blackmail, mugging, or other forms of demanding money with menaces. Under this doctrine, certain kinds of dictators, whose control over their own country and military establishment seems unshakeable and absolute, come to be seen as public enemies in the sense in which the FBI of J. Edgar Hoover first popularized the term. At the moment, international action against such states and persons can only draw on an inadequate repertoire of responses, each with a price tag that involves political as well as budgetary consequences for those governments that propose such action. It is hardly surprising that in these circumstances the advocates of victory through airpower, enhanced by the allegedly pinpoint accuracy of the latest airborne missiles, have found a new voice. Bombardment by air, accompanied by such measures as boycott and blockade as geography makes possible, seems the least hazardous of choices.

Until the conclusion of the latest agreement over Serb military withdrawal from Kosovo, they do not seem to have had a very successful track record. (Over Kosovo, the evidence is still being collected.) The best that can be said of blockades and boycotts, as in the cases of South Africa and Rhodesia after a Unilateral Declaration of Independence (UDI), is that the verdict on their effectiveness is still pending. They certainly offer no short-term remedy (unless applied as they were in November 1956 to Britain).

FACTORS IN POSTMODERN CONFLICT SINCE 1945

The Increasing Cost of Weaponry

Advances in weapons technology since 1945 have led to an enormous increase in the cost of all but the lightest of arms, such as automatic rifles and land mines, the weapons of the guerrilla and the terrorist. National economies now face a regular weight of something like 40 percent or more of their gross national product (GNP) already sequestered to meet the costs of welfare, universal education, and public health services. There is no national reserve, as there was before 1914 when government expenditure stood at about 10 to 15 percent of GNP, to be devoted to rearmament on any scale. Inability to manage the escalation of missile technology costs necessary to match American intentions in the Star Wars field brought the Soviet leadership to despair and rendered Britain and France vulnerable to relegation out of the ranks of the First Division powers. In 1939, the United States had been suffering from an enormous degree of slack in its economy as a result of the persistence of the Great Depression. It was thus able to finance a two-ocean war and contribute significantly to the war efforts of Britain and the Soviet Union without needing in any significant way to ration the allocation of national resources. In fact, during the years 1941–1945, the United States enjoyed a boom in consumer goods that has never seriously flagged since.[12] By 1966, however, so much had the cost of waging high-technological, mass industrial war risen that the quasi-colonial war in Vietnam was costing the United States more per diem than the Second World War had. The cost of the Borneo "confrontation" broke the Indonesian economy. Denis Healy, then British minister of defense, said a year after the end of the conflict that Britain could not afford another such exercise.

The changes in military technology also greatly altered the ratio of fighting force to "tail." Churchill had constantly complained during the Second World War at the size of the tail of British forces in North Africa, where three to four men were needed to keep one soldier in the line. In Vietnam the ratio between fighting forces and tail was more like one to eight. No other power could afford so great a disparity between men and women in uniform and front-line soldiery. But the need for a supply train (or fleet) to keep the weapons usable greatly enhanced the vulnerability of the British seaborne expedition against the Falklands and has led to an increasing civilianization of the war machine in the home country.

The Abandonment of Conscription

The rapid developments in the technology of warfare and the increasing need for the armed forces to be trained in their use and to be capable of action in small groups in situations that called for a great use of initiative by quite junior unit commanders made the use of conscription as a means of recruiting for the armed forces increasingly inefficient. Britain was the first to recognize this, abandoning conscription after the far-going rethinking of British defense policy involved in the 1958 Defense White Paper. The difficulties were expressed most clearly to me, however, in 1969 by a civilian adviser to the Socialist minister of defense for Western Germany, Helmut Schmitt. Even to train infantry in the new weaponry at unit level absorbed far too high a proportion of the long-term professionals in the armed forces and too much of the limited time in uniform served by the conscripts. The Soviet army avoided this dilemma by insisting on a minimum of three years in uniform for their draftees. But for the eighteen months to two years that was the maximum the Western democracies felt their electorates would tolerate, the effect of conscription was to leave only six months' service time once the recruits had finished their training. An army whose basic personnel changed every six months was hardly one likely to stand up to the stresses of the large-scale battles that could be expected from a conventional conflict in central Europe.

The possibility of tactical nuclear weapons being used from the outset of hostilities meant that the mobilization of reserves as practiced in two world wars seemed increasingly unreal an option. If this was true of the infantry, it was even truer of the armored and artillery forces. The British tradition of long-term professional armies meant that the abandonment of the conscription that had only been introduced in time of peace by the 1946 Defense Acts was psychologically easier than for those countries such as France, Western Germany, and the United States where service in the armed forces was regarded as an essential part of the citizen's duties and as a unifying force to be set against the natural centrifugal pulls of regions only unified by war against their neighbors. But economics and military logic gradually converted the military in the other major powers with the exception of China and the powers of the Middle East and the Third World. Smaller but more highly trained armed forces meant increased pay and rewards for the professional soldiers and a higher level of training and education. The abandonment of conscription was a relief to British opinion, though there had been no great opposition to its continuation in the conditions of 1946. Allegations that this abandonment had resulted in a deterioration in the respect held by the young for their seniors and a progressive demoralization of youth were not to surface for a decade or so after the abandonment. For the continental

European powers, the long-term social and psychological consequences of the abandonment of conscription are still undetermined.

The Development of Unusable Weapons for Threat Rather Than Employment

The drive for ever more technologically advanced weaponry led the military scientists of the most technologically advanced powers to two potentially counterproductive conclusions. The first was that the increasing cost of the more sophisticated weaponry reduced the scale at which they could be supplied to the armed forces and employed by them, particularly in training. It used to be a joke in Britain that in the end the British army would only be able to afford one example of the ultimate weapon and that the British army being what it is, this would be deployed to guard Buckingham Palace. The drill for the ceremonial changing of the Guard would have to be adapted to one in which the guard was changed, but the weapon remained in place.

More serious, however, was the realization that the most advanced weapons could only be deployed for purposes of deterrence, not employment. The nuclear missile developed and deployed by the hundreds, if not the thousands, by the Soviet Union and the United States gave the potential belligerents what was euphemistically, if inelegantly, described as an "overkill capacity." But it was much more than that; not only did its possible employment threaten the military and political leadership of its owners with personal annihilation in a way not seen in the civilized world since medieval kings ceased to lead their armies into battle from the front; not only did it ensure that even if the leadership survived the initial nuclear exchanges by burying themselves in deep, defended, and thoroughly provisioned bunkers, no organization could survive at ground level to answer the telephones with which the embunkered could communicate with the outside world, let alone execute their commands; the nuclear contamination of the atmosphere and the soil of the countries so embattled as a result of the bombardment of cities and the employment of tactical nuclear weapons would make the winning of land by battle meaningless. What profit is there in winning land made unusable by long-term pollution?

It is only now being realized that three other much more affordable types of weaponry present the same absolute unprofitability. These are chemical and biological weapons (CBWs) and land mines. In the last case, these have been used and great areas of land effectively sterilized. In the case of CBWs, we are still faced with a number of middle-ranking powers that in their cult of military machismo (all those heavily built soldiers with identical mustaches) have still to realize this; their admiring publics are even further away from such realization. What fervent Arab supporter of Saddam Hussein's defiance of the Satanic West ever cottoned onto the indifference of anthrax spores to whether their targets can be sorted into Israelis and Palestinians. None seem to realize, and the West has been ashamedly slow to tell them, that through the long-term pollution brought by CBWs even the Golden Mosque of the Mount in Jerusalem, one of the three holiest shrines in Islam, could be rendered unusable and unapproachable for half a century had one single biologically charged Iraqi missile gone off target. In the Second World War, Britain experimented with anthrax on the isolated Hebridean island of Gruinard. It was not judged safe for human settlement for the subsequent fifty years. Some of the gases now being developed have shorter but still substantial half lives. As for land mines, so cheap and easy to distribute, they will go on killing and maiming men, women, and children for decades in those parts of Africa and the former Yugoslavia in which they were so plentifully and irresponsible scattered.

Clandestine Warfare

The standoff between the major nuclear powers established in the 1950s still applies, although the Soviet Union is no more, as does the absolute prohibition placed by world opinion on the use of nuclear weapons against countries that do not possess them. The disparities between the military powers of the more expansionist-minded third-division powers and their first-division targets have resulted in the development by some of the third-division powers of disavowable special and guerrilla forces and of special reaction forces by the latter—and not only by the latter. (Israel has its own special reaction forces.)[13] One must, however, distinguish between two kinds of clandestine warfare. The first covers efforts to destabilize regimes by the provision of special forces to train and support local guerrillas, as practiced by the Central Intelligence Agency (CIA) and the Secret Intelligence Service (SIS) against Iran in 1954, against Indonesia in 1958–1959, and in the abortive invasion of Cuba in 1961 that ended so disastrously at the Bay of Pigs. The second is the development of rapid reaction forces in uniform such as those employed by the Israelis against the terrorist hijackers of an Israeli airliner to Entebbe in Amin's Uganda, the British Special Air Service's action against secessionist guerrillas in Oman in 1959, the West German rescue of their hijacked airliner, and the Soviet Spetznaz who spearheaded the Soviet invasion of Afghanistan by seizing the president of that unhappy country. The disaster that overtook the extraordinarily ambitious scheme to rescue the staff of the U.S. embassy in Teheran and the debacle in Somalia show that American military culture has had problems with rapid reaction forces. One of the first signs of the efficacy of such special forces has been the virtual disappearance of the hijacking as a weapon in the repertoire of the major revolutionary movements. Specialists in this kind of action, like professional revolutionary Ilich Ramirez Sanchez, alias Carlos the Jackal, who in his day enjoyed a good deal of financial and armed support as well as the provision of training facilities and sanctuary from the Soviet satellites, especially East Germany, found themselves an unemployable embarrassment to those countries on whose support they had once depended.[14] Special forces tend to be used less and less as force on their own and more and more as an auxiliary to more conventional armed action, much as their forerunners were used during the Second World War.

The Debate over Strategic Options in Postmodern War

The main debate today centers on the use of airpower for coercive purposes. Among the nuclear powers, the substitution of missiles for long-range bombers as a form of countercity bombardment seemed to condemn the separate air forces to a return to cooperation with the army commands in air to ground attacks in the extended battlefield, even if the air-carried air-to-ground missile was substituted for the free-falling bomb. Such battlefield usages as the denial of ground transport facilities to the enemy, the destruction of armor and military ground installations, and the dispersion or destruction of troop assemblies, however satisfying to the actual fliers, sat very uneasily with the doctrinal convictions of the air staff by forcing them into what seemed to be a role subordinate to the senior services in the formulation of strategy. Their resentment of this became particularly obvious in Britain after the movement for reform of the central policymaking machinery, having failed to secure an integrated central defense staff under the Sandys reforms of 1958, turned to the establishment of integrated command structures overseas in the eastern Mediterranean, Aden and the Gulf, and Southeast Asia.

These reforms, however, took the overseas commands satisfactorily through the interventions in Kuwait (1961), East Africa, (1964),[15] and Borneo. But the attempt to integrate the headquarters staffs that accompanied the abolition of the War Office, the Admiralty, and the Air Ministry in 1964 proved much less successful, and the fight for a new generation of aircraft carriers against the provision of land-based long-range fighter aircraft based on the few islands remaining in the Indian Ocean under British sovereignty ended with both going down in the wake of the decision to withdraw from east of Suez in 1958. In the United States, the air force faced similar problems with the abolition of Skybolt and the gradual obsolescence of the air forces's role in strategic deterrence. The air force retaliated with its attempt to win the Vietnam War by "bombing the country back into the stone age," a policy so redolent to the mindset of the American military and so irrelevant to the conditions on the ground that it is hardly surprising that it was no more successful than the army's reliance on firepower including the airborne firepower of the helicopter gunship.

Since 1990, advocates of victory through airpower have used the development of the so-called smart bomb and the even smarter air-to-ground missile to revive the 1920s idea of "imperial policing" (though such terminology is resolutely abhored) through the use of airpower. Once again, exaggerated claims as to the accuracy and efficacy of airpower employed on its own are far from having been shown to be justified. The alleged "smartness" of the missiles is vulnerable to electronic countermeasures, can be no smarter than the available target intelligence, and on the evidence of the film cameras carried in the American attacks on Tripoli, suffers from the instability of the launching platform if that is subject to hostile counterfire. Bismarck's famous adage "You can do anything with bayonets, except sit on them" still seems to retain its power even with the kind of modern missile of which it is said that you only need to write the address on its warhead, and it is certain to reach its target, something one wishes were true of the electronic postal services of today.[16] Critics, aware of these problems, found it easy to denounce the use of airpower alone against the recent Public Enemy No. 1, Saddam Hussein's Iraq, as a policy of gesture. In Britain, there was an equally bitter debate between those who thought the use of attack from the air against Milosevic Serbia without UN authorization immoral, cowardly, and wrong and those who felt that Serbian action against the Albanian majority in Kosovo put Serbian forces outside the boundaries applicable to civilized opponents and advocated the preparation of NATO ground forces for invasion.

SUMMARY

The nature and forms of international conflict have gone through a great metamorphosis in the twentieth century from bilateral traditional battlefield conflict through worldwide total war requiring the full mobilization of all the resources of the belligerent to the present much more controversial and divided picture. One side of this divide is filled with weapons of mass destruction so devastating and long-lasting in their effects as to make their employment of no advantage to those who possess them. The other side has itself divided again. One division leads to bilateral (and occasional multilateral) conflicts fought with weapons of ever-increasing sophistication and cost by middle-ranking powers (and occasionally between a middle-ranking power and a first-division power or powers). Others have led to conflicts of decolonization, neocolonialism, and military interventionism and increasingly to long, drawn-out civil wars where local patterns of society and the law and order that used to be based on them have disintegrated into permanent chaos, of the kind that the Greeks used to call "stasis."

These conditions have produced an equal bifurcation among the established first-division and would-be first-division powers. The one fork has led to the development at enormous expense of weapons that have no practical use in war but are acquired as a threat or as a deterrent to their use of others. The other leads to the development of cheap and nasty infantry weapons with a high rate of fire, special rapid intervention forces, and an unhappy absence of victory-winning strategies between the born troublemakers of the world and the UN-appointed police powers. In the twentieth century war as such became criminalized, and most conflicts fought under conditions that lacked any widely accepted legal basis such as had been established by treaty in the nineteenth century to obtain between civilized states. As a result, these latest of neomodern conflicts are accompanied, if not actually dominated, by measures against the nonmilitary populations that match the worst excesses of the total wars of the first half of the century—massacre, genocide, ethnic cleansing, the conscription and corruption of the young, the creation of armies of uncivilized condottiere, living by rape, loot, and extortion from disarmed and totally demoralized populations. There is very little glorious about war in the years before the millennium. But then they are not wars as the term was conceived in the year 1900.

NOTES

1. For a discussion of these issues, see Alfred Streim, "Das Völkerrecht und die sowjetischen Kriegsgefangenen," in Bernd Wegner, ed., *Zwei Wege nach Moskau: Vom Hitler-Stalin-pakt bis zum "Unternehmen Barbarossa"* (München, 1991), 291–308 and the sources therein cited.

2. Nigel West, *The Secret War for the Falklands* (London, 1997).

3. For details, see D. Cameron Watt, *How War Came: The Immediate Origins of the Second World War, 1938–1939* (New York, 1989), 541–42.

4. On the drafting of the Nuremberg indictment, see Bradley F. Smith *Reaching Judgment at Nuremberg* (New York: Basic Books, 1977). On the process at Tokyo, see D.C. Watt, Introduction to John R. Pritchard, ed., *The Tokyo War Crimes Trials* (New York, 1981). See also Arieh J. Kochavi, *Nuremberg; Allied War Crimes Policy and the Question of Punishment* (Chapel Hill, NC, 1999).

5. For a discussion of this point, see D. Cameron Watt, "1939 Revisited. On Theories of the Origins of Wars," *International Affairs*, 65.4 (Autumn 1989), 685–692.

6. Private information from the late Captain Steven Roskill, Royal Navy official historian of the *War at Sea*.

7. See Sean Maloney, *Securing Command of the Sea* (Annapolis, MD, 1989).

8. Sir Halford Mackinder, *Democratic Ideals and Reality* (London, 1909). Mackinder's work was reprinted during the Second World War and exercised a pro-

found influence over professional American thought when the confrontation with the Soviet Union seemed to be unavoidable.

9. Michael Dewar, *Brush Fire Wars: Minor Campaigns of the British Army since 1945* (London, 1984).

10. The preferred method of Ho Chi Minh's forces in the earlier stages of the war with the French in Indo-China, 1946–1950. See Dennis Duncanson, *Revolution in Indo-China* (London, 1966).

11. *Dewar, Brush Fire Wars*, passim. Colin McInnes, *Hot War, Cold War: The British Army's Way in Warfare 1945–95* (London, 1996). For a photographic record, see John Pimlott, ed., *British Military Operations 1945–1985* (London, 1986).

12. See John M. Blum, *V Was for Victory* (New York, 1976).

13. So too had the regime of Mr. Smith's Rhodesia. Barbara Cole, *The Elite: The Story of the Rhodesian Special Air Service* (London, 1984). This unit was employed to strike at the bases of Rhodesian nationalist guerrillas in the adjoining countries of Malawi, Botswana, Zambia, and Mozambique. The North Korean government has also developed special forces on the model of the Soviet Spetznaz and used them against South Korean targets.

14. On Carlos, see John Follain, *Jackal: The Secret Wars of Carlos the Jackal* (London, 1998).

15. D. Cameron Watt, "British Intervention in East Africa: An Essay in Strategic Mobility," *Revue Militaire Générale*, 5 (May 1966), 606–18.

16. As was noted earlier, the effectiveness of the use of high-level air attack against targets in Serbia and Kosovo in finally securing the withdrawal of Serb forces from Kosovo is still under investigation by the appropriate authorities.

CHAPTER 2

Disarmament, Arms Control, and Arms Reduction

Erik Goldstein

The twentieth century has been the most violent century, but, conversely, it has also witnessed the greatest efforts to control, reduce, or even abolish the tools of violence. Disarmament, arms control, and arms reduction are all variants of a common policy objective aimed at limiting or reducing the weaponry at the disposal of states. The twentieth century has seen arms races, first in naval weaponry and then in nuclear weaponry; the expense and potential destructiveness of these races led in turn to efforts at control. Two world wars were followed by attempts at disarmament of the aggressor states. If no century has survived more warfare than the twentieth, likewise none has made such efforts at control and disarmament.

The roots of disarmament are to be found in antiquity when it was commonplace to demand the disarmament of recently defeated foes in the interest of future security.[1] The Romans disarmed some of their defeated adversaries literally, on one occasion chopping off an arm from each captured Gallic soldier. History is replete with military mutilations, a product of times when the soldier was the weapon, and mutilations continue in parts of the world where this is still the case.

Napoleon can be considered the progenitor of modern disarmament, or rather of numeric disarmament. Prior to Napoleon it was a rarity to limit the size of a defeated state's army. In 1808 France imposed upon Prussia a limit of 42,000 soldiers, while in the following year a limit of

150,000 soldiers was imposed upon Austria.[2] At this stage in the history of disarmament the objective remained to limit the number of effective soldiers available to potential adversaries. This was to change as the industrial revolution increased the importance of weaponry, and the twentieth century in turn tried to extend disarmament efforts to weaponry as well as soldiers.

Arms control has a different genesis from that of disarmament, being primarily a twentieth-century phenomenon with some nineteenth-century antecedents. One of the earliest instances of attempts at arms control occurred in the aftermath of the Napoleonic wars when the Russian czar, Alexander I, proposed to the British foreign secretary, Lord Castlereagh, an international agreement on arms control. The proposal met with little enthusiasm, but it proved to be the beginning of a string of nineteenth-century efforts to deal with the issue of arms control.[3] In 1849 the new French government of Louis Napoleon Bonaparte proposed to Britain, as its first initiative, discussions on naval disarmament, an initiative that did not attract the interest of Lord Palmerston, the foreign secretary. In 1863 the now Emperor Napoleon III proposed a conference to discuss arms reduction, but, as this was linked to proposals to revise the map of Europe, this initiative too was dismissed.[4] The first substantive step toward arms control was proposed by Russian czar, Nicholas II in 1899 when he called together the first Hague Conference, part of whose remit was to discuss "the most effective means of assuring for all the peoples the blessings of real and lasting peace, and, above all things, for fixing a limit to the progressive development of present armaments."[5] The Russian initiative seized the public imagination, generating a popular enthusiasm similar to that witnessed during the Cold War with the peace movement and its attendant peace marches. In support of the czar's efforts, Wickam Steed, later to be editor of *The Times* (of London), organized a "Pilgrimage of Peace." It should be noted that the idea for the Hague Conference was not based upon pure altruism on the czar's part but was linked to concerns about a potential arms race with Austria-Hungary over new, quick-firing artillery, an arms race Russia could ill afford.[6] At the Hague Conference Russia did make arms control proposals, but these were rejected and the issue was left for further consideration. It is worthwhile to note that at the Hague Conference no technical advisers were present, a development that would only slowly become commonplace with the evolution of arms control efforts. The second Hague Conference, held in 1907, made attempts to limit the use of marine mines and torpedoes. Between them the Hague Conferences marked the beginning of substantive arms control efforts, though with limited success. The first Hague Conference agreed to prohibit dum dum bullets, though Italy would use them in Ethiopia in 1935–1936, and to prohibit the use of poison gas, though it would be used by Britain, France, and

Germany during the First World War; and it even attempted to control aerial arms by limiting the throwing of missiles from balloons. Looming behind the concerns of governments at the Hague Conference was a mounting concern with a new phenomenon—the arms race.

The increasing rate and quality of production of weapons systems, which technology had made possible, helped to spur the calls for arms control. The arms control talks of the first half of the twentieth century mostly concerned naval inventories, with naval vessels being to the pre-1945 world what nuclear weapons would be to the post-1945 world. The twentieth century thus started with a major arms race that can be viewed as the prototypical arms race of the century—the Anglo-German naval arms race. Beginning with the German decision in 1898 to build a high seas battle fleet, which could at least challenge British naval supremacy, its tempo increased as both sides escalated their rates of naval construction. This arms race escalated dramatically in 1906 with the launching by Britain of HMS *Dreadnought*, a major leap in naval technology that rendered existing battleships obsolete. Germany was soon able to compete with this technology, allowing an arms race for supremacy in numbers to ensue. This was the beginning of weapons counting, as in the missile races of the Cold War period, where power was assessed by the numbers of a particular class of weapon possessed. Winston Churchill recalled, "The Admiralty had demanded six ships: the economists offered four: and we finally compromised on eight."[7] Arms races, and their attendant expense, are the usual precursor and spur to efforts at arms control.

DISARMAMENT AND UTOPIANISM

One of the strands in the history of arms control and disarmament is the utopian vision of a world without armaments or armed forces. The emergence of a peace movement, which among its aims sought disarmament, had three points of origins: (1) pacifist religious movements, (2) utilitarians (e.g., Jeremy Bentham) who focused on economy and efficiency in society, and (3) radicals who saw the military as tools of governing regimes. All three retained a certain currency throughout the twentieth century.

Early publicists provided schemes for international peace. Notably Immanuel Kant, in his *Perpetual Peace: A Philosophical Essay*, proposed a scheme that would include the eventual disappearance of armies.[8] Jeremy Bentham likewise proposed severe arms reduction in his *Plan for an Universal and Perpetual Peace*.[9] Bentham wrote that "whatsoever nation should get the start of the other in making the proposal to reduce and fix the amount of its armed force, would crown itself with everlasting glory."[10] In 1843 the first Universal Peace Congress met in London, organized by the American and British Peace Societies.[11] The roots of these societies can be found in pacifist sects, such as the Quakers, though by the mid-nineteenth century these ideas attracted others as well, becoming in the process more internationalist. These early peace movements influenced thinking on international relations, and liberal thinking, with figures such as Richard Cobden favoring the abolition of weapons. In 1851 Cobden moved in the House of Commons the first ever resolution in a Parliament for arms reduction.[12] Such views were not confined to the political fringe. Sir Robert Peel, on the eve of becoming prime minister, told the House of Commons in 1841:

Is not the time come, when the powerful countries of Europe should reduce those military armaments which they have so sedulously raised? Is not the time come, when they should be prepared to declare that there is no use in such overgrown establishments? What is the advantage of one Power greatly increasing its army or navy? Does it not see, that if it possesses such increase for self-protection and defence, the other powers would follow its example? The consequence of this state of things must be that no increase of relative strength will accrue to any one power, but there must be a universal consumption of the resources of every country, in military preparations.

Peel concluded that "the true interest of Europe is to come to some one common accord, so as to enable every country to reduce those military armaments which belong to a state of war rather than of peace."[13] Organizations to promote peace flourished by the turn of the twentieth century, examples being the World Peace Foundation headquartered in Boston and the Carnegie Endowment for International Peace located in Washington. These ideas would find their way into aspects of the liberal political spectrum and later, through them, to successor political movements.

Liberalism was a potent force in the promotion of arms reduction. Arthur Link has observed that "all international liberals were convinced that the existence of large armies and navies was a prime cause of conflict."[14] They therefore advocated sweeping reductions in armaments. The First World War and the creation of a League of Nations provided an opportunity and a mechanism for attempting voluntary arms reduction and even disarmament.[15] The League of Nations spent a good part of its existence attempting to work out a scheme for general disarmament, very much in line with earlier liberal aspirations. The utopian dimension would also continue in tandem with applied efforts at arms control, such as during the Cold War era the popular campaigns to "Ban the Bomb."

The peace movement continued under various names and has remained a part of the political landscape, forming one of the many pressure groups governments have needed to be aware of. In Germany in 1998 a government was formed for the first time in a major state in which one of the coalition partners, the Greens, favored disarmament. The British Labour government formed in 1997 included several figures at one time associated with the Campaign for Nuclear Disarmament (CND).[16]

One aspect of the peace movement has been the attempt to make military force redundant through efforts to outlaw war. These efforts reached their culmination with the 1928 Kellogg-Briand Pact, signed at Paris, by which the signatories agreed to "condemn recourse to war for the solution of international controversies, and renounce it as an instrument of national policy in their relations with one another."[17] These liberal ideas also influenced more pragmatic efforts at arms control.

ARMS CONTROL: THE FIRST PHASE

The first phase of arms control efforts occurred from the turn of the twentieth century to the outbreak of the First World War. These attempts at arms control were part of the swansong of the liberal tide that had swept across Europe during the nineteenth century and that reached its high watermark in the years before the First World War, when liberal governments dominated most of the European world. The Liberal government in Britain, which governed from 1906 to 1916, sought to confront the problem of the arms race. The foreign secretary, Edward Grey, hoped to find a way to "control this enormous burden of expenditure which if it goes on increasing will undermine the financial position of the leading countries of Europe and impoverish them."[18] Britain sought to find a modus vivendi with Germany, to avoid an expensive arms race before embarking on a large construction program. These efforts ultimately failed and the naval arms race continued, its outcome being decided by the First World War and the destruction of the German high seas fleet. The end of the war saw a partial fusion for a period of the ideas of arms control and disarmament.

DISARMAMENT: THE INTERWAR EFFORTS

The cataclysm of the First World War caused a strong desire on the part of many to ensure that such a war could never occur again. One young British diplomat who attended the postwar Paris Peace Conference, Harold Nicolson, commented, "We were preparing not Peace only, but Eternal Peace."[19] As a first step toward ensuring international peace, the victorious powers sought to disarm Germany and its allies. In the Treaty of Versailles, Germany's forces were to be strictly limited, with its army not to exceed 100,000 soldiers, its navy limited to six battleships, and its air force to be abolished. The Treaty of Versailles was a landmark in disarmament negotiations, being the first time technical advisers assisted in the negotiations, and their imprint is to be found in the treaty's detailed limitations on all dimensions of the future German military establishment. One historian has observed that

> every essential problem connected with military power and armaments was covered in detail, including the question of conscription, the size of armies and navies, the problems of communication and blockade, the use of new instrumentalities of war, such as aeroplanes, wireless telegraph, poison gases, and submarines, as well as the principles of executing arms limitation.[20]

The negotiations over the disarmament of the Central powers would form the basis of arms limitation discussions in years that followed. It also saw the development of a professional group whose careers were mostly spent on arms control and disarmament.

Disarmament of the wartime Central powers was meant as a prelude to more general disarmament. Part V of the Treaty of Versailles opened with the statement, "In order to render possible the initiation of a general limitation of the armaments of all nations, Germany undertakes strictly to observe the military, naval and air clauses which follow." Aimed initially at eliminating German military power and ensuring the security of the victors, this preamble to the disarmament clauses also states the intention of using the enforced disarmament of the defeated states as a platform on which to erect a wider arms limitation regime. In their reply to Germany's observations on these terms, the Allied and Associated powers stated that these conditions were "the first steps toward that general reduction and limitation of armaments which they seek to bring about as one of the most fruitful preventives of war, and which will be one of the first duties of the League of Nations to promote."[21] While both the United States and Great Britain significantly reduced their military establishments, France in particular refused to do so, largely out of concern that Germany might not be fully adhering to the limits placed upon its forces.

The problem of verification was, and remains, one of the chief problems in implementing disarmament or arms control agreements. Verification of the Versailles obligations was to be accomplished through Inter-Allied Control Commissions supervising the military, naval, and air clauses. By Article 213 of the Versailles treaty Germany undertook "to give every facility for any investigation which the Council of the League of Nations, acting if need be by a majority vote, may consider necessary."

The League of Nations body for dealing with such matters was its Permanent Advisory Committee for Military, Naval, and Air Questions. By a resolution on March 14, 1925, commissions of investigation, which were always to be made up of experts of three different nationalities, were given extensive rights of entry and search and full diplomatic immunity and privileges.[22] This, however, was the apogee of attempting a rigorous verification regime.[23]

Germany, under both Weimar and Nazi regimes, sought to escape the restrictions imposed upon it.[24] Verification proved to be difficult to implement. The International Military Control Commission inspectors faced continual lack of cooperation and frequent popular hostility, and in 1924 some inspectors were even attacked by a mob. The inspectors' report sent to the Allied governments in February 1925 provided a list of breaches of Germany's obligations, including the militarization of the police, arms works that had not been converted to other uses, the effective reestablishment of a general staff, and military equipment retained in excess of permitted limits. This showed the difficulty "of preventing evasion of disarmament provisions, even when a Commission of Control was permanently resident in the country concerned."[25] Simultaneously with the Control Commission's investigations, Germany, under the guidance of Gustav Stresseman, adopted a policy of cooperation in foreign policy, a conciliatory approach that resulted in its rehabilitation and admittance to the League of Nations in the Locarno pact of 1925.

The diplomatic rapprochement of the western European powers that culminated in the Locarno pact of 1925 saw the effective winding up of the remaining control commission activity. Despite the International Military Control Commission's (IMCC) report, there is no trace of concern in British official circles. There was a firm belief that Stresseman's, and Germany's, intentions were good. In return for Germany's willing reaffirmation of its acceptance of the borders of western Europe, the International Military Control Commission was withdrawn from Germany. In December 1926 Germany successfully negotiated the termination of the IMCC with effect from January 31, 1927, despite the fact that in the week preceding the agreement *The Guardian* had published an exposé of German violations.[26] In its final report the IMCC states, "Germany had never disarmed, had never had the intention of disarming, and for seven years had done everything in her power to deceive and 'counter-control' the Commission appointed to control her disarmament."[27] Although the right of investigation remained, only one case was brought to the League's attention, when a shipment of five carloads of machine-gun parts, falsely marked "machine parts," was stopped by Austrian customs on its way from Italy to Hungary (January 1, 1928).

Control of German obligations slowly drifted. On June 18, 1935, Britain concluded a bilateral naval arms agreement with Germany fixing the ratio of their naval vessels at 35:100, in reality voiding the naval clauses imposed on Germany at Versailles. On March 8, 1936, in the first of what would become known as Hitler's weekend surprises, the reestablishment of the German air force was announced. When there was only muted reaction from the major powers a week later, Hitler announced the reintroduction of conscription, which would expand the army from 100,000 to 550,000 soldiers in the first instance. The League of Nations Council adopted a resolution condemning it but took no further action. In effect, by 1936 the clauses of the Versailles treaty mandating the disarmament of Germany had been made inoperative. While an argument might be made that it would be impossible to impose long-term restrictions on such an inherently powerful state, what was in fact collapsing was the will to maintain any part of the post–First World War disarmament regime. In 1938 the military, naval, and air restrictions on Bulgaria were likewise allowed to lapse. This raises the question of how long enforced disarmament can be maintained. The historical record does not provide examples exceeding sixteen years.

ARMS LIMITATION: THE INTERWAR PERIOD

The year 1899 saw the publication of I.S. Bloch's *The Future of War*, in which Bloch argues that technology now made war impossible, as war would be too destructive. The eve of the First World War witnessed the publication of Norman Angell's *The Great Illusion*, a bestseller that argued that war had been made obsolete. The First World War, however, while disproving the impossibility of war, bore out the arguments made in both books about the destructiveness of modern warfare. In Britain the war led to the founding of the Union for Democratic Control (UDC), which was dominated by radical liberals and socialists such as Norman Angell, E.D. Morel, and Arthur Ponsonby. As part of their program for a postwar order, they proposed general disarmament. These, or similar views, can be found in the pronouncements of the American president Woodrow Wilson.

Wilson, a transatlantic Gladstonian liberal, was concerned about the general level of armaments and was an advocate of arms control. During the First World War he observed, in the context of the problem of freedom of the seas,

It is a problem closely connected with the limitation of naval armaments and the cooperation of the navies of the world in keeping the seas at once free and safe. And the question of limiting armaments opens the wider and perhaps more difficult question of the limitation of armies and of all programmes of military preparation. . . . The question of armaments, whether on land or sea, is the most immediately and intensely practical question connected with the future fortunes of nations and of mankind.[28]

It is therefore not surprising to find in his speech of the Fourteen Points, outlining his scheme for a postwar order, that point four calls for "Ad-

Disarmament

equate guarantees given and taken that national armaments will be reduced to the lowest point consistent with domestic safety."[29] After the war, Article VIII of the Covenant of the League of Nations recognized that "the maintenance of peace requires the reduction of national armaments to the lowest point consistent with national safety," and the Council was charged to "formulate plans for such reduction."

The interwar period saw two types of approach to arms control, in part because of American nonadhesion to the League of Nations. The first was type-specific, through either bilateral or small group multilateral negotiations, and the second was general comprehensive negotiations intended for universal application. This is a pattern that has continued in varying degrees ever since. The type-specific negotiations began almost immediately while the League of Nations was finding its feet and getting established. The drive for arms control continued, with discussions outside the League, in part because of U.S. nonmembership.

TYPE-SPECIFIC ARMS CONTROL

In the aftermath of the First World War, with other adversaries removed, the United States and Britain found themselves facing a new naval arms race, at a time when both governments wanted to cut expenditure. Ships were by far the most costly defense expenditure, and if a solution could be found that met their security concerns, the resultant savings would be welcome.

The Washington Naval Treaty of 1922 and the follow-on London Naval Treaties of 1930 and 1936 faced very similar difficulties to those posed during the Cold War in United States–Soviet strategic arms limitation negotiations.[30] The Washington Conference solution was to set a ratio between the capital ships of the major naval powers, the United States, Britain, Japan, France, and Italy, of 5:5:3:1.7:1.7. This ratio related to upper ceilings in total tonnage of capital ships, allowing for a ceiling of 525,000 tons, 315,000 tons, and 175,000 tons. A maximum tonnage for individual ships was set at 35,000, with no guns to exceed sixteen inches in caliber.

Hedley Bull identified several similarities between the Washington process and the Strategic Arms Limitations Talks (SALT), which help to provide a baseline in understanding the necessary ingredients of an arms control negotiation.[31] (1) The naval treaty was the result of realistic efforts to establish formal limitation of a particular category of armaments of major strategic importance. Here a parallel can be drawn with the SALT talks, which produced results, rather than with the desultory and ineffective attempts during 1946–1960 for general arms control.[32] Bull suggests that part of the lesson is accepting partial arms limitation rather than comprehensive limitation. (2) The naval treaties were concerned with quantitative limitations, which were dealt with at the Washington Conference by employing a ratio. This caused difficulties, as Japan was unhappy with the implied inferiority of its lower ranking, with one diplomat complaining that a ratio of 5:5:3 sounded similar to Rolls Royce: Rolls Royce:Ford. (3) In attempting to deal with the ratio problem the concept of parity was used, as it was later used in SALT. (4) The negotiations concerned the major powers, but the armaments of lesser powers affected assessments of the major powers. (5) The naval arms negotiations, as with SALT, were part of a wider and longer effort. (6) The naval arms negotiations, as with SALT, assumed verification would not require formal inspection. Winston Churchill, a veteran of several arms races and arms control efforts, warned in 1959, "We must above all resist any temptation to rush into agreements which do not provide a workable system of inspection and control. Not to be firm on this principle would be a fatal error."[33]

Walter Lippmann summed up the approach of the Washington Conference as, "Big warships meant big wars. Smaller warships meant smaller wars. No warships might mean no wars."[34] The United States and Britain took advantage of the Washington–London Conference system to reduce spending, and overall spending fell almost immediately and did not reach pretreaty levels until 1938–1939. Attention, however, was shifted to other classes of vessel. In 1927–1928 Anglo-American cruiser competition was developing, which required further talks to resolve. During the period of the Washington Conference system the major naval states would actively continue building in allowed categories, the United States constructing 16 ships, Britain 37 ships, and Japan 116 ships. Japan would use its now higher actual number of noncapital ships in the next round of talks at London in 1930 to achieve a better deal. It demanded, and got, a ratio in cruisers of 7:10 rather than the 6:10 of Washington. Its active naval building meant that by 1934 the Imperial Japanese Navy had reached 80 percent of that of the U.S. Navy, and indeed by 1941 it had achieved parity with the U.S. Navy and the Royal Navy in the Pacific. These developments were happening against a wider political backdrop with changing strategic circumstances, to which both the United States and Britain were slow to react.

The Washington and London naval treaties of 1922 and 1930 were the only serious attempts to limit important classes of weaponry until the SALT agreement of 1972. The Washington and London talks were even more complex, as they involved five states rather than only two. The legacy of the Washington and London talks is still a matter of debate.

GENERAL ARMS CONTROL

Efforts at general arms control agreements, done for the most part through the League of Nations, enjoyed some success. One example was the 1925 Geneva Protocol, which prohibited the use of poison gas and bacteriological weapons. The chief effort of the League, though, was what is commonly known as the Geneva Disarmament Conference, though its official title was the Conference for the Reduction and Limitation of Armaments. The difference in the title indicates how readily the nomenclature was mixed. This conference was preceded by a Preparatory Commission to lay the groundwork, which first met in 1926 and completed its work in 1930.[35] The conference itself held its first meeting in 1932 and adjourned without a result. It then spent half of 1932 trying to reconcile differences, met again for the first half of 1933, but was then adjourned for the World Economic Conference. Its last session met in October 1933 and it finally adjourned on June 11, 1934, without result. One subcommittee of the conference reportedly "used 3,750,000 sheets of typescript, 'enough to enable the Polish or Swedish delegation to walk home on a path made of League paper.'"[36]

Lord Stanhope, one of the British delegates, reported to the prime minister, Stanley Baldwin, in 1932 of progress in the disarmament talks at Geneva,

I always thought that I was rather a master at wasting time, but I have learned that I was a mere tyro. Our committee on guns spent 2 hours in discussing whether we were justified in discussing a subject they had been talking about for 2 days, but even this was beaten by another committee who required a definition of the word "definition." The chemical warfare committee is going quite well, as the scientists forget that they are French or German or what-not, & so discuss things on reasonable lines. I think that they will produce a unanimous report. The Air Committee still up in the air & likely to remain there. The Naval people are drafting their report which I gather will be a wishy-washy document. The Budgetary people & the "Effectives" are both deep in figures & will be old men before they produce anything at present rate of progress. The Land Committee is marvelous. There are some 55 nations, most of whom attend, & most of them bring 3 or 4 delegates. We sit under the Presidency of a Uruguayan who, as a matter of fact, is quite a good little fellow. On *every* question they divide into 3 or 4 groups or, perhaps I ought to say 4—the Soviet for abolishing everything—their Delegate is a nasty-looking piece of work.... Then comes the German-Austrian-Hungarian group (with Italy) for abolishing everything they themselves are not allowed, and at the other end the French & their group who wish to abolish nothing & make constant allusions to a League Army. We & the Yanks come between the last 2 big groups. The result is 4 separate recommendations to the General Commission.[37]

Alfred Zimmern, an active and perceptive analyst of international affairs in this period, observed of the final failure of the conference, "To expect to arrive at a Disarmament Treaty between fifty States, or between the Great Powers alone, upon a competitive basis of this kind was to expect to succeed in squaring the circle."[38]

QUALITATIVE DISARMAMENT

One important idea that was tested at Geneva, as an attempt to break through the logjam of difficulties that were immobilizing the general conference, was that of qualitative arms control. This was proposed by British Foreign Secretary Sir John Simon. The Preparatory Commission had thought in quantitative terms, while the Simon proposal looked to prohibiting the types of weaponry that could be considered offensive, rather than defensive. Initially well received, it foundered on the delegates' inability to agree on what was an offensive, as opposed to a defensive, weapon. For example, the United States and Britain saw battleships and submarines as defensive, while many other states saw them as offensive. It has been observed that "the category to which a weapon could be assigned depended upon the end of it at which one was standing."[39]

The idea of qualitative disarmament was one, though, that retained a certain attraction for some politicians. Then British Prime Minister Neville Chamberlain, in 1937, explained:

As for disarmament I believe we should do much better if we tried for qualitative rather than quantitative restrictions of material. An agreement to do away with tanks & aeroplanes over a certain weight or guns over a certain calibre on the lines of the Washington Naval Agreement would be easier to achieve & to supervise than any limitation of numbers.[40]

He also knew it was easier for the general public to understand and therefore more useful to advocate. Land mines are the more recent focus of such efforts, with most states able to agree that they are offensive weapons and should be banned, but the United States has utilized large numbers of such mines to protect South Korea from North Korea and argues for their utility as defensive weapons, at least in this instance. As a result, it is impossible to achieve consensus on this matter.

ARMS CONTROL: THE INTERWAR YEARS

Hitler's rise to power in 1933 effectively ended hopes of achieving agreement on arms reduction. Soon it would be a matter of *rearmament* in a different strategic climate. The arms control efforts of the 1920s achieved some limited success on naval matters, but none when it came to land and air forces. In the more stable international climate then prevailing, the United States and Britain took the opportunity to reduce their armies to about 100,000 soldiers each, but the other Great Powers, such as France and Italy, did not do so.

The 1920s saw liberal democracy emerge as the predominant international ideology, while the 1930s saw a transition to authoritarian regimes in many countries. This, in turn, altered the political-strategic realities and resulted in a growth in armaments. The arms control process lingered on while the transition from democracies to autocracies became evident, slowly tailing off. Winston Churchill, who in the safer climate of the 1920s had advocated sharp reductions in armaments, was one of many political leaders who now adapted their views to the new international climate, as rearmament became a necessity of national security.

DISARMAMENT: POST–SECOND WORLD WAR ERA

The aftermath of the Second World War saw a brief return to enforced disarmament, in this instance of the defeated Axis powers.[41] Germany was disarmed in 1945 through 1954, though some restrictions remained in place until 1984. Japan was likewise disarmed in the 1945–1950 period. Washington informed General MacArthur as he went to assume command in Tokyo in 1945, "Disarmament and demilitarization are the primary tasks of the military occupation."[42] It was felt in the case of Japan that the militaristic nature of society had to be changed, and demilitarization was part of this process. The 1947 Japanese constitution, drafted by American-Japanese agreement, enshrined the concept of a demilitarized Japan. This, however, was later modified to allow for the creation of a Japanese Self-Defense Force.

More recently, in the wake of the 1990–1991 Gulf War, Iraq became the object of an attempt at enforced disarmament. The terms for the cessation of hostilities, laid down for Iraq in UN Security Council resolution 687 of April 3, 1991, included the destruction of any nuclear, biological, or chemical weapons. Iraq's possession of such weaponry should have already been precluded by earlier international agreements, as biological weapons were banned by the 1925 Geneva Protocol and the 1972 Biological Weapons Convention, while Iraq was also a signatory to the 1968 Nuclear Non-Proliferation Treaty. The United Nations provided personnel for the verification of Iraq's compliance with the terms of the cease-fire agreement. The result of efforts to maintain enforcement of the disarmament provisions of the cease-fire, and the necessity of using inspectors for verification, has led to a series of crises and confrontations as Iraq probes the durability of the powers' willingness to maintain the sanctions regime. Iraq's attempts to circumvent the terms imposed upon it, and its unhappiness at the presence of the UN inspectors, bear a close resemblance to that experienced by the inspectors deployed in Germany after the First World War. It was a taxing game of cat and mouse in full play at century's end.

ARMS CONTROL: SINCE THE SECOND WORLD WAR

The main attempts at arms control after the Second World War focused on nuclear weapons and the systems related to them. Although the U.S.-Soviet nuclear arms race began to escalate in the 1950s, it was not until the early 1960s that serious efforts were made at arms control. As had happened previously the various arms races of the Cold War in turn led to efforts at arms control. The work of such analysts as Albert Wohlstetter that marked the beginning of a new phase in the study of arms control now focused on the issue of nuclear weaponry.[43] The United States established an Arms Control and Disarmament Agency in 1961 and began to spawn a whole new discipline of arms control that fed into the policy process.

Sometimes, though, states cannot wait for the long process of arms control talks to reach fruition, particularly if serious economic problems confront them. Soviet leader Mikhail Gorbachev attempted at the 1986 Reykjavik summit with President Ronald Reagan to end the Soviet-American arms race that threatened to cripple the Soviet Union if it continued. When that failed, Gorbachev, seeing lengthy and highly technical talks stretching out into the future, was forced to begin a series of deep cuts to the Soviet military.[44] In effect the Soviet Union was forced to opt for unilateral arms reduction. After the final collapse of the Soviet Union in 1991 the pace of such unilateral arms reduction increased among many of its successor states. The once vaunted Red Navy was left, due to insufficient funds for maintenance, to gently, if toxically, rust at anchor. One indicator of the changed atmosphere in the absence of any nuclear arms race was the decision by the United States in 1999 to wind up its Arms Control and Disarmament Agency.

DISARMAMENT: VOLUNTARY AND GENERAL

Voluntary disarmament by a state is very rare but has occurred. Lichtenstein's army was allowed slowly to disappear through no new recruitments and finally ceased to exist on the death of its last soldier. Costa Rica made the decision in 1949 to abolish its military. Ukraine, after independence in 1991, found itself the heir of a portion of the former Soviet nuclear arsenal. These were decommissioned and Ukraine became a nonnuclear state in 1996. Iceland, though a member of the North Atlantic Treaty Organization (NATO), has pursued since independence a policy of nonarmament and has never possessed a military force. These instances, though, are unilateral decisions by the states concerned and were not the result of any multilateral arrangement.

ARMS CONTROL AND DISARMAMENT BY INTERNATIONAL ORGANIZATION

Arms control, disarmament, and peacekeeping operations with arms control responsibilities utilizing international organizations, particularly the United Nations, have become more common since the end of the Cold War.[45] The United Nations has mandated arms embargoes, examples being those imposed upon Libya and Haiti. The terms of the embargo on Libya called upon all states to

[p]rohibit any provision to Libya by their nationals or from their territory of arms and related material of all types, including the sale or transfer of weapons and ammunition, military vehicles and equipment, paramilitary police equipment and spare parts for the aforementioned.[46]

A UN committee was established to monitor the embargo. Peacekeeping operations in parts of the former Yugoslavia included blockading weapons and arms collection. Disarmament has been part of the task assigned to UN peacekeepers operating in Cambodia and Mozambique, as well as the more extensive operation concerning Iraq.

DEMILITARIZED ZONES

Demilitarized zones, that is, areas from which the deployment of any soldiers or military weaponry have been banned, are usually brought about as an aspect of enforced disarmament. The Rhineland was demilitarized 1919–1936 as part of the terms imposed upon Germany by the Treaty of Versailles. Its remilitarization by an unopposed, unilateral German decision was an important step in the general unwinding of the enforced disarmament of Germany. The Rhineland crisis of 1936 raised the issue of how much force, and for how long, the signatories of the Versailles treaty were willing to use force to maintain the settlement. The same problem arises in all cases of enforced disarmament when the state in question wishes ultimately to see such strictures eliminated. More recently, the issue has arisen with the no-fly zones over Iraq from which the Iraqi air force is banned. In this case, the powers enforcing the UN resolution have taken action when Iraq has sought to violate the cease-fire terms. One factor in determining the willingness of states to maintain such enforced disarmament agreements is the economic climate. It is far easier for the United States, at the peak of its strongest-ever economic boom, to decide to take action against Iraq, when necessary, than for the Allied powers to maintain the Treaty of Versailles in the depths of the economic depression of the 1930s.

GEOGRAPHICALLY DEFINED ARMS CONTROL

The oldest example of a geographically defined arms control regime is the 1817 Anglo-American Rush-Bagot agreement that limited the deployment of naval vessels on the Great Lakes to four vessels each, not to exceed 100 tons, with cannon not to exceed eighteen pounds. This agreement was later revised and updated as circumstances and technology changed but otherwise remains in force as the longest-running such agreement.[47] The 1936 Montreux Convention sought to limit the deployment of ships in the Black Sea of nonlittoral states. There were four key points relating to this: (1) The aggregate tonnage of ships was not to exceed 30,000 tons (later increased to 45,000); (2) no nonlittoral state could deploy ships with a gross tonnage of more than two thirds of this figure; (3) the Turkish government could on humanitarian grounds allow in ships, provided they did not exceed 8,000 tons; and (4) no warship was to remain in the Black Sea for more than twenty-one days. The convention's classification of warships was copied verbatim from the 1936 London Naval Arms Limitation Treaty. Although the Montreux Convention was generally ignored during the Second World War, and it expired in 1956, states have continued to act as if it were in force.[48]

The Nyon Agreement of 1937 was an attempt to control submarine deployment in the Mediterranean. It was signed by nine states, and Britain and France were given the right to conduct patrols to verify adherence.[49] It proved to be ineffective in the growing tensions leading up to the Second World War and ended with the outbreak of the war. Britain and France never seriously exercised their rights of inspection. Other attempts at achieving arms control through setting geographical parameters include a discussion between American President Richard Nixon and Soviet leader Leonid Brezhnev in 1974 to denuclearize the Indian Ocean.[50]

Geographical arms control has proven to be successful in several instances, though the existence of a mare clausum, or an almost closed sea, is an important aspect in the success of such agreements. As with all agreements, its maintenance will always depend on the condition of relations between states.

CONCLUSION

Disarmament started as an attempt to limit the size of armies and was later extended to include weapons, until by the end of the twentieth century, as can be seen in the case of Iraq, weapons had become the predominant area of concern. No attempt was made in the 1991 ceasefire agreement to limit the size of the Iraqi army. With the end of the Cold War the international political environment is again closer to that of the post–First World War era. The states of the G7 that dominate the international arena are all liberal democracies. Once again the political currency operates on the basis of liberal democratic ideas, one of which is that democracies are unlikely to go to war with one another. This is seen as an opportunity for arms reduction, and most of the G7 states that maintained significant military forces have greatly reduced them since the end of the Cold War. Current efforts at arms control are aimed at preventing or limiting the spread of highly dangerous categories of weapons, especially nuclear, chemical, and biological weapons. It is one of the paradoxes of the transition in international relations since the end of the Cold War that the desire to achieve arms control and disarmament is itself the justification for military action in Iraq and could conceivably occur over North Korea's nuclear potential. John Maurer has observed that "the plea of disarmament advocates—namely, that weapons themselves cause war—might come to have a new, more ominous meaning."[51]

Arms control, arms reduction, and disarmament have proven to be complex problems on which much effort was expended in the twentieth century, though with only limited success. When Czar Alexander I proposed arms reduction in 1816, Castlereagh responded that such a scheme "presents a very complicated question of negotiation."[52] Henry Kissinger similarly observed that arms control is "so esoteric that it multiplied the anxieties of both policymakers and the public at large."[53] Arms control and disarmament became, at times, a major concern of twentieth-century diplomacy, and the problems of implementation as diplomatists from Castlereagh to Kissinger have observed remain a conundrum for policymakers. Disarmament continues to be a sanction that the international system seeks to impose upon states that have threatened the equilibrium, while arms control and reduction, a much newer phenomenon of international relations, has slowly been evolving as a practicality rather than an aspiration.

NOTES

1. Philip Towle, *Enforced Disarmament from Napoleon to the Gulf War* (Oxford, 1997).

2. Treaty of Paris between France and Prussia, September 8, 1808; Treaty of Vienna between France and Austria, October 27, 1809.

3. Alexander to Castlereagh, April 2, 1816, FO 65/105/private, Foreign Office Papers, Public Record Office, London. See also Alan Palmer, *Alexander I: Tsar of War and Peace* (London, 1974), 354–55; C.K. Webster, *The Foreign Policy of Castlereagh*, vol. 2: *1815–1822: Britain and the European Alliance* (London, 1963), 97–103.

4. William Echard, *Napoleon III and the Concert of Europe* (Baton Rouge, 1983), 193–210.

5. *Annual Register*, 1898 (London, 1899), 149.

6. Thomas Ford, "The Genesis of the First Hague Peace Conference," *Political Science Quarterly*, 51(1936), 354–82.

7. Winston Churchill, *The Great War* (London, 1933), 1:13.

8. Immanuel Kant, *Perpetual Peace: A Philosophical Essay*, M. Campbell Smith, ed. and trans. (London, 1903); originally written in 1795 as *Zum ewigen Frieden*.

9. John Bowring, ed., *The Works of Jeremy Bentham*, vol. 2 (New York, 1962), 546–60.

10. Ibid., 551.

11. F.H. Hinsley, *Power and the Pursuit of Peace: Theory and Practice in the History of Relations between States* (Cambridge, United Kingdom, 1963), 95–96.

12. William Harbutt Dawson, *Richard Cobden and Foreign Policy* (London, 1926), 154–55.

13. W. Cooke Taylor, *Life and Times of Sir Robert Peel* (London, 1851), 3:149.

14. Arthur Link, *Wilson the Diplomatist* (Baltimore, 1957), 92–93.

15. Patrick Glynn, *Closing Pandora's Box: Arms Races, Arms Control, and the History of the Cold War* (New York, 1992), 49–57.

16. Tony Blair, the prime minister, was a member of parliamentary CND until 1986 and the secretary of state for defense; George Robertson was also an active CND supporter.

17. Robert Ferrell, *Peace in Their Time: The Origins of the Kellogg-Briand Pact* (New Haven, CT, 1952). See also J.W. Wheeler-Bennett, *Information on the Renunciation of War, 1927–1928* (London, 1928).

18. Quoted in Andre Sidorowicz, "The British Government, the Hague Peace Conference, and the Armaments Question," in B.J.C. McKercher, ed., *Arms Limitation and Disarmament: Restraints on War, 1899–1939* (Westport, CT, 1992), 3, from FO 800/61, Grey to Lascelles (Berlin), November 12, 1907.

19. Harold Nicolson, *Peacemaking 1919* (Boston, 1933), 32.

20. Gerda Richards Crosby, *Disarmament and Peace in British Politics, 1914–1919* (Cambridge, United Kingdom, 1957), 104.

21. Department of State, *The Treaty of Versailles and After: Annotations of The text of the Treaty* (Washington, DC, 1947), 309.

22. Ibid., 363.

23. The Aeronautical Control Commission was withdrawn in March 1922, although an Aeronautical Committee of Guarantee functioned until August 9, 1926, the Naval Control Commission until September 30, 1924, and the Military Control Commission until January 31, 1927.

24. J.H. Morgan, *Assize of Arms: The Disarmament of Germany and Her Rearmament, 1919–1939* (New York, 1946); John W. Wheeler-Bennet, *The Nemesis of Power: The German Army in Politics, 1918–1945* (London, 1964).

25. C.A. Macartney et al., eds., *Survey of International Affairs, 1925*, (Oxford, 1928), 2:17n.

26. *The Guardian* reports were published on December 6, 1926.

27. Cf. Hans Gatzke, *Stresemann and the Rearmament of Germany* (Baltimore, 1954).

28. Speech to the U.S. Senate, January 22, 1917, in Arthur Link, ed. *The Papers of Woodrow Wilson*, vol. 40: *November 20, 1916–January 23, 1917* (Princeton, NJ, 1982), 538.

29. Arthur Link, ed. *The Papers of Woodrow Wilson*, vol. 45, *November 11, 1917–January 15, 1918* (Princeton, 1984), p. 537.

30. Erik Goldstein and John Maurer, eds., *The Washington Conference, 1921–22: Naval Rivalry, East Asian Stability, and the Road to Pearl Harbor* (London, 1993).

31. Hedley Bull, "Strategic Arms Limitation: The Precedent of the Washington and London Naval Treaties," reprinted in Robert O'Neill and David Schwartz, eds. *Hedley Bull on Arms Control* (New York, 1987), 131–51; originally published as an Occasional Paper of the Center for Policy Study, University of Chicago, 1971.

32. Some agreements of course were reached, as some public display was needed, for example, the Partial Test Ban Treaty, the Outer Space Treaty, the Non-Proliferation Treaty, but these were not of the same level of strategic importance to the key powers.

33. Martin Gilbert, *"Never Despair" Winston S. Churchill, 1945–1965* (London, 1988), 1301.

34. Walter Lippmann, *U.S. Foreign Policy: Shield of the Republic* (Boston, 1943), 54.

35. John Wheeler-Bennett, *Disarmament and Security since Locarno, 1925–1931: Being the Political and Technical Background to the General Disarmament Conference, 1932* (1937; reprinted, New York, 1973).

36. Alfred Zimmern, *The League of Nations and the Rule of Law, 1918–1935*, 2nd ed. (London, 1939), 338.

37. Stanhope to Baldwin, May 25, 1932, Baldwin 118, Baldwin of Bewdley Papers, University Library, Cambridge.

38. Zimmern, *The League of Nations*, p. 338.

39. G.M. Gathorne-Hardy, *A Short History of International Affairs, 1920–1939* (London, 1950), 348.

40. Neville Chamberlain to Ida Chamberlain, November 26, 1937, NC 18/1/1030, Neville Chamberlain Papers, University of Birmingham Library, Birmingham.

41. Churchill advocated full disarmament of the Axis to Roosevelt, Churchill to Roosevelt, February 2, 1943, in Warren Kimball, ed., *Churchill & Roosevelt: The Complete Correspondence*, vol. 2: *Alliance Forged* (Princeton, NJ, 1984), 129.

42. R. Buhite, ed., *The Dynamics of World Power: A Documentary History of United States Foreign Policy, 1945–1973* (New York, 1973), 12.

43. Albert Wohlstetter, "The Delicate Balance of Terror," *Foreign Affairs*, 37.2 (January 1959), 211–34.

44. See Henry Kissinger, *Diplomacy* (New York, 1994), 791–92.

45. See Stuart Croft, *Strategies of Arms Control: A History and Typology* (Manchester, 1996), chap. 6.

46. UNSC Res 731 (January 21, 1992).

47. See also C.P. Stacey, "The Myth of the Unguarded Frontier, 1815–1871," *American Historical Review*, 56 (1950), 1–18.

48. Harry Howard, "The Turkish Straits and the Great Powers," *Foreign Affairs*, 13 (October, 1936), 199–202; idem, "The Turkish Straits after World War II: Problems and Prospects," *Balkan Studies*, 11.1 (1970), 35–60; Cyril Black, "The Turkish Straits and the Great Powers," *Foreign Policy Reports*, 23.14 (1947), 174–82; Ferenc Vali, *The Turkish Straits and NATO* (Stanford, CA, 1972); A.L. Macfie, *The Straits*

Question, 1908–36 (Thessaloniki, 1993). See also Richard Burns and Seymour Chapin, "Near Eastern Naval Limitation Pacts, 1930–1931," *East European Quarterly*, 4.1 (1970), 77–87.

49. It was signed by Britain, France, Bulgaria, Egypt, Greece, Romania, the Soviet Union, Turkey, and Yugoslavia. Italy subsequently joined.

50. Barry Blechman. *The Control of Naval Armaments: Prospects and Possibilities* (Washington, DC, 1975), 34, 64–71.

51. John Maurer, "Disarmament," in Robert Cowley and Geoffrey Parker, eds., *The Reader's Companion to Military History* (Boston, 1996), 134.

52. Quoted in Hinsley, *Power and the Pursuit of Peace*, 209.

53. Kissinger, *Diplomacy*, 715.

CHAPTER 3

The Economic Foundations of the Cold War Alliance Systems, 1945 to 1953

Lawrence R. Aronsen

One of the ironies of the early Cold War period, at least from the Soviet perspective, was the stabilization and successful integration of the capitalist economies of the Western bloc nations. Marxist theory, as it was interpreted by Stalin and his inner circle, suggested that the United States and the other capitalist powers, driven by the need to avert a return to the 1930s depression, would quickly become adversaries over the struggle for the redivision of markets and resources after the war.[1] On the other hand, one of the unexpected developments, not anticipated by Western analysts, was that the imposition of total Soviet control over the European East bloc nations did not maximize Soviet power. The subjugation of the Eastern allies only set in motion tensions that would culminate first in the East German uprisings of 1953 followed by the 1956 rebellions in Poland and Hungary. The impact of these rebellions in turn caused the Soviets to reassess their East bloc policies. Trade and investment concessions were offered that by the late 1950s reversed the course of empire by turning the satellites into economic liabilities.[2]

To date, the work on the economic aspects of the early postwar Sovietization of eastern Europe, one of the most egregious examples of exploitative imperialism in modern history, has been surprisingly limited.[3] The literature on the Americanization of the West bloc in comparison has been quite extensive.[4] Scholars of the "Stalinization" process have paid close attention to politics, especially the imposition of Communist Party control. There is some debate, however, about when Stalin decided to establish total control over the East bloc and whether or not Soviet actions were a defensive consolidation in response to the encroachment of the West.[5]

The following study starts from certain basic premises. First, the foreign economic policies of the Soviet Union and the United States were defined within a specific ideological context and reflected basic national security objectives. Second, both superpowers in 1945 had an asymmetrical relationship within their respective alliance systems. The United States and the Soviet Union always enjoyed a favorable advantage in terms of population, territory, economic resources, and military power in relation to their allies. The two superpowers also used a variety of bilateral and multilateral mechanisms to establish control and influence within their spheres of influence. How the United States and the Soviet Union behaved given their unique and unchallenged position is particularly revealing of the character of their political systems during the period of greatest confrontation and crisis. As a contemporary issue that is discussed in the popular media, questions can be raised about the moral equivalency thesis regarding the exercise of political power, a viewpoint most recently presented in the CNN series on the Cold War.[6]

This study will focus on the core countries within the respective alliance systems. These countries were selected on the basis of their relatively advanced resource and industrial defense production and importance to the strategic plans of the bloc leaders. In the East bloc, Germany, Poland, Czechoslovakia, and Hungary emerged as the critical client states. On the Western side, several countries were important to the United States, but above all Canada and Great Britain formed a "special relationship" sometimes referred to as the North Atlantic Triangle.[7] The economic relations within the North Atlantic Triangle were much different from the Soviet bloc at least in terms of capital flows from the center to the periphery, the extent of technology transfer across borders, and the relative absence of restrictions on the flow of trade.

For the purposes of organization and analysis, three periods can be identified. From 1945 to 1946 the Soviet occupation forces in eastern Europe were primarily concerned with taking over and rebuilding war-torn industries and the extraction of reparations from Hungary and East Germany. The other bloc countries, Poland and Czechoslovakia, were confronted with the reality of the first stage of direct economic control, notably the imposition of unequal bilateral trade treaties and the creation of joint stock companies. At the same time the United States was less concerned with establishing economic control over its allies than achieving economic stabilization through the creation of the Bretton Woods financial systems and the implementation of a humanitarian relief program through the offices of the United Nations Relief and Rehabilitation Administration (UNRRA).

In the second period from 1947 to 1949, the Soviets consolidated their dominant position through the imposition of currency controls, the imposition of centralized planning, and the nationalization of what remained of the private sector throughout the East bloc. The uncooperative regime in Yugoslavia was subjected to an economic embargo, while the remainder of the East bloc satellites were reduced to a closed autarkic economic system under the restrictive dictates of the Council for Mutual Economic Assistance (COMECON). In this period the United States entered a transition phase. On the one hand, efforts were continued to create a multilateral trading system under the 1947 General Agreement on Tariffs and Trade (GATT), but on the other hand, foreign economic policy became more focused on the containment of further communist expansion on the European continent. The Marshall Plan was designed as an emergency aid program to ensure European access to foodstuffs and critical manufactured products while trade with the Communist bloc was restricted under the guidelines of the Coordinating Committee (CoCom).

Throughout the period 1950 to 1953, the fighting of a limited war in Korea heightened the prospects of mobilization for nuclear war. From the perspective of the leaders in Moscow and Washington, their allies were increasingly seen in terms of what contribution each could immediately make to the fighting of a conventional war in Korea and what economic assets the bloc allies had that would be useful in the preparation of the air-atomic arsenals of the superpowers in the event of fighting a total war. The industrial defense production of the bloc allies including armored vehicles, transports, electrical and electronic equipment, and small arms production was most useful in the fighting of a limited convential war. What received the highest priority in the preparation for a total nuclear war was the acquisition of strategic resources such as aluminum, titanium, and uranium.

THE ORIGINS OF SOVIET ECONOMIC CONTROL OF EASTERN EUROPE: THE PUNITIVE PEACE, 1945–1946

The course of early postwar Soviet economic relations with its captive neighbors to the east was determined by several factors. Not the least was Stalin's capricious personality and preference for Machiavellian subterfuge. Added to this was an element of pure revenge that was interpreted through certain Marxist principles regarding the power of the economic base over the political superstructure. Translated into policy this meant that while the Soviets did not immediately impose direct political control, they wielded significant influence over the domestic and foreign economic policies of the satellites. The reasoning of Marxist theoreticians in the Kremlin was that economic dependence would eventually lead to political dependence.[8] The record is particularly clear that the extension of Soviet economic control in this period was not a reaction to Western aggressiveness. Finally, economic policy was calculated as an asset to furthering Soviet national security objectives. In the immediate postwar period the Malenkov faction within the Kremlin was particularly concerned with assuring maximum postwar economic recovery to avert a possible insurrection at home. Soviet military planners also argued that the postwar armaments modernization program would greatly benefit from the removal of skilled personnel and the most technologically advanced industries in the captive nations.[9]

The exercise of Soviet economic power in eastern Europe was complicated in that the degree of exploitation was uneven and the means of control varied from country to country. In Hungary and Germany the dominant authority was the occupying Red Army. Elsewhere throughout the East bloc there were several examples of the Kremlin directly controlling the appointment of people in key economic positions. Also by 1946, over 250 joint stock companies (SAGs—Sowjetische Aktiengesellschaften) were set up, of which some 213 concentrated in East Germany, the rest in Hungary and Czechoslovakia. Poland was spared this particular form of Soviet influence but did not escape being subjected to other means of control. Although the term *SAG* implied joint control, in reality these companies reported directly to the Ministry of Foreign Trade in Moscow. SAGs were most prevalent in strategic and defense-related industries: chemicals, vehicles, electrical, and liquid fuels.[10] An equally effective means of control was the use of bilateral trade treaties first imposed on Poland in 1945, followed by Czechoslovakia and Hungary in 1947.

The demands imposed by the Soviets were uneven; former Axis bloc enemies Germany and Hungary were singled out for special retribution. In short, the Soviets were not uniformly exploitative, but there was very little to temper the excesses of their policy toward nonenemy states. Poland, for example, was not a former Axis bloc ally but received almost equally harsh economic and political subjugation as former Soviet enemies. Nowhere did Moscow officials practice what could be described as enlightened self-interest. Despite some aid being given to Poland and East Germany to address the conditions of near starvation, most of the emergency relief came from the American-sponsored UNRRA program.[11]

The Soviet-occupied zone in Germany stands out as the most severe example of economic exploitation by a victor nation, far surpassing what the Allies imposed on that country after the First World War. For the most part, the West stood idly by and even helped set the framework for Soviet exploitation under the terms of the Potsdam Agreement in

July 1945. It was at Potsdam that the Soviets secured reparation from Germany totaling $10 billion. Also a formula was worked out that the Soviets would get 15 percent of the industrial equipment removed from the western zones in exchange for food and raw materials and an additional 10 percent without any exchange commitment to the West.[12]

Yet the Soviets faced a dilemma: how to maximize reparations while at the same time building a new socialist utopia in the heart of Europe? The most recent evidence suggests that the Soviets planned to unify all the occupation zones of Germany and then draw the new socialist state into the Soviet sphere of influence. In the spring of 1946 Stalin reassured Milovan Djilas, "All of Germany must be ours... that is Soviet Communist."[13] But in the end this longer-term vision of a new east European proletarian order characterized by solidarity among socialist states was compromised by shorter-term Soviet economic interests.

The systematic economic denuding of the East German economy was first undertaken by the occupying Russian Red Army. The looting began at the local level when communist troops, unrestrained by their commanding officers, randomly seized the possessions of German families. The next stage was the removal of German industrial equipment by specialized units known as the "trophy" battalions. On orders from the highest occupation authorities, vast quantities of German military equipment, scientific laboratories, printing presses, communications technology, and transportation equipment were shipped eastward. By the time the trophy brigades stopped the looting in August 1945, they had seized 1.2 million tons of materials and 3.6 million tons of equipment for shipment to the Soviet Union.[14]

The final stage was the removal of reparations through the administrative mechanism of the Soviet Military Administration (SMAG), which was put in charge of the day-to-day operation of the economy. The basic objective of SMAG was to obtain as much strategic industrial equipment as possible without completely paralyzing the economy but at the same time weaken Germany so that it would not pose a military threat for many years. The Soviets were driven in part by revenge and the immediate need to address the problem of restoring their war-damaged economy. It has been estimated that at least 17,000 cities and towns and 70,000 villages were devastated, and 70 percent of industries and 60 percent of the Soviet transportation systems were destroyed.[15]

In addition to the factor of revenge and the need to help rebuild war-torn industries at home, the transfer of plants and technical equipment and workers was dictated primarily by national security considerations. Immediately after the war the Soviets began reducing the size of the Red Army but continued to give a high priority to the development of new weapons systems, notably the development of the atomic bomb, the intercontinental ballistic missile (ICBM), and a new generation of fighter-interceptors. What they took from East Germany was the highly valued rocket works program at Peenumunde, several dozen prominent rocket scientists, and a vital segment of the aircraft production program. In total about 6,000 German engineers and technicians were removed to the Leningrad area in 1946. These highly skilled workers were an important asset in the development of the first generation of postwar Soviet rockets, notably the R-3, that later became operational intermediate range ballistic missiles (IRBMs).[16]

Less publicized than the seizure of the German rocketry program but well known at the time by Western intelligence agencies was the consolidation of Soviet control over East German uranium production. After the war the Russians gave the highest priority to their atomic bomb program headed by KGB director Laventri Beria. In the latter part of 1945 the Red Army had seized over a hundred tons of processed uranium from the Auer Company, a German mining operation. The major operation was at the Erzgebirge mine in the mountainous region bordering on Czechoslovakia. The approach to uranium extraction nicely encapsulates the whole approach to Germany in the first period—a total preoccupation with immediate Soviet national security interests coupled with a complete disregard for the interests of the Germans. The treatment of the German proletariat was a case in point. Over 100,000 workers were drafted for work in the mines and exposed to hazardous radiation and substandard living conditions. This operation, described as a "death march" in one recent account, continued to be the Soviets' leading foreign supplier through the 1950s.[17]

Clearly the Soviets were in a position to arbitrarily exercise their will over the prostrate East Germans in the pursuit of their own self-interests. However, two major problems developed that were not anticipated. Often when the Soviets removed German plants to be reassembled elsewhere, there was no appreciable immediate economic advantage that was gained. Intelligence reports and other sources indicated that there were several examples of equipment that sat indefinitely on railway cars exposed to the elements and consequently became damaged beyond repair. There were other examples of equipment from German industrial operations that arrived in Russia only to malfunction because of inadequate reassembly.[18]

The Soviets continued their occupation policies for the time being, unaware of any consequences related to the indiscriminate industrial stripping of the East German zone. By May 1946 it was becoming clear that the occupying Red Army was depriving the East Germans of the economic means to sustain themselves. Moreover, even the Soviets came to recognize by the summer of 1946 certain ideological inconsistencies with their policies. This unfolded in the above-cited debate between the Georgi Malenkov and Andrei Zhdandov factions within the Kremlin.

Economic Foundations 71

The former wanted to relentlessly pummel Germany and extract as much as possible, whereas the Zhdandov group preferred to create some semblance of a model socialist state in East Germany. Molotov later noted, "What would those people [East Germans] think of us if we had taken everything from their country? ... After all, we were taking from the German communists who wanted to work with us."[19] But if the Russians slightly modified their policies in the years ahead, this cannot be interpreted as a new appreciation of the economic interests of their eastern satellites.

Hungary was also subjected to a military occupation by the Red Army and the imposition of an economically punitive peace settlement. In some respects Hungary's fate was not as harsh as Germany's in that a mass rape was not visited on the female population. Nor did the country suffer the deportation of slave laborers to Russia. The economic demands were nonetheless quite imposing and not without consequence.

By the autumn of 1944 the Red Army totally occupied the country but withdrew by the summer of 1945. Although Hungary held relatively democratic elections in 1945, the Soviets were able to influence foreign economic policy through their dominant position on the Allied Control Commission.[20] It was through this mechanism that the Peace Treaty was imposed, calling for the payment of reparations over a period of six years. Under these terms, Hungary was required to pay $200 million per year at 1938 prices—which amounted to 37.5 percent of the Hungarian budget in 1946.[21] The Hungarian economy was also subjugated through the joint Soviet-Hungarian state-controlled companies in the key economic sectors of air transport, shipping, bauxite, and oil production. There is some evidence that the Soviets in this early period wanted to deliberately impose harsh conditions, creating a situation whereby the Hungarian Communist Party, then in a coalition government, would be able to expand and take advantage of the crisis.[22] Despite the unusually poor harvest in the summer of 1945, producing near-starvation conditions across the country, the Soviet director of the Allied Control Commission refused food aid offered by UNRRA. Consequently, food rationing was introduced, further destabilizing the domestic political scene.[23]

Although Poland was not a former Axis bloc ally, it became the focal point of Soviet security concerns in postwar eastern Europe. While a semblance of a multiparty coalition government was tolerated, Poland enjoyed little in the way of economic independence.[24] The Soviets made it clear from 1945 onward that they would be the final arbiter of the state of Polish foreign economic policy.

How the Soviets imposed control over Poland is of some significance for the comparative study of the behavior of the two superpowers. Historian Vojtech Mastny has argued that there was never any intention of allowing for the unfettered operation of a liberal democracy.[25] The Soviets exercised direct control through the dominant position held by the Communist Party within the coalition government. At the time, the Polish Communist Party was led by Bolesleaw Bierut, one of the most ingratiating and humorless of the satellite apparatchiks. Zbigniew Brzezinski recalls an incident when Bierut went so far as to suggest to Stalin that the Polish national anthem be replaced with something in keeping with the higher calling of proletarian solidarity. Stalin, somewhat startled by this outburst of socialist sycophancy, remarked, "It's a good song. Leave it for a while."[26]

As the Soviet army moved across eastern Poland, industries were nationalized and production was appropriated by Kremlin authorities. The next step involved the large-scale siphoning off of capital equipment in the newly acquired former German territory in the west. This seizure of German industry, which was presumably to be awarded to Poland for compensation for losing the territory east of the Curzon line, was a serious setback to postwar economic development. In 1945 the Poles effectively inherited a shell of an industrial economy.[27]

The most telling piece of evidence that Bierut would govern only as a Soviet apparatchik, especially on economic issues, was the signing of the April 1945 Trade Treaty. The Polish coalition government, under the influence of the Communist Party, obligingly signed a trade agreement that was officially presented as an example of proletarian solidarity. According to what the Preamble described as a Treaty of Friendship between Poland and the Soviet Union,

the High Contracting Parties, convinced that the interests of the security and prosperity of the Soviet and the Polish peoples call for the preservation and strengthening of a stable and permanent friendship in time of war and after the war ... to achieve these aims the High Contracting Parties will participate in a spirit of most sincere collaboration.[28]

The Poles were quick to learn the real meaning of the Soviet conception of "sincere collaboration" among socialist allies, especially as it was applied to the export of coal. The Soviets insisted that Polish coal had to be delivered at a price that amounted to less than one tenth of the price reached in coal export agreements with western European countries. When Stanislaw Mikolajcyk, the noncommunist vice-premier raised questions, he was vehemently denounced for disrupting Soviet-Polish relations. Under the terms of the 1945 agreement, Poland was forced to export 12 million tons of coal at $1.25 a ton. At the same time, it cost $5 to $6 to mine the coal. Moreover, the international price offered by the capitalist countries was as high as $16 a ton.[29] "They take our wheat," angrily mused one Pole, "and we send them our coal."[30]

Czechoslovakia offers a unique example in that it sought to become Moscow's "favorite protégé."[31] On several issues the Benes government preferred to acquiesce in the face of Soviet demands. For example, in 1945 Prague officials agreed to the establishment of Soviet direct control of the uranium mines in the Jachymov region near the border with Saxony. The pricing for the uranium was determined by the Soviet formula, which included the cost of mining the ore, plus 10 percent for commercial profit. Years later the Czechs expressed some discontent about the contract but to no avail.[32] There was little room for the Czechs to maneuver as the Soviets directly monitored their uranium production through the creation of a Joint Stock Company.[33]

In the first stage, the Soviets dominated but did not exercise total control on all matters related to trade and postwar economic recovery. They did, however, establish a "stranglehold" over the East bloc economies long before direct political control was imposed. There is little evidence to suggest that in this early period the Soviets were reacting to Western pressure to expand in the region. In fact, the Western influence was minimal, confined largely to postwar emergency relief programs. Even this aid was unevenly distributed and closely monitored by the Soviets. The largest recipients were Poland ($481 million) and Czechoslovakia ($270 million).[34] An economic iron curtain had come down across eastern Europe even before Winston Churchill's famous warning made in his Fulton, Missouri, address that a political iron curtain descended from Stettin in the Baltic to Trieste in the Adriatic.

THE IMPLEMENTATION OF AMERICAN FOREIGN ECONOMIC POLICY, 1945–1946

American foreign economic policy was similar to the Soviet Union in that it was based on considerations of national security and ideology. At the most general level the United States sought the stabilization of the economies of the primary industrial producing nations, thereby avoiding a return of the 1930s depression and the resulting international crisis. Throughout the process of reconstructing this new economic order, what most separated the United States from the Soviet Union was the relative absence of coercion. Indeed, what is most remarkable according to historian Geir Lundestad was the pressure exerted by the Western allies to create an "empire by invitation."[35] With some exceptions about the timing and extent of tariff reductions, the Western allies welcomed and encouraged the creation of a liberalized international economic order based on specialization determined by comparative advantage. Toward this end, the United States pursued a "freer" trading system within a clearly defined multilateral organization outlining basic rules and regulations. "Sound and healthy trade, conducted on equitable and nondiscriminatory principles" was, in President Truman's opinion, "the keystone in the structure of world peace and security."[36]

The United States acted as the undisputed leader of the Western allies but always sought to forge a consensus regarding the major financial issues, including the creation of the Bretton Woods agreement dealing with international finance, the financing of emergency relief through UNRRA, and the extension of postwar loans. The search for consensus also underlined the Truman administration's approach to trade and commercial issues: the creation of the GATT to reduce trade barriers, the Marshall Plan program to reconstruct Europe, and the establishment of CoCom to restrict trade exports to the Communist bloc.

Washington officials only briefly considered the imposition of a punitive peace on the defeated Axis bloc nations, Japan and Germany. In the case of Germany, the controversial Morgenthau Plan, named after Roosevelt's secretary of the treasury, called for the dismantling of the heavy industrial base and the reduction of the economy to a nineteenth-century agricultural base.[37] This proposal was strongly opposed by the State Department and quickly dropped by the Truman administration in the summer of 1945. Instead, General Lucius Clay, the commander of the occupation, dictated that a viable economy combined with a liberal democratic political system was the most advantageous long-term strategy to promote security in that region.[38]

Although the Western allies generally supported American initiatives, Washington did rely on an "inner sphere" of support from Britain and Canada regarding its foreign economic policy objectives. This amicable relationship was essentially an outgrowth of the special relations of the North Atlantic Triangle partnership dating back to the early twentieth century.[39] All the Western allies agreed with the American premise about the connection between economic internationalism and postwar security. While there was a consensus on the basic postwar economic objectives, difficulties nonetheless arose. If fact, it is the way in which difficulties were handled that highlights a significant difference in the respective integration of the West and East bloc economies.

The first major step toward reconstructing the postwar international economy was taken at the July 1944 Bretton Woods Conference. Delegates representing the Western allies dealt with the difficult issue of stabilizing international currencies, a necessary measure to prevent a repetition of the destructive competitive devaluations characteristic of the 1930s. These efforts culminated in the creation of the International Monetary Fund and the International Bank for Reconstruction and Development. Throughout the course of the conference the United States worked most closely with its "special relationship" allies Canada and Great Britain. At times the British representative, Lord Keynes, and his American counterpart, Harry Dexter White, expressed disagreements, but a consensus was forged on all the outstanding issues. Despite the fact that these initiatives were taken by the leader of the capitalist bloc, the Soviet Union did not, for the time being, hesitate to approve the Bretton Woods principles as well.[40]

The second major initiative the United States took to encourage postwar international economic stabilization was the creation of UNRRA as a UN agency designed to provide emergency food and medical supplies to liberated nations. This mandate was later broadened to include help for displaced persons from the Axis countries. Again the Soviets cooperated but were clever enough to relabel UNRRA aid packages with the inscription "from the Russian people" and then redistribute this Western capitalist largesse to Poland and Czechoslovakia.[41] While Britain played a key role in the creation of the UNRRA, Canada played an even greater role in its funding and day-to-day operations. It is important to note that Canada's wartime shift to a liberalized international economic order was not in response to pressure from its southern ally; in fact, there was none. Instead, Canada's new international commitment was largely a reflection of the Dominion's status as a rising middle power coupled with an expanding export-oriented economy.[42]

The United States generally encouraged a multilateral approach to foreign economic relations yet at the same time favored its long-standing English-speaking allies, Canada and the United Kingdom. To avoid a repetition of the extended recession Canada faced after the First World War, the United States paid special attention to the reconversion of the Canadian economy. In 1945, it extended the provisions of the 1941 Hyde Park Agreement whereby the northern Dominion could continue importing scarce materials on the same priority basis as American companies. Canada in turn was allowed to maintain controls on the export of what it deemed key commodities for its own domestic consumption. To avoid the shock of canceling war production orders, provisions were made to help the disposal of surplus equipment produced by Canadian industries. The State Department noted in a classified memo that the provisions of the 1945 Hyde Park extension "constituted an extremely valuable concession to Canadian industry . . . and it is unfortunate that we are not prepared at this moment with specific requests for concessions from Canada."[43]

The "special relationship" with Britain encountered some obstacles that were eventually resolved through compromise and extension of some concessions from Washington. Part of the problem Washington officials faced was dealing with state interventionist policies of nationalization and subsidization adopted by the new social democratic government of Prime Minister Clement Attlee.[44] Moreover, concern was expressed that Britain was far too protectionist-minded in preserving the old Imperial Preference Trading System that conflicted with the multilateral preferences of the United States. There was the additional problem of some British resistance to the coordination of European economic integration through the Marshall Plan. These efforts to make Europe economically interdependent and less reliant on the United States stand in contrast to the Soviet policy of restrictive bilateralism and autarky.

On occasion British and American ideological differences spilled over into the occupation policies on the European continent. For example, in 1946 there was some tension over the Labour government's encouragement of the German labor union movement and imposition of statist economic policies in its German occupation zone.[45] Yet the need to restore the North Atlantic trading system after the war overrode these problems, and the Truman administration moved to stabilize the British currency through the extension of a $3.75 billion loan in 1946.

THE SOVIET UNION AND THE ISOLATION OF THE EAST BLOC, 1947–1949

The lack of significant progress toward economic recovery coupled with the growing political threat posed by the communists within western European coalition governments prompted the Truman administration to offer massive financial assistance through the European Recovery Program (ERP). The Soviets responded by rejecting this offer and resorted to ideological warfare through the creation of the Cominform, an international organization that controlled and coordinated the activities of foreign Communist Parties. One specific objective of the Cominform was to order the French and Italian Communist Parties to withdraw from the postwar coalition governments and cause as much disruption as possible at a time when the capitalist economies were most unstable. Within his own sphere of influence, Stalin implemented a more sophisticated but equally inequitable system of control. It now became clear to authorities in Moscow that greater coordination over resources and the adoption of large developmental projects in the East bloc would be more advantageous to Soviet security than simply pillaging the local economies.

Some historians have interpreted the provocative nature of the Marshall Plan as the catalyst for Stalin's crackdown on eastern Europe.[46] Others such as Vojtech Mastny have concluded that Stalin, as early as the spring of 1946, believed that the wartime cooperation with Britain and the United States had ended.[47] Therefore, total Sovietization was inevitable, and it was simply a matter of timing. Still another consideration was that by 1947 the Soviets became increasingly disturbed with the initiatives East bloc countries had taken to set up a number of joint planning committees to promote economic ties with each other.[48] These manifestations of East bloc national self-interest such as Bulgaria's plans for trade and industrialization in the region had to be quickly contained and replaced with the Soviet version of proletarian internationalism.

The rhetoric of proletarian internationalism conveniently served the national interests of the Soviet Union in the second period of East bloc history from 1947 to 1949. If western Europe was going to pursue the course of rapid economic expansion, the Soviet bloc was compelled to follow suit. From the perspective of Kremlin economic planners, accelerated economic growth was best achieved through the application of the Stalinist model of the 1930s. That approach emphasized heavy industrial development over consumer production. The Soviet Union would supply the necessary raw materials, which at that time were generally unsaleable on world markets.[49] In effect, the Soviets imposed a kind of reverse imperialism, forcing high raw materials prices on its satellites and buying at the lowest possible price their industrial production. The next objective was to limit bilateral economic initiatives among the satellites and tie each of them into a dependency relationship with the Soviet Union. Finally, the Soviets moved to drastically reduce trade with the Western bloc, especially that of Czechoslovakia and Poland.

The first indication that the Soviets were going to redefine economic relations within their sphere of influence came in July 1947. Foreign Minister Molotov led the Soviet delegation out of the Marshall Plan talks in Paris, insisting that the American proposal was an act of economic aggression designed to divide Europe. Moscow quickly ordered the Czechoslovakian, Polish, and Hungarian Foreign Offices not to participate as well. What is interesting is that even before the final consolidation of communist authority in the February 1948 coup, the Soviets dictated to the coalition government in Prague the proper course of foreign economic policy. In no uncertain terms the Benes government was informed that participation in the ERP would be "construed as an act that infringed on our ties of alliance with the Soviet Union."[50]

Throughout the second period, 1947–1949, the Soviets tightened their mechanism for imposing economic control. A new series of bilateral trade agreements were imposed. Officially referred to as Treaties of Friendship and Mutual Cooperation, agreements were signed with Czechoslovakia in December 1947, Hungary in February 1948, and an updated treaty was presented to Poland in January 1949.[51] To ensure compliance, Soviet embassies directly monitored all economic developments within the bloc. Also, the Soviets worked directly through economic ministries by appointing their own advisers. All the key sectors of the domestic bloc economies were affected.

Shortly after the 1948 Czech coup Stalin informed east European leaders, "World War III is inevitable in three to four years."[52] Thus it was for reasons related to national security rather than improving the lot of the east European proletariat that the final assault on the capitalist order was undertaken. Under the new conditions of socialist industrialization, East bloc workers soon found themselves toiling in the new factories for longer hours and less pay than in the prewar period.[53] Between 1947 and 1949 virtually all industrial operations of over fifty workers were put under state control in Poland, Hungary, and Czechoslovakia. Virtually all foreign enterprises were nationalized without compensation. Banking systems in eastern Europe, previously under state control, were organized according to the Soviet model and placed under the Ministry of Finance.

The primary blueprints for industrialization were the multiyear plans. The first one to appear was a three-year plan in Hungary that was drafted in 1948. The following year five-year plans were adopted in Poland and Czechoslovakia. The Soviets monitored the plans again by way of requiring planning officials to report directly to the Soviet embassy in their respective countries.[54] In keeping with national security priorities the objective was to accelerate the pace of industrialization with specific reference to capital or producer-goods industries.

A new socialist division of labor was imposed on eastern Europe, beginning in the summer of 1948. The satellites were required to industrialize in selected sectors—iron, steel, and heavy machinery production—regardless of the supply of natural resources at home. In fact, Moscow authorities preferred that they become dependent on Soviet resources that were conveniently priced above the world market. In return the satellites would reexport their finished products at below-market prices. Viewed in a larger historical context, the Russian satellites essentially adopted the classic turn-of-the-century approach to industrialization that was reflected in the priorities of the first Soviet five-year plan. The communists were not subtle in their efforts to promote the necessary changes. Economist Ivan Berend suggests that after the execution of Hungarian and Czech Titoists "all obediently imitated the first Soviet year Plan in their own plans."[55]

From 1947 to 1949 the trade patterns throughout the East bloc changed dramatically. The Soviets were able to control the course of intrabloc commerce by placing representatives in the foreign trade ministries in each of the satellites. East Germany was an exception in that trade was controlled directly by the occupation forces (SMAG) until 1949. Until 1948, West Germany was the largest trade partner, but by the summer of that year, SMAG dramatically reduced commercial ties with the West in favor of the Communist bloc. That year 45 percent of East German trade was with other bloc members and reached 75 percent by 1950.[56] Under the new trading regime Hungary and Czechoslovakia were required to buy Soviet grain and export machinery, oil piping, chemicals, clothing, and sugar. Poland was forced to import Soviet ores, oil products, and raw cotton and export coal, textiles, railway rolling stock steel, and cement. Moscow trade officials consistently underpriced imported goods and overpriced their own exports. On some occasions the Soviets even reexported East bloc goods to "hard currency" countries at higher prices than for what they were purchased.[57]

The creation of COMECON in January 1949 was the culmination of socialist reforms designed to facilitate the economic integration of the Soviet satellites. Negotiation and compromise were not the hallmarks of the new multilateral socialist economic order. There is surprisingly little reference to COMECON in the standard literature on the Cold War suffice to say that it was explained as a reaction to the intrusiveness of the Marshall Plan.[58] But the perceived threat of the Marshall Plan is only a partial explanation of the motives behind this new Soviet initiative. In fact, COMECON was also designed as an instrument to coordinate the Communist bloc boycott of the dissident Tito regime in Yugoslavia.[59] Still another useful function was that COMECON stopped once and for all any efforts on the part of individual satellite countries to take further initiatives to improve economic relations with each other.[60]

From 1949 to 1955 COMECON engaged in statistical research, technical exchanges, and the promotion of bilateral trade treaties. Trade was planned by annual agreements that in 1951 were extended for longer periods. In the end, the basic objective officially stated in the charter was

> to unite and coordinate the efforts of the member countries in order to improve the development of socialist economic integration; to achieve more rapid economic and technical progress in these countries, and particularly a higher level of industrialization in countries where this is lacking; to achieve a steady growth of labor productivity; to work gradually towards a balanced level of development in the different regions, and a steady increase in standards of living in the member states.[61]

The reality of COMECON was that it reinforced the pattern that began in 1947 based on autarky and the adoption of the Soviet model of industrialization. In contrast to the West there was no division of labor based on supply and demand or reciprocal economic advantages. There were no negotiated settlements and therefore no compromises.

COMECON did little to improve economic relations between East Germany, Poland, Czechoslovakia, and Hungary. In the end, it only existed to reinforce the bilateral relationship between these individual countries and the Soviet Union. Not surprisingly, COMECON reproduced all the deficiencies inherent in bureaucratic planning—goods that were of low quality, short in supply, and unsuitable for what they were originally designed. Some of the communist apparatchiks in the satellites remained eternally grateful for participation in this new socialist order. After signing an updated trade agreement with the Soviets in 1950, Czech Foreign

Trade Minister Alexander Gregor described it as "guaranteeing us a free and independent existence," in contrast to "trading transactions imposed by Wall Street on the nations of the Marshallised countries."[62]

AMERICAN FOREIGN ECONOMIC POLICY AND THE CONTAINMENT DOCTRINE, 1947–1949

The onset of the Cold War by 1947 marks a transition stage in American foreign policy. Washington officials, increasingly preoccupied with communist expansion in Europe, continued the pursuit of multilateral nondiscriminatory trade objectives through the 1947 GATT negotiations at Geneva. At the same time there was a clear recognition that foreign economic policy would have to serve more specifically designed national security objectives, notably the containment of communist expansion. The basic pattern established during the Roosevelt administration of forging a consensus through the use of formal and informal negotiations continued into this new period.

The institutional framework for the early discussions leading up to the creation of the GATT in 1947 was the United Nations Social and Economic Council (UNSOC). Support for UNSOC initially came from the group known as the "Big Three," Canada, Great Britain, and the United States. Within this group, Canada, with 30 percent of its gross national product (GNP) derived from exports, had the most to gain from American multinational initiatives. The British were supportive in principle, but the dramatic run on the pound and the serious decline in currency reserves throughout 1947 undermined their commitment to multilateralism. In the end, the United States did not gain much British cooperation to significantly reduce preferential tariff barriers, the elimination of discriminatory quantitative restrictions, or the control of export subsidies. Richard Gardner, the historian of Anglo-American commercial relations, thus concluded the new GATT system provided "little practical benefit" to American trade.[63]

The devastating winter of 1946–1947, the decline in industrial production, and the termination of the UNRRA, set against the backdrop of rising communist movements in France and Italy, forced the United States to reconsider its commitment to liberal democracy on the continent of Europe. The State Department recognized that certain economic initiatives were necessary to stabilize the political situation that were best achieved through cooperation and consensus building. Canada and Britain were considered to be within the inner sphere of an embryonic North Atlantic alliance and therefore received special considerations. Through the use of effective and well-timed diplomatic pressure on Washington, Canada was able to gain significant trade concessions by way of offshore purchases by European Recovery Plan recipients.[64] Britain, despite its unwillingness to give total commitment to the GATT and dismantle the Imperial Preference System, would receive the largest appropriation of Marshall Plan money.

To be sure, American motives for the Marshall Plan were a mixture of economic self-interest and the pursuit of a favorable balance of power on the European continent.[65] The primary intention of Washington officials was that the program be kept within a clearly defined time period and that some concessions from the Western allies would be forthcoming. For example, ERP recipient countries were committed to buy American goods with the aid, which in turn was to be shipped only on American vessels. To determine the amount of aid received, host countries had to make available their economic statistics and allow for some American inspection. In contrast to the Soviet effort to reduce economic relations to a dominant one-on-one bilateral arrangement, the intention of the authors of the Marshall Plan was to encourage Europeans to take the initiative and organize their own regional economic union. Thus in April 1948 the Organization for European Economic Cooperation (OEEC) was created, which evolved into the European Coal and Steel Community in 1952.

As the Cold War unfolded, the United States took some initiative to control the direction of trade within the Western alliance, notably by encouraging more inter-European trade through the OEEC. These initiatives were welcomed by the West bloc generally. The most contentious issue, however, arose when the Truman administration attempted to restrict trade involving strategic materials with the East bloc. Consequently, some diplomatic arm twisting ensued, but in the end the Americans did not achieve very much. Even their closest ally Great Britain was not deterred from exporting Rolls Royce Nene engines to Czechoslovakia in 1948 that eventually ended up in the hands of Soviet aircraft engineers. The United States considered using the threat of cutting off aid if the Europeans did not comply, but Secretary of State Dean Acheson concluded that this would ultimately be counterproductive.[66] The best the United States could do was to set up a voluntary agency, the Coordinating Committee, otherwise known as CoCom. In the end, CoCom attempted to restrict export of the most obvious defense-related commodities. Much to the dismay of the Truman administration, western European countries adopted a definition of strategic commodities that was much more relaxed that the American.

INDUSTRIAL DEFENSE PRODUCTION AND STRATEGIC RESOURCES, 1950–1953: THE COMMUNIST BLOC

In November 1950 Stalin issued orders that all the East bloc leaders were to convene a special meeting in Moscow. The Soviet leader pointed out that the highest priority should be immediately given to increasing the defense production of the COMECON economies. He issued a dire warning that within the next three to four years the communist countries would be in a position to deal a decisive blow against western Europe. Consequently, military spending was to rise as high as 40 percent of the annual budgets in some of the satellite countries.[67] Precise statistics are not available during this period in part because nationalized industries provided a convenient mechanism to conceal the real defense burden that was imposed on the Soviet allies.[68]

Zbigniew Brzezinski notes that Stalin's admonitions quickly had an impact on defense production of the COMECON countries.[69] Special attention was paid to determining the overall budget allocations for defense materiel and the type of equipment that was needed by the communist armed forces. Part of these responsibilities were assumed by a new subbureaucracy within COMECON, designed to coordinate economic mobilization. Given the priorities the Soviets attached to eastern Europe for defense-related industries, one recent study indicates that COMECON during these years was more important than previous historians had realized.[70] At times Soviet authorities directly oversaw the industrial production process, and they were only removed after the Korean War had ended.

The task of mobilizing industrial defense production became a major undertaking because most industries in Poland and Czechoslovakia had been destroyed during the war and had to be completely rebuilt. The reconstruction of defense industries was complicated by the fact that the Czech Communist Party recommended the wholesale transfer of these operations to the Soviet Union. After the 1948 coup this suggestion was dropped, however.[71] Despite the inevitable bureaucratic wrangling, considerable progress was made in the modernization of arms production. One of Europe's leading arms producers, the Skoda Works, for example, was 75 percent destroyed in 1945 but shortly after 1950 was totally reconstructed.[72]

The defense production of the East bloc was unevenly distributed and evolved on an ad hoc basis. Most notable was the fact that there was a virtual absence of industrial defense production in East Germany except for the increased output of uranium ore. In the first stage of mobilization during the early years of the Korean War, Poland, for no apparent reason, was ordered to assume a heavier share than the other bloc countries. Polish authorities later estimated that 11 percent of all industrial investment during the period 1951–1955 went into the expansion of defense production capacity.[73] Hilary Minc, head of economic planning, recalled the one-sided nature of the defense production decision-making process. The Soviets "skimmed the cream of output." The country was therefore left with a negligible consumer-based economy and by 1953 was burdened with "a half-war economy."[74]

The shipyards at Gdyania produced smaller naval vessels in line with Soviet specifications. The production of tanks, armored vehicles, and other heavy weapons was located in Gliwice, while the truck plants at Starachowice produced military transportation equipment. Similar to the guidelines that were issued to other East bloc satellites, production was to be determined by where there were shortages in the Soviet Union and type of industries that would require the least amount of industrial defense technology transfer. This last point was notable in the development of a limited Polish aircraft industry that was restricted to the production of smaller trainer aircraft.[75]

The new priority assigned to defense production had a ripple effect on more traditional industries, most notably in the area of steel production. When direct national security considerations were paramount, the Soviets in some cases provided engineers and economic advisers. The best example was the upgrading of the Polish Nowa Huta Steel Works by the end of 1953. But despite the assistance from Soviet engineers, the Nowa Huta plant did not quite achieve the efficiencies originally anticipated. The upgraded Gottwald Works in Czechoslovakia produced about the same amount of steel as the Polish plant but with 3,000 fewer employees.[76] Elsewhere throughout the bloc, in response to the Korean War mobilization, there was modernization of the Stalin Works at Dunapentele in Hungary, which became operational in 1952.[77]

Czechoslovakia also emerged as a key player during the Korean War mobilization. In fact, by the signing of the Warsaw Pact in 1955, that country had come to replace Poland as the largest armaments producer in eastern Europe. In November 1950 the Czech Communist Party committed the country to a new defense production agreement with the Soviet Union that was expanded on in February 1951. There were rumors in the Western press of this new agreement, but for the most part, the details were shrouded in secrecy. Later information indicated that arms spending rose from 1 percent before the Korean War to over 10 percent of gross industrial production, absorbing up to 30 percent of engineering production by 1953.[78]

Arms production in Czechoslovakia remained a branch operation dependent on Soviet technology. In the case of major weapons systems the Soviets restricted the satellites to the production of component parts. Czechoslovakia was significant during this period in that it became the supplier of the most advanced parts for weapons systems. Jet engines built to Soviet specifications were produced for the MIG 15, but full assembly of this fighter was not allowed until after 1953 when it was becoming obsolete.[79]

The expansion of defense production facilities in Czechoslovakia and the other allies offered several advantages to the Soviet Union. In contrast to the experience of the Western allies there were few problems regarding standardization that had to be resolved by way of diplomacy and compromise. Another advantage was the nature of labor markets in totalitarian states. After the outbreak of the Korean War the Czechoslovakian government stepped up operations at the Jachymov uranium mines, making good use of a new class of mining workers. This involuntary proletariat was largely composed of those accused of being associated with the Rudolf Slansky wing of the Communist Party, the unfortunate victims of the 1949 nationwide purge. While more communists were killed between 1948 and 1953 by the new Stalinist regime than were executed during the Nazi occupation, several thousands did survive only to be used as slave laborers in the uranium mines.[80] Given the quality and diversity of Czech small arms production, the Soviets were confident that communist revolutionaries abroad would be well equipped. Moreover, by working through Czechoslovakia, ostensibly an independent state of the Soviet Union, that country became a convenient conduit for the export of arms to further unrest in the Middle East and Guatemala.[81]

Hungary offers a useful example of the changing role of the Soviets in the state planning process of the satellite nations. Compared to the Hungarian Three-Year Plan of 1947, the 1950 Five-Year Plan was designed to directly serve the industrial defense production interests of the Soviet Union. Under this plan nearly half of the increased expenditures were allocated for industrial expansion related to defense. Consequently, industrial consumer goods production remained almost nonexistent until the 1960s. Traditional sectors such as agriculture and the service industries were also seriously neglected.[82]

Arms production was concentrated on armored vehicles, small arms, and ammunition assembled at Godolloi Gepgyar plant. This operation was the largest defense production facility in the country and was directly controlled by the Ministry of Defense. One analyst observed the beginning of an electronic communications equipment industry, which by the 1980s would constitute 75 percent of total military output.[83] As for strategic materials the highest priority was given to Hungarian bauxite production, the country's primary natural resource. After 1950 processing plants were expanded in Inota, Ajka, and Slmasfuzito. The alumina extracted at these sites was then sent by river and sea to the Soviet Volgograd aluminum plant, which in turn was used primarily for aircraft production.[84]

THE UNITED STATES AND THE PREPARATION FOR WAR: MOBILIZATION OF DEFENSE PRODUCTION AND STRATEGIC RESOURCES, 1950–1953

The Korean War, the limited mobilization of American armed forces in response to the recommendations of NSC #68, and the rearmament of NATO forced the Truman administration to reconsider what and how much military equipment was to be produced for itself and its allies abroad. The coordination of defense production within the Western alliance was conducted under the auspices of NATO's Defense Production Board. Canada, Great Britain, and the United States largely determined the division of defense production during the early 1950s. Britain, for example, was to produce for itself and supply weapons systems such as the Centurian tank to the allies on the European continent. Canada and the United States produced about two-thirds of the output of goods and services of the NATO member nations and therefore became the primary "arsenal of democracy." In an effort to rationalize the continental division of production a special bilateral arrangement was worked out under the terms of the 1950 Washington Agreement.

The "invitation to empire" thesis, developed by Geir Lundestad, nicely captures the essence of the Canadian-American relationship during the Korean War buildup. Canada generally took the initiative to promote greater American reliance on its strategic resources and defense-related industries. The United States was accommodating for the most part, largely because it made sense to diversify industrial defense production for strategic reasons related to Soviet targeting. Moreover, it would help reduce the pressing dollar gap problem in Canadian-American trade. If questions were raised by skeptical isolationists in Congress about dispensing favors to their northern neighbor, the Truman administration usually responded by pointing out that American multinationals in Canada stood to benefit the most from the continental integration of defense production.

The United States assumed a leadership position within the Western alliance but did not always gain strategic advantages at the expense of its allies. When strategic considerations of the Western alliance conflicted with Canadian domestic budgetary priorities, Ottawa usually held its ground. This was certainly the case when Ottawa officials resisted American pressure on Canada to increase defense spending and provide greater military support to the NATO alliance.

Conversely, Canadian pressure on the United States had some impact, a case in point being the Department of Defense's (DOD) use of a "creative interpretation" of the procurement process. By circumventing the "Buy America" Act the DOD was able to significantly increase the import of Canadian defense equipment. Almost immediately Canadian electronic and automobile industries landed new contracts south of the border, which greatly contributed to their bottom line. In an all-out effort to revitalize the Canadian electronics industry, long-term contracts were let by the DOD for over $100 million for proximity fuses, amplifiers, navigational devices, and radar sets. Additional contracts were awarded to Canadian automobile manufacturers for 6,600 military vehicles, which were in turn shipped to the NATO allies under the Mutual Security Aid program.[85]

During the Korean War one of the most effective weapons in the field was the North American Aviation F-86 fighter. There was great demand for this weapons system not only by the U.S. Air Force but by the Canadian Air Force as well. The problem facing Ottawa officials was a serious balance-of-trade deficit with the United States that restricted further imports from the United States. The best workable solution was to expand production and license out the production design of the F-86 to the Canadair plant in Montreal. The United States also shared the latest jet engine technology with its northern ally. The result was the production of the Sabre V equipped with Canadian-made, state-of-the-art Orenda engines. There were 1,550 of these aircraft that rolled off Canadian assembly lines, of which over 600 were acquired by the United States and the NATO allies in Europe.[86] What was of some significance about this arrangement was that the United States extended such highly classified technological information on advanced weapons systems, an advantage that the East bloc allies enjoyed on a much more limited basis.

The United States also turned to Canada for a wide range of strategic resources, but it was the Canadians that usually took the initiative to negotiate long-term contracts. The United States was generally accommodating to the Canadians, given the demands of the stockpiling program and Korean War mobilization. To assure adequate supplies of Canadian titanium the U.S. Department of Mines made available the results of its most recent research on the smelting, fabricating, and processing of titanium.[87] Washington officials made every effort possible to extend concessions on price, volume, and long-term contracts and the reduction of tariff restrictions. The Truman administration also overcame pressures at home to buy more from domestic producers. Again considerations of national security explain American behavior.[88]

One of the best examples that highlights the nature of the American approach to mobilizing the Western alliance was the issue of uranium production and procurement. Like the Soviets, American defense officials gave the highest priority to the acquisition of uranium ore for the atomic bomb program. But the approach was considerably different. In the case of relations with Canada the United States negotiated a series of contracts extending through the Korean War to buy uranium oxide at a price that was higher than that given to competitive foreign producers like the Belgian Congo. To ensure that production proceeded as quickly as possible, the Americans relied less on expanding the labor force (the use of draft labor in the case of the Soviet Union) and more on introducing technological innovations. Consequently, the American government offered advanced and highly classified technical assistance for geological surveys, exploration, and final processing. To ensure the security of supply the United States in 1951 negotiated a new contract raising the price ceiling to $11.25 per pound, and the period of guaranteed purchase was extended to 1962. Despite some criticism from Congress, the Atomic Energy Commission gave technical advice on certain irradiation projects at the Chalk River research facility in northern Ontario.[89]

CONCLUSION

By way of reparations, trade treaties, and the operation of joint stock companies, the Soviet Union from 1945 to 1955 was able to extract an estimated $14 billion from its satellites.[90] Ostensibly this could be viewed as a direct asset to Soviet security, but there were some complicating factors. As noted above, there were numerous incidents involving the removal of industrial equipment that simply did not reach its intended destination, or if it did, there was improper reassembly upon arrival in the Soviet Union.[91]

The USSR did succeed in dramatically reducing the economic dependency of its eastern European sphere on the West. At the time the negative consequences of imposing the Soviet economic model were not immediately apparent. By the early 1950s, however, there was clear evidence indicating duplication of effort, overproduction of unsalable products, and an underproduction of much needed equipment. Despite the rhetoric about the equality of the socialist alliance, the East bloc overall was characterized by uneven economic development between countries and sectoral distortions within their domestic economies. It was generally a one-sided zero-sum economic game in which the Soviets benefitted from the acquisition of selected war materials such as uranium and bauxite, component parts of weapons systems, transportation vehicles, and armaments. But on the other hand, recent evidence suggests the Soviet Union did not gain much by absorbing excessive quantities of coal and steel from its satellites.[92] A major problem never resolved was the rational determination of exchange values by the operation of market forces. Instead, value was determined arbitrarily by Soviet trade planners and for the most part did not approximate the more reasonable exchange conditions of the Western alliance.[93]

Marx observed that the appearance of things did not always correlate with the essence of things. The ruling elite in the Kremlin, often unaware of the limits of totalitarian state control, confirms this Marxist insight. The earliest sign that the Soviet search for security through empire was not going to produce the desired results appeared in Czechoslovakia, the most Stalinist of the east European regimes. After communist authorities stepped up defense production at the Skoda works in Plzen in 1951, the plant was faced with a massive strike of 20,000 workers who proceeded to shut down all operations.[94] Unrest continued into 1953, and the police responded by clubbing and shooting several dozen workers.[95] Similarly, Hungary throughout 1952 and 1953 faced outbreaks by workers in the Matyas Rakosi steelworks in Csepel outside Budapest and in industrial operations in Ozd and Diosgyor. Across the border to the north, sporadic outbursts of worker unrest were reported in Poland.

The most serious uprising within the people's democracies broke out in the Soviet-occupied zone of East Germany. In 1952 Stalin ordered a reduction in the production of consumer-related goods further complicated by a production speedup in the heavy industrial sector, notably chemicals, steel, and electrical machinery. Again the proletariat faced a new round of intensive labor production targets that would be implemented indefinitely without compensation. The result was not the one anticipated in Moscow. Almost immediately the number of Germans fleeing to the western zones increased, and the stage was set for a massive protest by strikers and demonstrators in June of 1953. The Soviets, who were confident that worker unrest could only be instigated by foreign subversives, responded by dispatching troops sent in to restore order.[96]

It was only after the 1953 riots that the Soviets recognized the limits of the Stalinist model of total economic control of their German satellite. Moscow moved cautiously and later that year provided some assistance to the ailing East German economy. East Germany welcomed the annulment of the remaining $3.2 billion in reparations payments and received a modest loan of $125 million. These gestures were a step in the right direction but did not stem the outflow of the population to the West. From 1949 to 1961 an estimated 2.5 million fled to West Germany.[97] Nor were the Soviets able to avoid another round of nationalist unrest throughout Poland and Hungary in 1956.

The outcome of eight years of American economic leadership in the Western bloc stands in contrast to the exercise of Soviet power over its sphere of influence. Like the Soviet Union, the United States took the initiative to create a new economic order within its sphere of influence. However, as the above discussion suggests, there were significant differences in the approach and the substance of policy. The search for security in the Western alliance was different in that the United States relied on a series of bilateral and multilateral organizations and the occasional use of personal diplomacy. Thomas Zeiler, in a recent study of Cold War foreign economic policy, emphasizes the point that the search for security was nearly always achieved through consensus. Most notably, concessions were extended to the British who were significantly at odds with the multilateral and laissez-faire policies of William Clayton and other free traders within the State Department.[98] In short, the United States understood how its national security interests overlapped with the economic interests of its key allies. The evidence suggests that in the West there was a sense of "enlightened capitalist internationalism" in contrast to the inconsistencies of "proletarian internationalism."

The record of how the United States pursued security interests while attending to the economic interests of its allies from 1945 to 1953 was not unimpressive. After four years of Marshall Plan assistance, European agricultural and industrial output was up 10 and 35 percent, respectively, over prewar levels.[99] This aid, calculated to improve American exports and the fortunes of East Coast shipping companies, and not the least, the protection of a favorable balance of power in Europe, was described by Winston Churchill as "the most unsordid act in history."[100] Great Britain governed by an occasionally troublesome social democratic government was the largest beneficiary of Marshall Plan aid ($3.2 billion). By the early 1950s its economy had recovered significantly and GNP was well beyond the prewar highs. Despite some wrangling over Imperial Preferences, the British trade position had improved, and its currency reserves were healthy. By the early 1950s the United States was able to restore a trading balance within the North Atlantic Triangle. Overall for the Western alliance there was a dramatic improvement in defense production and general economic prosperity. In the long term the European economy would emerge as a serious competitor to the United States, but in the period 1945–1953 the primary objectives of maintaining political stability and containing communist expansion were achieved.

The American impact on Canada was in many respects even more dramatic. From 1945 to 1953 total U.S. investments amounted to $3.9 billion, about one-third of which was concentrated in the high-technology defense-related industries. This investment helped to diversify the Canadian industrial sector, improve the balance of trade through increased exports, and strengthen the Canadian dollar. Throughout the postwar period, growth rates were generally higher in Canada than in the United States. In several leading economic categories—level of employment, rate of increase in per capita income, and the strength of its currency—Canada surpassed the United States.[101]

The Soviet record indicates that there were few restraining influences standing in the way of total domination of its sphere of influence. There was certainly little sense of proletarian internationalism or a realization that a common Slavic heritage should enlighten policy beyond the immediate calculation of self-interest. Clearly the impulses of revenge cannot be discounted in the case of East Germany and Hungary. But Georgi Malenkov underscored the point that above all Stalin's regime sought to "strengthen our might, strengthen our air force, strengthen our socialist state, strengthen our glorious Red Army, and Navy."[102] In the end, Stalin's relentless pursuit of national security only heightened suspicions in the West and stirred discontent among its allies. Not only was it ruthless, Stalin's quest for security was insatiable, at least in the opinion of George Kennan, the former State Department official and noted Sovietologist. "Nothing short of complete disarmament, delivery of our air and naval forces to Russia and resigning of powers of government to American communists" would in Kennan's opinion be enough to appease Stalin.[103]

On the American side the economic foundations of the Western alliance were influenced by immediate considerations of national security related to the fighting of the Second World War and the Cold War. In economic terms the modern "special relationship" stands in contrast to the narrow isolationism on the part of Washington officials to address the financial and commercial difficulties of Britain and Canada after the First World War. But in addition to war and Cold War the "special relationship" was also facilitated by a common cultural heritage and intangible factors such as personal ties between Mackenzie King, Winston Churchill, and Franklin Roosevelt that extended into the postwar period. Nor can the common vision of the North Atlanticists, who made up the second tier of officials within the Foreign Ministries of the three allies, be underestimated as well.

The key promoters of North Atlantic ties in the Truman administration—George Kennan, William Clayton, Dean Acheson, and George Marshall—were crucial in that these farsighted diplomats were able to translate general notions about the "special relationship" into specific policies. One of the best examples of the American approach to building the economic foundations was the Marshall Plan. One official recalled that "the whole thrust of U.S. policy was to insist that Europeans collectively make their own decisions."[104] That way, the United States would win over in the long run the goodwill of its allies while at the same time having the ERP monitored by its recipients to make the program as efficient and expeditious as possible. Of course, the historical record is clear that enlightened self-interest did not always inform American relations with Central America as the numerous military interventions in the twentieth century testify. But on the other hand, there is no enduring legacy of COMECON's socialist reconstruction that the current eastern European nations fondly recall.

NOTES

1. Vladislav Zubok and Constantine Pleshakov, *Inside the Kemlin's Cold War* (Cambridge, 1996), 34–35, 50–51; Bruce Franklin, ed., *The Essential Stalin: Major Theoretical Writings, 1905–1952* (New York, 1972), 472–73.

2. Valerie Bruce, "The Empire Strikes Back: The Transformation of the Eastern Bloc from a Soviet Asset to a Soviet Liability," *International Organization*, 39 (Winter 1985), 1–46; Victor Winston, "The Soviet Satellites—Economic Liability?" *Problems of Communism*, 7 (January–February 1958), 14–20.

3. Recent studies include Lee Kendall Metcalf, "The Creation of a Socialist Trading System," *East European Quarterly*, 29 (January 1996), 465–85; Bruce, "The Empire Strikes Back," 1–46.

4. For examples of two dissenting views of this process, see Joyce Kolko and Gabriel Kolko, *The Limits of Power* (New York, 1972); Robert Pollard, *Economic Security and the Origins of the Cold War*, 1945–1950 (New York, 1985).

5. Geoffrey Swain and Nigel Swain, *Eastern Europe since 1945* (New York, 1993), 28–47; Joseph Rothschild, *Return to Diversity: A Political History of East Central Europe since World War II* (New York, 1993), 76–124.

6. Jeremy Isaacs and Taylor Downing, *Cold War: An Illustrated History, 1945–1991 Companion to the CNN TV Series* (New York, 1998).

7. John B. Brebner, *North Atlantic Triangle: The Interplay of Canada, the United States and Great Britain* (New York, 1945).

8. Helen Carrere D'Encausse, *Big Brother: The Soviet Union and Soviet Europe* (New York, 1987), 47–71.

9. V.M. Sokolov, *Soviet Use of German Science and Technology, 1945–1946* (New York, 1955).

10. Beate Ruhm von Oppen, ed., *Documents on Germany under Occupation, 1945–54* (London, 1955), 141.

11. R. Judson Mitchell, "A Theoretical Approach to the Study of Communist International Organizations," in Jan F. Triska, ed., *Communist Party-States* (New York, 1969), 93.

12. "Potsdam Conference (1945)," in John Findling, ed., *Dictionary of American Diplomatic History* (New York, 1989), 426.

13. Milovan Djilas, *Conversations with Stalin*, Michael B. Petrovich, trans. (New York, 1962), 153.

14. Norman M. Naimark, *The Russians in Germany: A History of the Soviet Zone of Occupation, 1945–1949* (Cambridge, MA, 1995), 167.

15. Derek Aldcrott, *The European Economy, 1914–1970* (London, 1978), 135.

16. John Prados, *The Soviet Estimate: U.S. Intelligence Analysis and Russian Military Strength* (New York, 1982), 53–54; Steven J. Zaloga, *Target America: The Soviet Union and the Strategic Arms Race, 1945–1964* (Novato, CA, 1993), 115–21.

17. Norman M. Naimark, *The Russians in Germany: A History of the Soviet Zone of Occupation, 1945–1949* (Cambridge, MA, 1995), 238–50.

18. Ibid., 178–83.

19. Molotov quoted in Zubok and Pleshakov, *Inside the Kremlin's Cold War*, 49.

20. Charles Gati, *Hungary and the Soviet Bloc* (Durham, NC, 1986), 22–27; Stan-

ley Max, *The United States, Great Britain, and the Sovietization of Hungary, 1945–1948* (Boulder, CO, 1985), 19–32.

21. Zbigniew Brzezinski, *The Soviet Bloc: Unity and Conflict* (Cambridge, MA, 1967), 125.

22. Joseph Held, "1945 to the Present," in Joseph Held, ed., *The Columbia History of Eastern Europe in the Twentieth Century* (New York, 1992), 204–11; Andras B. Gollner, "Foundations of Soviet Domination and Communist Political Power in Hungary, 1945–1950," *Canadian-American Review of Hungarian Studies*, 3 (Fall 1976), 85–94.

23. Susan Glanz, "Economic Platforms of the Various Political Parties in the Hungarian Elections of 1945," *Hungarian Studies Review*, 22.1 (Spring 1995), 31–45.

24. Vojtech Mastny, *The Cold War and Soviet Insecurity: The Stalin Years* (New York, 1996), 19–20.

25. Vojtech Mastny, *Russian's Road to the Cold War* (New York, 1979), 180–82.

26. Stalin quoted in Brzezinski, *The Soviet Bloc*, 113.

27. Stanley J. Zyzniewski, "The Soviet Economic Impact on Poland," *American Slavic and East European Review*, 18.2 (April 1959), 206–9.

28. Stephan Horak, ed., *Poland's International Affairs, 1919–1960: A Calendar* (Bloomington, IN, 1964), 182–83.

29. Stanislaw Mikolajczk, *The Pattern of Soviet Domination* (New York, 1948), 158–59; Victor Winston, "The Polish Bituminous Coal-Mining Industry," *The American Slavic and East European Review*, 15 (February 1956), 55–56.

30. Irwin Isenberg, *The Soviet Satellites of Eastern Europe* (New York, 1963), 25.

31. Vojtech Mastny, "Eastern Europe and the West in the Perspective of Time," in William E. Griffith, ed., *Central and Eastern Europe: The Opening Curtain?* (London, 1989), 25.

32. David Holloway, *Stalin and the Bomb* (New York, 1994), 109.

33. Jan Wszelaki, *Communist Economic Strategy: The Role of East-Central Europe* (Washington, DC, 1959), 69.

34. Hugh Seton-Watson, *The East European Revolution* (New York, 1971), 223–34.

35. Geir Lundestad, *The American "Empire"* (New York, 1990), 54–62.

36. President Truman quoted in Thomas Paterson, *Soviet-American Confrontation: Postwar Reconstruction and the Origins of the Cold War* (Baltimore, MD, 1983), 5.

37. Warren Kimball, *Swords or Plowshares? The Morgenthau Plan for Defeated Nazi Germany, 1943–1946* (Philadelphia, 1976).

38. Even left-revisionist critics have described the American occupation of Japan as being "fundamentally progressive." With respect to social reform and economic development, see, for example, John W. Dower, "Occupied Japan and the Cold War in Asia," in Michael Lacy, ed., *The Truman Presidency* (New York, 1991), 379.

39. Brebner, *North Atlantic Triangle*. For an update of some of the themes developed by Brebner, see B.J.C. McKercher and Lawrence Aronsen, eds., *The North Atlantic Triangle in a Changing World: Anglo-American-Canadian Relations, 1903–1956* (Toronto, 1996).

40. Robert Hathaway, "Economic Diplomacy in Time of Crisis," in William

H. Becker and Samuel F. Wells, Jr., eds., *Economics & World Power* (New York, 1984), 23–32; Raymond F. Mikesell, "Negotiating at Bretton Woods, 1944," in Raymond Dennett and Joseph E. Johnson, eds., *Negotiation with the Russians* (Boston, 1955), 101–12.

41. Charles S. Maier, "Alliance and Autonomy: European Identity and U.S. Foreign Policy Objectives in the Truman Years," in Michael J. Lacey, ed., *The Truman Presidency* (New York, 1989), 277.

42. John Holmes, *The Shaping of Peace: Canada and the Search for World Order, 1943–1957* (Toronto, 1979), 1: 229–95.

43. Quoted in Lawrence Aronsen, "From World War to Cold War: Cooperation and Competition and the North Atlantic Triangle, 1945–1949," in B.J.C. McKercher and Lawrence Aronsen, eds., *The North Atlantic Triangle in a Changing World: Anglo-American-Canadian Relations, 1903–1956* (Toronto, 1996), 195.

44. Gregory A. Fossedal, *Our Finest Hour: Will Clayton, the Marshall Plan, and the Triumph of Democracy* (Stanford, CA, 1993), 184–90.

45. Carolyn Eisenberg, "Working Class Politics and the Cold War: American Intervention in the German Labor Movement, 1945–49," *Diplomatic History*, 7 (Fall 1983), 283–306.

46. See, for example, Kolko and Kolko, *The Limits of Power*, 361–64, 385–87.

47. Mastny, *The Cold War and Soviet Insecurity*, 23–29.

48. M. Kaiser and J.G. Zielinski, *Planning in East Europe* (London, 1970), 24–25.

49. Paul Marer, "Soviet Economic Relations with Eastern Europe," in Sarah Meiklejohn Terry, ed., *Soviet Policy in Eastern Europe* (London, 1984), 159–60.

50. Chairman of the Czech Social Democratic Party quoted in Lee Kendall Metcalf, "The Creation of a Socialist Trading System," *East European Quarterly*, 29 (January 1996), 469.

51. Robert M. Slusser and Jan F. Triska, eds., *A Calendar of Soviet Treaties 1917–1957* (Stanford, CA, 1959), 240, 245, 256.

52. Enro Gero quoted in Ivan T. Berend, *Central and Eastern Europe, 1944–1993* (Cambridge, UK, 1996), 36.

53. Brezezinski, *The Soviet Bloc*, 91–92, 102–3.

54. F.L. Pryor, *The Communist Foreign Trade System* (Cambridge, MA, 1963), 200–201.

55. Berend, *Central and Eastern Europe*, 79.

56. Heinz Kohler, *Economic Integration in the Soviet Bloc with a East German Case Study* (New York, 1965), 27–37.

57. Seton-Watson, *The East European Revolution*, 260–81.

58. See, for example, Thomas G. Paterson, *On Every Front: The Making and Unmaking of the Cold War* (New York, 1991), 87; Walter LaFeber, *America, Russia, and the Cold War, 1945–1990* (New York, 1990), 69–70.

59. Alan Palmer, *Dictionary of Twentieth Century History 1900–1982* (New York, 1983), 97; J. Robert Wegs, *Europe since 1945* (New York, 1984), 39–40.

60. Adam Zwass, *The Council for Mutual Economic Assistance* (Armonk, NY, 1989), 3–8.

61. "Council for Mutual Economic Assistance," in Thomas S. Arms, ed., *Encyclopedia of the Cold War*, (New York, 1994), 142–43.

62. Alexander Gregor quoted in Martin Myant, *The Czechoslovak Economy 1948–1988* (New York, 1989), 15.

63. Richard N. Gardner, *Sterling Dollar Diplomacy: Anglo-American Collaboration in the Reconstruction of Multilateral Trade* (New York, 1969), 360.

64. Ottawa officials advised the Truman administration on how to use the national security issue to gain congressional support for the Off-shore Purchases Clause of the Marshall Plan under which the Canadians were able to export to Europe. See Memorandum of conversation between Ambassador Wrong and Mr. Andrew B. Foster concerning the Canadian dollar problem, September 25, 1947, *Documents on Canadian External Relations 1947* (Ottawa, 1993), 13: 1428–29.

65. Pollard, *Economic Security and the Origins of the Cold War, 1945–1950*, 133–67; Randall B. Woods and Howard Jones, *Dawning of the Cold War: The United States' Quest for Order* (Athens, GA, 1991), 153–73.

66. Michael Mastanduno, "Trade as a Strategic Weapon: American and Alliance Export Control Policy in the Early Postwar Period," in G. John Ikenberry, David A. Lake, and Michael Mastanduno, eds., *The State and American Foreign Economic Policy* (London, 1988), 135–36.

67. Mikhail Heller and Aleksandr Nekrich, *Utopia in Power: The History of the Soviet Union from 1917 to the Present* (New York, 1982), 504–5.

68. Michael Checinski, "Warsaw Pact/CEMA Military-Economic Trends," *Problems of Communism* 36 (March–April 1987), 16–17.

69. Brzezinski, *The Soviet Bloc, Unity and Conflict*, 128.

70. Wlodzimierz Brus, "1950 to 1953: The Peak of Stalinism," in M.C. Kase, ed., *The Economic History of Eastern Europe 1919–1975* (Oxford, 1986), 4.

71. Condoleezza Rice, "Defense Burden-Sharing," in David Holloway and Jane M.O. Sharp, eds., *The Warsaw Pact: Alliance in Transition?* (Ithaca, NY, 1984), 65–66.

72. Yudit Kiss, *The Defence Industry in East-Central Europe: Restructuring and Conversion* (Oxford, 1997), n. 28, 42.

73. Andrezej Korbonski, *The Politics of Socialist Agriculture in Poland: 1945–1960* (New York, 1965), chap. 8, 10.

74. Hilary Minc quoted in Paul Marer, "The Political Economy of Soviet Relations with Eastern Europe," in Sarah M. Terry, ed., *Soviet Policy in Eastern Europe* (New Haven, CT, 1984), 158.

75. R.E.H. Mellor, *COMECON: Challenge to the West* (New York, 1971), 37–38.

76. Richard F. Staar, *Poland 1944–1962: The Sovietization of a Captive People* (New Orleans, 1962), 95–96.

77. Kiss, *The Defence Industry in East-Central Europe*, 123–25.

78. K. Kaplan, *The Overcoming of the Regime Crisis after Stalin's Death in Czechoslovakia, Poland and Hungary* (Cologne, 1986), 6–7; John N. Stevens, *Czechoslovakia at the Crossroads* (New York, 1985), 49–50.

79. Rice, "Defense Sharing Burden," 66–67.

80. Richard Crampton and Ben Crampton, *Atlas of Eastern Europe in the Twentieth Century* (London, 1996), 157.

81. Ernest Bock, "Soviet Economic Expansionism," *Problems of Communism*, 7 (July–August 1958), 32–33.

82. Berend, *Central and Eastern Europe*, 80–81.

83. Yudit Kiss, *The Defence Industry in Eastern Europe, 1944–1993* (Cambridge, UK, 1996), 80–81.
84. Mellor, *COMECON: Challenge to the West*, 47–48.
85. Lawrence Aronsen, *American National Security and Economic Relations with Canada, 1945–1953* (Westport, CT, 1997), 89–94.
86. "Super Sabres," *Aviation Week*, August 27, 1956, 37–38.
87. U.S. Bureau of Mines, *Minerals Yearbook, 1953* (Washington, DC, 1953), 1165.
88. Aronsen, *American National Security*, 142.
89. Ibid., 122–23.
90. Mastny, *The Cold War and Soviet Insecurity: The Stalin Years*, 58.
91. V. Yershov, "The First Phase of the Occupation, Confiscation and Plunder by the Army of Occupation," in Robert Slusser, ed., *Soviet Economic Policy* (New York, 1953), 1–14.
92. Michael Kaser, *Comecon: Integration Problems of the Planned Economies* (London, 1967), 20–21.
93. Robert S. Jaster "CEMA's Influence on Soviet Politics in Eastern Europe," *World Politics*, 14.3 (April 1962), 508.
94. Crampton and Crampton, *Atlas of Eastern Europe*, 169.
95. Sharon L. Wolchik, "Czechoslovakia," in Sabrina P. Ramet, *Eastern Europe: Politics, Culture and Society since 1939* (Bloomington, IN, 1998), 39–40.
96. Helene Carrere D'Encause, *Big Brother: The Soviet Union and Soviet Europe*, George Holoch, trans. (London, 1987), 132–36; S. Brant [pseud.], *The East German Rising 17th June 1953* (London, 1955).
97. Arthur M. Manhardt, Jr., "The German Democratic Republic," in Teresa Rakowska-Harmstone, ed., *Communism in Eastern Europe* (Bloomington, IN, 1984), 148.
98. Thomas W. Zeiler, *Free Trade Free World: The Advent of GATT* (Chapel Hill, 1999), 105–25.
99. "Marshall Plan," in Arms, *Encyclopedia of the Cold War*, 383–85.
100. Winston Churchill quoted in Michael Kort, *The Columbia Guide to the Cold War* (New York, 1998), 151.
101. "Canada's Economic Boom," *U.S. News & World Report*, June 4, 1954, 110.
102. Georgi Malenkov quoted in Caroline Kennedy-Pipe, *Stalin's Cold War: Soviet Strategies in Europe, 1943 to 1956* (New York, 1995), 94.
103. George Kennan quoted in James Chace, *Acheson: The Secretary of State Who Created the American World* (New York, 1998), 153.
104. Richard Bissell quoted in *The New York Times*, June 7, 1987.

CHAPTER 4

Containment, "Disease," and Cold War Culture

Geoffrey S. Smith

> World communism is like a malignant parasite, which feeds on diseased tissue.
>
> *George F. Kennan*[1]

> It's like a germ. It can spread. Communists are a danger when they talk to ignorant people. Ignorant people can be used by Communists to get more converts. I think ignorant people are most likely to become Communists.
>
> *New Jersey housewife*[2]

> Is your washroom breeding Bolsheviks?
>
> *Advertisement for ScotTissue Towels*[3]

Until recently American social and diplomatic historians traversed different paths. The former stressed elite decisionmaking, cause-and-effect explanations, and great decisions for war and peace. The latter considered grassroots phenomena, often microcosmic in scope and viewed "from the bottom up," and focused on change over time and the way diverse segments and wholes fit together.[4] The phenomenon of postmodernism also influenced the split between the two disciplines. Under the influence of such French theorists as Michel Foucault and Jacques

Derrida, cultural studies challenged the notion of an objective historical past existing independently of observers and the texts they perceive.

But postmodernism with its emphasis upon interrogating discourse and rhetoric in relations between dominant and complicit social groups also converges with a key concern of foreign relations scholarship. Increasingly, issues of power in interrelated foreign and domestic policy questions demand not only careful reading of official public documents and discussions but also the unraveling of class, gender/sexual, and racial/ethnic components resting beneath, influenced by and often influencing, policy outcomes.[5]

Although some traditional diplomatic historians regard this new emphasis as a new barbarism,[6] scholars in fact have much to gain from insights garnered from cultural studies. The unifying theme of this chapter, borrowed from policy planner George F. Kennan's "long telegram" of March 1946 and President Harry S Truman's subsequent uncompromising Soviet policy, focuses upon the theme of "containments" in postwar America—buttressed by key intersecting metaphors of disease and gender. Both biomedical tropes figured prominently in U.S. policy toward the Soviet Union in Washington's locating and reinforcing boundaries in the developing Great Power conflict[7] and on the domestic front. Figures of speech in both instances provided Americans images to look for in their "culturally encoded experience," in order to determine how to interpret Cold War perils.[8] In the fifteen years following V-J Day, pronouncements about maintaining the health of the state exerted significant influence at home and abroad.

Ironically, given the primacy of American strategic power immediately after the Second World War, citizens during this period displayed deep anxiety about unseen products of the material world created during and after the war.[9] This apprehension belies the popular image of the 1950s as a placid decade, peopled by happy families, and it permeated society from elite sanctums of power to Main Street, generating genuine concern for the health of the Republic in a disordered world.[10] These anxieties—often expressed in graphic metaphor—reflected the desire to contain the pathology of Marxist-Leninist "international communism," as well as domestic cultural productions deemed harmful by the dominant security culture.[11]

Many Americans, including President Truman, Attorney General J. Howard McGrath, and Federal Bureau of Investigation (FBI) Director J. Edgar Hoover, linked metaphors of disease and gender to describe and proscribe the communist threat.[12] Truman's self-image as a "tough guy" engaged in a high-stakes game of international "poker" against a sinister adversary set the tone for the Cold War: This scenario left scant room for ambiguity, let alone accommodation.[13] Real men stood up for their beliefs, and poker was a game with winners and losers. Both themes resonated deeply in American history and culture.[14] The extent to which these metaphorical analogies helped structure American policy toward Europe and the world as enshrined in the Truman Doctrine, and later NSC-68, remains debatable.[15] Yet they gave Americans a succession of "regulative fictions," or ways of thinking of themselves at a critical juncture in world history, when the international milieu suddenly had to be rehypothesized.[16]

Opposing binary categories of a healthy and vigorous free world resisting a diseased slave world owed much to the Republic's triumph in the Second World War over European fascism and Japanese militarism.[17] Indeed, the Soviet Union inherited much of the cultural pathology imputed to fascism.[18] But where goose-stepping fascists had been immodestly visible, communists were different. They accomplished their nefarious work through stealth—through espionage and Fifth Columns, much like unseen germs and viral agents—threatening to infect debilitated areas, especially those parts of Europe devastated during the war.[19] As with all viruses, which know no boundaries, one could not be certain where the pestilence might appear—only that it would appear.[20] The tendency to treat the Soviet Union as a diseased "Other" and to use this template to identify and negate suspicious domestic groups became a permanent cultural force after the Second World War—a goad to shore up the economic health and security of Europe through the Marshall Plan and North Atlantic Treaty Organization (NATO) and a powerful mechanism to recreate at home an imagined community of perfection, to maintain links forged during the war between the body and the state, and to secure internal borders and eliminate ambiguity from the Republic's victory culture.[21]

By 1951, establishment use of spliced metaphors of disease and gender to marginalize Americans who did not embrace cultural orthodoxy reached high tide. Cold War liberals set the stage for the use of "regulative fictions" of gender and disease to pinpoint targets deemed alien, subversive, dirty, or sick.[22] Having employed gendered rhetoric in discounting the claim to masculinity of Henry Wallace's Progressive Party and leftists generally in the 1948 election, Arthur M. Schlesinger, Jr., allowed that if several critics of American Cold War policy were not servants of Moscow, unfortunately, none "objected very much to Communism." "They are," the historian continued, connecting infirmity, effeminacy, and radicalism, "the Typhoid Marys of the left, bearing the germs of infection even if not suffering obviously from the disease."[23]

Cold War security culture at home was the flip side of Washington's foreign policy of containment. In seeking to prevent the spread of the ideological pathogen of Soviet Marxism, that culture grew from the premise that secrecy—both protecting but especially crusading against the unseen (or barely glimpsed) enemy—comprised the basic means to protect security and win the Cold War abroad and discipline the body politic at home.²⁴ The consequences of this assumption proved enormous for Americans on all levels. The disease metaphor was applied by security state scientists striving to achieve a "clean" hydrogen bomb (in contrast to the "dirty" Soviet bomb); by FBI and Central Intelligence Agency (CIA) operatives endeavoring to cleanse the body politic and the world of communists, radicals, leftists, and neutralists; by military authorities and political leaders seeking to eliminate gays and lesbians from the armed services; by corporate presidents and advertising executives striving to foster a consumer-oriented society after two decades of depression and war-generated deprivation; by chemical corporations like Du Pont working to develop new and more powerful pesticides to destroy microbes and insects; by physicians pursuing a "magic bullet" for sexually transmitted disease and other illnesses like polio; and by psychiatrists, psychologists, and educators endeavoring to enable Americans to assimilate, rather than challenge, social and gender norms. Metaphors of disease and illness in the first years of the Cold War helped create a binary cultural framework where boundaries approximated the boundary between democracy and totalitarianism.²⁵

A binary culture leaves scant room for uncertainty. Either one is something or one is not. So to traverse borders between categories or to inhabit parts of both, Americans had to cross terrain carefully, lest they be deemed aberrant. Here the Cold War emphasis on secrecy provided citizens who wished to stroll near, or cross, boundaries, the privacy to do so. Secrecy also allowed people to hide what psychiatry came to call "the enemy within," and it provided the bond linking the "cult of domesticity" within nuclear families (whatever went on in the home was "nobody's business") to national and international security arrangements. The political economy of the nuclear family—the key unit in the postwar domestic cultural arrangement—in fact resembled the fledgling national security state.

Early Cold War culture often contained irreconcilable dualisms. Seeking to "reconcile the cult of domesticity with the demand for domestic security," narratives emanating from the mythic nuclear family "made personal behavior part of a global struggle with communism at the same time they personalized the international struggle with communism."²⁶ Television, that key projection booth for the corporate discourse of normalcy, reminded Americans that while the Soviets were godless, "the family that prayed together, stayed together," even if mom and dad inhabited separate beds.²⁷ In the new national security state, personal behavior comprised a key weapon in the arsenal of democracy against communism.²⁸

The peril of global nuclear holocaust after 1949 both girded and jeopardized the American vision of unbridled power.²⁹ If the "American Century" in fact endured a mere four years, it remained a compelling commemorative illusion.[30] In 1949, when the Soviet Union got the bomb, a grim metanarrative emerged, remaining submerged by its triumphal counterpart. Now, Russian nuclear capacity threatened instantaneous annihilation. Despite the much-touted "Atoms for Peace" program, and official assurances that the U.S. testing program was safe, the dangers of radiation quickly mounted, providing another problematic secret. This bad news was not part of the victory narrative; it was suppressed, together with related ill tidings, for years.[31] It remains today bitterly contested terrain, as illustrated by the aborted Smithsonian Institution exhibition in 1996 on the *Enola Gay*'s mission at war's end.[32]

Nonetheless, connections drawn between Russian communism and fascism, together with the powerful domestic alloy of traditional anticommunism, Judeo-Christian religious tenets, democratic capitalism, technological might, and militarization, bolstered the nation's claim to global authority.[33] Embracing these standards, explicit in class symbols, civic religion, and canons of sexual conduct and gender expression, allowed participation in the broader American chronicle.

Diplomat George Kennan's famous essay on containment, written in July 1947, set the early parameters of Washington's policy toward the Soviet Union, as well as influencing official mind-sets on domestic arrangements.[34] This article reiterated themes from his earlier "Long Telegram" from the Moscow embassy on February 22, 1946, which constructed Soviet-American conflict in classic Cold War binaries. Less than two weeks later, at Fulton, Missouri, British leader Winston Churchill had warned about creation of a Soviet "Iron Curtain," behind which the virus of Marxism-Leninism would intensify and proliferate. Both Churchill and Kennan construed the Soviet threat in biomedical tropes. Kennan especially saw the conflict as "a sexualized narrative of courtship and rivalry: the Other and the Same, the virile and the impotent, the satisfied and the frustrated." His analysis also "equated the containment of communism with containment of atomic secrets, of sexual license, of gender roles, of nuclear energy, and of artistic expression."[35]

Kennan's emotional call to repel Soviet "penetration" of Europe, a motif reiterated five times in his 8,000-word telegram, underlined the need for a calm and rational response to a pathological, unpredictable adversary.[36] In his view the war's devastation rendered Europe vulnerable to Marxism-Leninism. Advocating the West's need to apply quickly a mix of political and economic prophylaxis, Kennan warned of potential Soviet international wantonness. His rhetoric here, and in other writings, asserted the viral/bacterial potential of Moscow's paranoiac ideology. From this characteristic flowed, amoebalike, "many of the phenomena which we find disturbing in the Kremlin's conduct of foreign policy: the secretiveness, the lack of frankness, the duplicity, the wary suspiciousness, and the basic unfriendliness of purpose." There was no way to tell when Marxism-Leninism, through Soviet agents and spies, would move across adjacent or distant borders. Kennan sensed Russian Marxism's "seminal quality" and argued that "containing the flow long enough [would] make Soviet impotence apparent or cause a mutation."[37] The United States should seek to restrain its circulation through "a long-term, patient but firm and vigilant containment of Russian expansive tendencies."[38]

The Truman administration quickly embraced Kennan's suggestion of "firm containment designed to confront the Russians with unalterable counterforce at every point where they show signs of encroaching upon the interests of a peaceful and stable world." This approach would "increase enormously the strains under which Soviet policy must operate ... and in this way ... promote tendencies which must eventually find their outlet in either the break-up or gradual mellowing of Soviet Power." Moscow could not "face frustration indefinitely without eventually adjusting itself in one way or another."[39]

On the surface, Kennan portrayed himself as composed and logical—an avatar of the masculine style that came to dominate the public behavior of American leaders through the entire Cold War. He emphasized the need to keep "cool nerves, and [to maintain them] consistently, not in a provocative way but in a polite way, a calm way, persevering at all times with our own strength and firmness but never blustering or threatening, always keeping the door open for them to come in." The United States had to treat Russia "with the same courage, detachment, [and] objectivity ... with which a doctor studies unruly and unreasonable individuals."[40] In Kennan's medicalized frame of reference, the Soviet Union was a pathological entity—insecure, crossing into the dangerous realm of mental illness.

Yet beneath his unruffled exterior Kennan concealed deep anger toward Joseph Stalin and even deeper concern with the direction in which the United States appeared headed.[41] His story is a strange one, reflecting a mix of hope and disillusionment, of ambition and hubris, and the anxiety of a man as personally agitated as any cold warrior.

In the honeymoon period after Washington recognized the Soviet Union in 1933, as a diplomat Kennan enjoyed almost a "frat-house" atmosphere in the Moscow embassy, with bonds of male homosocialty flourishing until around 1937. He, along with Charles Bohlen and William Bullitt, among other personnel, partied with Russian women (especially the ballerina and ardent communist Irena Chanodskaya), savored access to Stalin and Politburo bureaucrats, and developed a paternal attitude toward the untutored ("adolescent") yet promising Russian people. But the fun and Kennan's hope that the United States had something to learn from the vibrant Russian people died with Stalin's purges and his abrupt edict cutting foreigners' access to Russians. Embittered, Kennan spent the next decade pondering the promise denied the Russian populace and the defects of American culture.[42]

By 1944 Kennan's distaste for Americans' excessive materialism, consumerism, and extreme individualism led him to believe they could neither act collectively nor responsibly to solve "community problems".[43] No less than a national catastrophe would rebuild real community and "carry away something of this stuffy individualism and force." In Kennan's view, this new community would take its cue from male elites, who would take the vote away from immigrants, African Americans, and women. Sounding much like the writer Philip Wylie, he felt that the war had transformed the nation into a "crumbling matriarchy." Female war workers and "emasculated war workers who have been corrupted and spoiled by high wages and easy working conditions" threatened gender inversion—masculinized women and feminized men. Indeed, women now exercised so much power in social, economic, and political affairs that politicians "tremble[d] at their approach." The presence of women in public life had placed "enormous power in the hands of lobbyists, charlatans, and racketeers." Moreover, he lamented, American females had "become, in comparison with the women of other countries, delicate, high-strung, unsatisfied, flat-chested and flat-footed." Family life also had suffered, as confirmed by soaring rates of juvenile delinquency. Elites, he told staff officers in June 1944 at the U.S. Legation in Lisbon, Portugal, would have to play a key role in solving "some of the really crucial internal problems." Kennan's list included defending "things like independence of speech and thought, honesty, and courage of public life, dignity, and the quiet and serenity of the home and family."[44]

Kennan was not yet a policymaker when he made these observations. Within two years, of course, the Long Telegram propelled him to the head of the Policy Planning Staff in Washington. Although one may not determine the exact impact of his alarmed view of domestic American culture upon the subsequent containment policy that he sired, his anxiety about the Soviet Union included impassioned feelings about the threat to national safety posed not only by Moscow but also by American women who ventured outside the home, aliens, and minorities. Proper gender arrangements *were* important to the nation's health.

Kennan's brand of elite, liberal anticommunism differed fundamentally from populist anticommunism.[45] Where through background and training elites believed that they alone should manage the Soviet challenge, they felt that Americans generally should not. Here was the juncture at which Kennan's realist disdain for the *vox populi*, with its class and misogynist overtones, emerged. This was not surprising, as populist anticommunism often targeted the diplomatic aristocracy that men like

Kennan comprised. The Truman administration encountered this problem during the two perjury trials of New Dealer Alger Hiss, whose Harvard education, Ivy League demeanor, and condescending attitude toward his accusers struck conservative Republicans as evidence, as Senator Joseph R. McCarthy put it, that Hiss belonged to that "lace-handkerchief crowd."

Kennan's ironic insistence that the United States avoid an overly emotional response to the Soviet Union dovetailed with his disdain for "the hysterical sort" of anticommunism in America, which, he felt, resembled the degeneration of political life in the Soviet Union.[46] In his view the militarization of containment with the enactment of NSC #68 in 1950 perilously upped the ante on Soviet-American conflict and converted the reasoned policy of 1947 into an ideological, militarized crusade. This helped open the domestic political realm to anticommunist populists like McCarthy. Ironically, viewed from Kennan's elite promontory, and given accepted gender norms in 1950, the Wisconsin senator appeared to exemplify attributes that were putatively feminine. His anticommunist drive exhibited illogic, irrationality, intuition—and bordered on hysteria.

Against the background of worsening Soviet-American conflict, a domestic struggle developed between elite liberals and their conservative Republican adversaries to lay claim to healthy American masculinity and the political leverage it provided. With the foreign policy setbacks of 1949–1950—the Hiss perjury trials, the Soviet bomb, the "fall" of China, and the Korean War—the liberal establishment became vulnerable to charges of being unable to stand up to the communists.[47] It would remain so, feminized by its political opposition for its imputed failures, until McCarthy's abrupt downfall during the army-McCarthy hearings of 1954. This event sounded a death knell, for the next decade, of the claim by Republican conservatives to masculine virtue and the ability to check presidential foreign policy.[48]

Along with Soviet-American conflict and the sharpening gender war at home, the Federal government along with its supporters and adversaries sought cultural authority to distinguish between national and international security realms and between perilous and nonhazardous domestic activities. Truman's decision to hold its monopoly over the atomic bomb and all it symbolized held huge implications. For one, the choice necessitated perpetual scrutiny, not only of those Manhattan Project scientists who might compromise the great secret but of the American populace generally. As Robert Corber points out, "[O]ne of the ways that Cold War liberals tried to contain the increasing heterogeneity of American society was by linking questions of gender and social identity directly to questions of national security."[49] The politicization of marriage and family life, for example, of gay and lesbian identity, and of cultural production generally attested to the security state's determination to locate and contain cultural aberrations. The possibility of pathology within national borders also helps explain the determination of foreign policy-makers to identify neutralism and nationalism, especially in the decolonizing Third World, as evidence of communist infection. Not only did scrutiny abroad become a key to unlocking anticommunist strategy (perceptions of the global balance of power mattered more than reality), but the interlocked phenomenon of McCarthyism fed and reflected approval of the surveillance state, both on elite and grassroots levels.[50]

While ferreting communists from Hollywood, the universities, and labor unions made headlines for congressmen and self-appointed red hunters, gazing at neighbors became a patriotic act for average citizens. One by-product of this dynamic was the furnishing of modern "closet epistemology" as a symbolic refuge furnished by the dominant Cold War culture.[51] As suburban homes featured new amenities (including ornate large closets), the metaphorical "closet" became a private sanctum where personalities and behaviors emerged and family dynamics developed— temporarily free from direct security-state intrusion.

The Andersons, Cleavers, Nelsons, and other happy families notwithstanding, the entire nuclear family home served after 1945 as a sort of closet, a metaphorical venue to contain tensions between social norms and individual rebelliousness, between loyalty and subversion, and between allegiance and disaffection. Here was the site where family "anomalies" like insanity, homosexuality, senility, alcoholism, bankruptcy, illegitimacy, adultery, cancer, spouse battering, and divorce might be contained.[52]

Eavesdropping in Cold War America in no way approached the level of surveillance existing in the Soviet Union. Yet middle-class perceptions of loyalty depended upon adherence to tenets of consumer capitalism, which increasingly assimilated the lofty ideals of freedom and democracy. "Keeping up with the Joneses" resonated as a domestic echo of the country's larger containment policy.[53] Americans in the 1950s marked a general shift in leisure from public spaces to the privacy of the home, do-it-yourself projects and subduing the crabgrass frontier. "No man who owns his own house and lot can be a Communist," suburban developer William J. Levitt observed in 1948, even as he assured that minorities would not live in his new tract development. "He has too much to do."[54]

Uncovering duplicity constituted the order of the day on many levels. Deciding who and what were dangerous comprised the work of myriad individuals and groups besides Levitt—President Truman's Loyalty Board, Hoover's FBI, the University of California Board of Regents, congressional enforcers of the Smith Act, McCarthy's Permanent Senate Subcommittee on Government Operations, Martin Dies's House Committee on Un-American Activities, and baby Houses on Un-American Activities

(HUACs) in states like Washington, Florida, and California.[55] Left-wing subversion, a columnist argued in an American Legion journal, was a social disease, "like a cancer. . . . Allowed to grow, it affects the vitals of the organism in such a way that its removal is a critical and sometimes fatal operation."[56]

Biomedical tropes of containment also proved powerful in popular culture. Many films and novels embraced the dominant Cold War narrative that separated friend from enemy, partner from rival, and self from Other. Security state concern with phoniness, for example, animated J.D. Salinger's protagonist Holden Caulfield in *Catcher in the Rye*. Rather than an archetype of the alienated baby boomers who became radicals in the tumultuous 1960s, Alan Nadel argues, Caulfield epitomized the many excommunists and "friendly" witnesses of the postwar era. His veracity, like theirs, rested ironically upon "the evidence of his deceitfulness."[57] Throughout the novel Holden uses the signifier "really" to distinguish what he *does* mean (he is, he reiterates, quite a deceitful chap) from the subversive rhetorical artifices of other characters in the novel.[58] His deceptions mirrored in literary form those of numerous participants in what historian Stanley I. Kutler terms "the American inquisition" and underscores the link between state- and body-related discourses.[59] Only by confessing, snitching, informing, and recanting could one reenter the church of America regnant.

The nexus between Holden Caulfield's troubled adolescence and domestic life generally underscores the importance of exploring other gender-related texts for cultural meaning. Here, invariably, grisly images of Soviet communism contrasted with attractive portraits of healthy men and women and happy children in America. The organization of American culture in the late 1940s and 1950s served the need to maintain the larger victory narrative. Under fire for its role in promoting the wartime romance with the Soviet Union, Hollywood did an about-face once investigators charged that communists were at work in the celluloid capital. Soviet domestic and family life had appeared bucolic and heroic in pro-Russian wartime films like *Mission to Moscow* (based on Ambassador Joseph Davies' experience from 1936 to 1938), *Song of Russia* (1944), *The North Star* (1944), and two 1942 B-films, *Miss V from Moscow* and *Three Russian Girls*.[60]

After the war, as the Soviet Union expanded westward, Hollywood concocted films that were as mindlessly anticommunist as wartime cinema had been uncritical. Invariably, they bombed. RKO offered the lurid *I Married a Communist*, while *The Red Menace* (1949) also underlined the deceitful role played by single, "liberated" women seeking to recruit red-blooded American males into the Communist Party. Illustrating Hollywood's use of firm gender standards to celebrate red-blooded American masculinity were celebrations of the patriotism of Matt Cvetic of Pittsburgh and Herbert Philbrick of Boston. Both men came in from the cold in 1949 to testify against and help convict several Communist Party USA (CPUSA) members for violating the Smith Act. Cvetic was a heavy drinker whose life resembled novelist Mickey Spillane's hardboiled anticommunist detective Mike Hammer. Pittsburgh celebrated "Matt Cvetic Day" to mark Warner Brothers' release of his story, *I Was a Communist for the F.B.I.*, which starred iron-jawed Frank Lovejoy and gained an Academy Award nomination as "best documentary" of the year. Philbrick, meanwhile, became even more renowned for his *I Led Three Lives* (1952), an exposé that quickly became a TV series. Both men fingered more than 500 communist agents, many of them, it turned out, FBI operatives.[61]

By mid-1947, popular anticommunism developed a pornographic aspect, based upon fantasies of Soviet invasion and enslavement of the Republic. These images often aimed at children—and families—and equaled in violence the mainstream comic books that drew congressional censure several years later.[62] Even romance comics in the late 1940s and early 1950s took time to note the red menace, with story titles like "Communist Kisses," "Behind the Romantic Curtain," and "Priority Kisses."

The link between wayward women, sexual deviance, and domestic peril gained strength in 1948 when Judith Coplon, a Justice Department employee in the Foreign Agents Registration Section, ran afoul of an FBI sting operation. J. Edgar Hoover had known for some time that Coplon, a double agent, had passed secrets to her lover Valentin Gubitchev, Soviet UN Secretariat attaché. Rather than simply order him back to the Soviet Union, Hoover—with the impeccable sense of timing of an accomplished voyeur—determined to nab Coplon en flagrante delicto. This the FBI accomplished on March 4, 1949, and the Cold War had its Mata Hari. Few observers cared that Hoover had arrested the pair without warrants and organized illegal wiretaps before, during, and after her two trials.[63]

If furtive lovers endangered national security, seemingly normal husbands and wives also needed watching. The trial and execution of Julius and Ethel Rosenberg for passing atomic secrets to the Soviet Union captured headlines between 1951 and 1953 and revealed intertwined gender, ethnic, and class themes. Ethel's dowdy appearance, her dreadful hats and singing voice, and the run-down, working-class Lower East Side neighborhood in which she lived—all intersected with questions of disloyalty in the early 1950s as unstated subtexts to the trial, as did her Jewishness and unwillingness to embrace a proper feminine role.[64] Although recently released VENONA documents confirm ("apodictically," historian Eduard Mark writes) Julius Rosenberg's involvement in the Los Alamos espionage ring, they do not incriminate Ethel, who nonetheless became the focal point of the trial.[65] Judge Irving Kaufman blamed her for her husband's weakness, deemed her a "full-fledged partner in his crime," and damned her as a woman who had sacrificed her two young sons. Worse, in Kaufman's eyes, Ethel was a mother who declined to inform to save her sons from becoming orphans.[66]

As in the Rosenberg affair, treacherous women and unsettled family situations played a central role in Cold War popular culture. Wearing trousers in the nuclear family comprised dad's primary masculine role. No film underlined this obligation, nor revealed the vulnerability of the family unit, as did *My Son John* (Paramount, 1952), the film that "came closest to blaming mom for communism." Far from safeguarding the nation from the external menace of communism, the film suggested that domestic ideology "generated aliens from within its bosom."[67] Directed by Leo McCarey, a "friendly" witness for HUAC who joined Cecil B. DeMille in 1950 to try to force all members of the Screen Actors' Guild to sign a loyalty oath, "John" politicized family privacy in the desire to protect it. Nourished by the troubling realities of the Coplon and Rosenberg spy cases, the film became in fact a gendered celluloid affidavit. Patriotic Hollywood could not tackle issues of class or race; hence McCarey "pursued the logical consequences of the only dramatically plausible alternative," the family itself, "the traditional institution that best justified the remorseless struggle against Communism."[68]

"John Jefferson," actor Robert Walker (who died during production), played a twin brother whose father (Dean Jagger) was unable to catch a football because he "was a tackle in college" and who proved ineffectual in dealing with both his boys and his wife (Helen Hayes). No matter how hard he tried, mom always was late for church and also flirted habitually with her sons. Unlike his brothers, who soon went to fight in Korea, John was an intellectual (Alger Hiss? Owen Lattimore? Adlai Stevenson?) who stayed home to deride his father for the latter's knee-jerk patriotism and American Legion uniform. Aloof from his family, John rejected his father's oft-iterated warning that communists were no longer foreigners but internal subversives who ridicule patriotic Americans like himself.

Ultimately John's father attempted to force him to swear that he was not a communist. The attempt failed, and the outraged father slammed the Bible on John's head. But mom intervened and promised to set matters right: "I'll make you cookies, pies, cake, and jam if you'll learn Matthew, Mark, Luke, and John." This peculiar offer shrouded the horrible truth—John *was* a communist, primarily, the film avers, because of his mother's permissiveness and sexual availability. John, Michael Rogin observes, "has imbibed his mother's naive humanitarianism and, to distance himself from her, taken it in a sinister direction." He has betrayed his mom.[69]

Here was evidence of journalist Philip Wylie's earlier warning (and George Kennan's) about the perils of "momism."[70] John's mother erred in only living for, and through, her son. Moviegoers soon learned that John was more than a communist—he was a spy (which his mother intuited). When John inadvertently left the key to his female communist accomplice's apartment in the pocket of a pair of trousers destined for charity, his mother discovered the dreadful secret. Then, good patriot herself, she delivered John to the FBI. In a soliloquy that mimicked the testimony of "friendly" HUAC witnesses, she asked John to confess after denouncing him to an FBI agent. When John refused, his mother collapsed on a sofa and bellowed to the agent, "Take him away! He has to be punished!" At the last moment, though, John had a change of heart and decided to confess. But before he recanted, communist thugs murdered him—on the steps of the Lincoln Memorial. Yet John still had the last word. He left a taped speech that he planned to deliver at his alma mater's convocation ceremony. In that valedictory, played for shocked graduands, he warned posthumously that "even now, the eyes of the Soviet agents are on some of you. . . . I am a living lie. I am a traitor. I am a Native American. Communist. Spy. And may God have mercy on my soul."[71]

My Son John warned that bookishness (his mother noted that John "had more degrees than a thermometer") would make a young man vulnerable to harmful political tendencies, inimical to masculinity.[72] Young men who looked bookish were not trustworthy. The film also questioned the ability of religion and parents to save a family that had propagated a communist. The FBI agent, Steadman, did this when he rejected John's father's agitated advice ("both barrels"), undercutting parental authority in favor of the secular expertise of the security state. John's mother, meanwhile, clearly valued the FBI more than her family and thus undermined the emotional loyalty that lay at the core of family life.[73] John's was the sort of mother about whom George Stoddard, president of the University of Illinois, warned in 1949—a woman who failed to set her children upon the right career path. Stoddard told the National Commission on Children and Youth that as well as shunning home economics at college for "miscellaneous liberal arts courses which usually leave her an expert on nothing," too many mothers grew easily bored. Women, he observed, failed "to make the home a center of culture for the family. In how many American homes do you find a mother teaching her children anything artistic or trying to instill in them an appreciation of good music? Instead she sends them to the movies."[74]

Under this dreary panorama of enforced traditional femininity and homophobia, there did exist activism on several fronts, including the abiding interest in labor and civil rights issues of Betty Friedan, subsequent author of the influential book *The Feminine Mystique* (1963).[75] Yet because of the dominant security culture's power, white middle-class women, from their teen years, generally hewed to the public line.[76] Patriotic American moms stayed home and kept their homes clean. Spinsters and career women—isolated from the taming alchemy of marriage and its consumer delights—were risky, as were career-oriented women generally.[77] Cold War femininity dictated full use of the corporate arsenal of lipsticks, hair coloring, girdles (and cornstarch), crinolines, garters and stockings, cigarettes, Betty Crocker cake mixes, TV dinners, Tupperware, and a variety of cleansers.[78]

Journalist Craig Thompson underlined the danger of filth in 1953 when he scorned the Jefferson School of Social Science in New York, the alleged "training school" for "doltish fledgling" Marxists. "The hallmark of communist enterprises is squalor," he wrote in *Look*, echoing elite disapproval of the Rosenberg's neighborhood and anticipating criticism of the Beat Generation, "and the Jefferson School bears the approved stamp. Peeling paint hangs from its walls, the floors are bare and scuffed, the furniture nicked and rickety and the windows gray with grime."[79] The connection between dirt, contagious disease, and Marxist ideology was clear in the minds of many Americans, especially FBI Director Hoover, with his lifelong phobia about germs.[80] Hoover's dread of germs juxtaposed well with corporate advertisers who literally ordered patriotic moms to "chase dirt." Grime was not a simple matter, as even "indoor odors" were "nearly as disturbing and pervasive as germs." Freshening products allowed housewives to cope with " 'so many chances to offend.' Cooking, bathroom, perspiration, smoking, and refrigerator odors were only a few of many that might embarrass or disgust family and friends."[81]

Many products allowed consumers to keep secrets—a hidden tummy bulge here or cellulite thighs there, or the fact that "only her hairdresser knows for sure." These were politically correct links to the secret-saturated security culture. Graceful dresses, effective foundation garments, and high heels, which highlighted feminine allure and concealed problems, gained new importance for setting American women apart from their dowdy Soviet counterparts. Soviet women were reputed to have thick ankles, dig ditches, and wear sacks—not from Fifth Avenue.[82] A 1952 issue of *Life* heralded "the Iron Curtain Look" ("high priced, wide shouldered, not very handsome") and pointed out that "the slender gams of the girl above (the wife of a former U.S. ambassador in Moscow) gives her away as American." The *Life* writer also disparaged "an anatomically unique [Russian] bra, shaped like a double-barrelled shotgun, and knitted bloomers of a shade one observer calls 'NVD blue' because it is the color of a Russian secret policeman's cap."[83] A good-looking woman wearing makeup in Moscow was "one of three things: a foreigner, an actress or a prostitute. . . . The majority of statues of women in Russian parks wear brassieres and gym pants! Needless to say, there is no 'Miss U.S.S.R.' "[84]

There was, of course, "Miss America," the female icon who from her inception in 1929 celebrated physical allure while maintaining neo-Victorian cultural borders—"emerging in all her pulchritude, in a specific setting." The addition of talent competition and college scholarships did not lessen the event's continuing emphasis upon physical beauty.[85] The popularity of beauty contests in Cold War America served as a means to enforce gender and sexual boundaries.[86] Here, again, hawking items women "could not do without" and supporting these contests, corporate sponsors assayed a key role in merging patriotism, notions of security, and ideas about femininity.

Unprecedented prosperity in the 1950s created great opportunities for entrepreneurs. They confronted a demographic bulge comprising the last of the alleged "silent generation" and the first of the baby boomers (born after 1946) in the first era of abundance since the 1920s. Nowhere was this tryst between retailers and youthful consumers, especially teenage girls, so powerful as in the popular music market.

Nowhere did the convergence of youth and money hold more meaning than the emerging popular music market. In the late 1940s and early 1950s, what became known as rock 'n' roll seemed to have shifted from the serious world of loss and angst rooted in traditional blues to an ethereal, make-believe cosmos that in its themes struck many observers as mindless fantasy.[87] Yet on two levels rock music seemed subversive in the eyes of custodians of security state culture. For one thing, as rock 'n' roll colonized popular music, it foregrounded black and working-class artists who often conveyed rebellious attitudes—which young white, middle-class Americans, with money in their pockets, embraced.[88] These boundary-disturbing crossovers provoked much moralizing by defenders of high culture and produced "cover" recordings in which such white artists as the Crew Cuts, the McGuire Sisters, and Pat Boone domesticated the primal, folk-derived raunchiness (and authenticity) of black artists like the Chords, Spaniels, Penguins, "Little Richard" Penniman, and Antoine ("Fats") Domino. "Cover" records sought to shore up the boundaries of Cold War musical culture, and they sold far more copies than works by the original artists. Condemnations of Cold War rock 'n' roll intersected with alarm about race mixing and juvenile delinquency. Not a few critics twinned "communism" and disease when damning the new musical form. Crooner Frank Sinatra thought it "a rancid-smelling aphrodisiac," while cellist Pablo Casals termed it "poison put to sound."[89] The psychiatric establishment (a Connecticut physician) deemed it a virulent, "communicable disease." "If we cannot stem the tide of rock 'n' roll with its waves of rhythmic narcosis and waves of vicarious craze, we are preparing our own downfall in the midst of pandemic funeral dances." According to the *Encyclopedia Britannica*, rock 'n' roll amounted to "instant savagery."[90] Within this censure stood the deeper Cold War concern that the music threatened borders of race, gender, and class while glorifying deviance and immaturity.

Yet a significant irony existed in rock 'n' roll. Widely viewed as an evil, alien force in 1950s America, this music in fact buttressed the values of containment culture. Its dreadful lyrics embraced Cold War sex/gender expectations of the young. Gone were the earthy laments of the blues. In their place one found such themes as "angels, paradise, weddings, eternal love, heaven, etc."[91] Even if the messengers were suspect, their message fit within prevailing cultural confines, especially its celebration of monogamy, heterosexual love, early marriage, and parenthood—all with God's blessing.[92] Rock 'n' roll lyrics sang paeans to domestic norms.

Yet in revisiting this music, one recognizes that its neanderthal litany of "doos" and "wops" comprised a youthful glossolalia arrayed mocking the saccharine ballads of singers like Perry Como, Eddie Fisher, and Rosemary Clooney.[93] Indeed, there is some truth to the argument by Stewart Kessler that the gap between the (square) *Lucky Strike Hit Parade* and Dick Clark's (hip but clean) *American Bandstand* exhibited youthful dissatisfaction with domestic Cold War arrangements. This unease, Kessler argues, knit 1950s rock 'n' roll to subsequent civil rights and student movements.[94] Songs like "Yakety Yak" and "Charlie Brown" by the Coasters, "School Day" by Chuck Berry, "Wonderful World (Don't know much about history)" by Sam Cooke, and "Get a Job" by the Silhouettes (which featured ten *shas*, thirty-five *das*, six *mums*, and eight *yips*)[95] shrouded questions about, discontent with, and alienation from the institutions of the liberal security state.[96]

Deconstructing the lyrics of these songs, therefore (and the reader is spared the agony), reveals a mixed message. Despite the proto-protest inherent in the structure of rock 'n' roll, and in some of its songs, virtually all singers and groups of the era yearned less for Peggy Sue, Julie, or Diana than for acceptance within the prevailing socioeconomic consensus. This was especially true for African American performers and working-class, often Italian American a capella groups. This desire for approval, which anticipated and accompanied the integrationist thrust of the early civil rights movement, helped catapult young artists through the golden door of the burgeoning consumer culture.[97] It also fit well within the borders of Cold War cultural expression. Historian George Lipsitz notes that 1950s singers and the young public that purchased their records confirmed that "capitalism's efficiency as an economic order and its legitimacy as a way of life" depended on "convincing people that material goods [did] not conflict with moral goals, [and] that personal happiness [could] best be achieved in the context of capital accumulation."[98]

But popular success did not bring most performers a surfeit of riches.

White singers earned more than their black contemporaries, and record companies ensured that access to the lucrative market came on corporatist terms. Even disk jockeys had to toe the line, or invent new identities. Many DJs who sounded black were in fact white; and blacks still faced difficulty securing radio jobs.[99] The payola scandal at the end of the 1950s, climaxed by the conviction of Alan Freed, the Jewish DJ who did so much to bring black music to white audiences in New York, owed much of its animus to the music establishment's reaction against rock 'n' roll's perceived subversive image. Freed, the famed "Moondog" was arrested several times for disturbing public order with his concerts.[100] Ultimately, like the Hollywood Ten, fired professors, and others who transgressed Cold War boundaries, Freed paid for his trespass by being excommunicated from the industry.

Tension between rebelliousness and the desire for acceptance—and the saleability of defiance—became clear in the response accorded Bill Haley and the Comets' huge hit in 1954, "Rock Around the Clock." This song, which became an instant teen anthem, was reissued a year later to accompany *Blackboard Jungle*, the controversial movie that linked rock music, juvenile delinquency, and racial and sexual problems and implied the inability of adult institutions (and adults) to comprehend youthful truths. Ironically, Haley issued the recording as a cover for an earlier rhythm-and-blues version; and his country and western background influenced his rendition. But "Rock Around the Clock" became the first rock 'n' roll record to top the charts—in the United States and England.

As Americans debated ways to contain juvenile delinquents like those in *Blackboard Jungle*, Elvis Presley burst upon the music scene. Like the doo-wop artists who preceded him, Presley tested the cultural establishment. His performances drew immediate fire from custodians of cultural containment—musical artists, religious groups, PTA leaders, and the psychiatric establishment. But this critique was tricky. With his release of "Heartbreak Hotel" for RCA in 1956, Presley was definitely new, exciting, unstable—but above all, a valuable commodity. Haley's blending of country and western and rock 'n' roll may have sharpened class antagonism to the new music among highbrows, but Presley brought with him a unique cultural compound—a talent that knew no boundaries nor, apparently, limits. More than any other performer in this century, the working-class truck driver from Tupelo, Mississippi, imparted to teens—especially females—his unique mix of southern blues and black Methodist hymns, his aggressive and overtly sexual guitar-playing technique, his gaudy wardrobe of gold lame suits, and his vulnerable demeanor that belied his background in heavy machinery.[101] And, like America's other 1950s rebel heroes, Marlon Brando and James Dean, he didn't smile.[102]

Defenders of elite culture quickly branded Presley a renegade, a menace—even as they booked him for shows. Ed Sullivan, self-appointed minister of national culture and gatekeeper of new (and often bizarre) talent on his Sunday night TV show, ordered cameras to focus above Presley's waist when he first appeared, to deny visual access to the singer's spastic, gyrating pelvis. This raised the ante on the pelvis, transforming it and its owner into a commodified fetish for millions. Moralists resisted, but the market insisted. Presley quickly became an icon of corporatism, a living cover, and an artist who annihilated gender, race, and class boundaries. Establishing himself as the "King" of rock 'n' roll, a mantle he wore for a decade, he helped spawn a gargantuan economic empire, producing a spinoff much as Henry Ford had with his Tin Lizzie thirty years earlier. Through Presley fledgling, independent record companies like Sam Phillips's Sun label breached ramparts previously dominated by RCA and Columbia. Only this time the children of America—with as much disposable weekly income in their pockets as entire families managed fifteen years earlier—comprised the bulk of the market.[103]

More important, like Charles A. Lindbergh three decades earlier, Presley anticipated the emergent culture of modern celebrity and consequent destruction of the long-standing division between public and private lives. That border, a key point of intersection for the secluded American nuclear family and the neo-Victorian security culture, had shielded the powerful from the gaze of the masses. Yes, there had been fan clubs before, but Elvis's fans, spanning the globe, took Hollywood one further, demanding to know *all* about their idol. They created "Elvis environments" in their rooms at home, festooned their walls with his photographs, dressed like him and wore their hair Elvis duck-tail style, and they thronged to his live performances; they (males) mimed—or (females) swooned—at his sensual sneer. All this created a sacred market space that rivaled (or surpassed) in relevance church, school, and family.[104] Presley's stardom strengthened personality and style as key components of market capitalism, and in another decade—when Americans confronted Vietnam and Watergate—this development helped undercut the ability of politicians, themselves forced increasingly to become performers, to shroud private acts behind public pieties.[105]

Yet again, despite warnings about his pernicious impact upon youth, Presley remained at base a nice person who played by all the rules and, in fact, was very much his mama Gladys's boy. He addressed his elders with the honorifics "ma'm" and "sir."[106] No, Presley did not destroy Western civilization; in fact, he helped save it. He accepted induction in 1957 into the U.S. Army and traveled to Germany as part of NATO's free world shield against Soviet pestilence.

From Kennan of Foggy Bottom to Presley of Graceland, from dating rituals to bathroom cleansers, the containment of the pathogen of communism and related domestic agents loomed large in postwar foreign policy and popular culture. Yet during the decade 1947–1957, despite its apparent strength, the core of elite containment culture began to unravel. If the national unity produced during the Second World War persisted well into the 1960s, the American victory narrative excluded too many citizens who did not feel a part of the central culture and who slowly recognized that containment aimed at them as it did the Soviets. Gays and lesbians, blacks, working women, the Beats, peace workers, antinuclear activists, and a growing number of white, middle-class teens began to question the liberal cultural consensus, even as they sought to join and enhance it.

Ironically, in the long run the prime force that made so many Americans link perceived deviance with disease was neither the Soviet Union nor the ideology of Marxism–Leninism. No, evidence here suggests that the serpent in the Edenic garden was unleashed by the postwar marketplace and such things as long-play vinyl records, drive-in movies, and cheap gasoline, which generated a huge contradiction between the self-image of a virtuous people and a nation of consumers.[107] That contradiction would shortly generate a more somber narrative to contest that of the Republic triumphant.

NOTES

1. George F. Kennan, "Moscow Embassy Telegram #511," in Thomas H. Etzold and John Lewis Gaddis, eds., *Containment: Documents on American Policy and Strategy, 1945–1950* (New York: Columbia University Press, 1978), 63.

2. For several similar comments, see Samuel A. Stouffer, *Communism, Conformity, and Civil Liberties: A Cross-section of the Nation Speaks Its Mind* (Garden City, NY: Doubleday, 1955), 156–64.

3. Andrew Ross, *No Respect: Intellectuals and Popular Culture* (New York: Routledge, 1989), 45, 150f.

4. For a dubious assessment of the contribution of cultural analyses for diplomatic history, see Melvyn P. Leffler, "New Approaches, Old Interpretations, and Prospective Reconfigurations," in Michael J. Hogan, ed., *America in the World: The Historiography of American Foreign Relations since 1941* (New York: Cambridge University Press, 1995), 63–92. For a more benign view, see Michael Hunt, "The Three Realms Revisited," in ibid., 148–55. For the problem of fragmentation in much cultural and social history, see Thomas Bender, "Wholes and Parts: The Need for Synthesis in American History," *Journal of American History*, 73 (June 1986), 120–36.

5. An important recent dialogue between culture and foreign policy appears in "Culture, Gender, and Foreign Policy: A Symposium," featuring articles by Laura McEnaney ("He-Men and Christian Mothers" before the Second World War) and Emily S. Rosenberg (" 'Foreign Affairs' " after the Second World War) and six commentaries, in *Diplomatic History*, 18 (Winter 1994), 47–124.

6. Leffler, "New Approaches," 68–70; Stephen Pelz, "Commentary on

Sharon Rudy Plaxton, 'Emasculating the Antiwar Warrior...,'" SHAFR Conference, Annapolis, MD, 1995.

7. The best recent study of American perceptions of Soviet behavior and the requirements for U.S. international security is Melvyn P. Leffler's magisterial *A Preponderance of Power: National Security, the Truman Administration, and the Cold War* (Stanford, CA: Stanford University Press, 1992). Also influencing the author's thinking about Cold War culture on internal and external levels is Michael S. Sherry, *In the Shadow of War: The United States since the 1930s* (New Haven, CT: Yale University Press, 1995), which underscores the development of a militaristic American culture after 1941, while questioning the rationality and consistent influence of the "national security state."

8. Hayden White, *Tropics of Discourse: Essays in Cultural Criticism* (Baltimore, MD: Johns Hopkins University Press, 1978), 91.

9. American medicine, of course, did vanquish dreaded poliomyelitis, with the Salk vaccine in 1954–1955. See Alan M. Brandt, *No Magic Bullet: A Social History of Venereal Disease in the United States since 1880*, with a new chapter on AIDS (New York: Oxford University Press, 1987), 161–82; William H. McNeill, *Plagues and Peoples* (Garden City, NY: Doubleday, 1976), 288.

10. See Stephanie Coontz, *The Way We Never Were: American Families and the Nostalgia Trap* (New York: Basic Books, 1992), 8–67; Arlene Skolnick, *Embattled Paradise: The American Family in an Age of Uncertainty* (New York: Basic Books, 1991), 49–74; H.W. Brands, "The Age of Vulnerability: Eisenhower and the National Insecurity State," *American Historical Review*, 94 (1989), 963–89; Douglas T. Miller and Marion Nowak, *The Fifties: The Way We Really Were* (New York: Doubleday, 1977); Paul Carter, *Another Part of the Fifties* (New York: Columbia University Press, 1983).

11. Developments described here, of course, could not have occurred without the deterioration of the Soviet-American wartime alliance into a postwar relationship of suspicion and antagonism. This external environment provided the key catalyst in influencing the Republic's need to contain its adversary, both abroad and at home.

12. In 1946, as justification for the subsequent Federal Employee Loyalty Program, Attorney General McGrath noted, "Communists are everywhere—in factories, offices, butcher shops, on street corners, in private business, and each carries in himself the germs of death for society." This "poison of disloyalty" justified "a state-initiated counterepidemic of anti-Communism." Quoted in R.J. Goldstein, *Political Repression in Modern America from 1870 to the Present* (Cambridge, MA: Schenkman, 1978), 328–29. The author's view of connections between filth, disease, and ideology has been facilitated by Cindy Patton, *Sex and Germs: The Politics of AIDS* (Boston: South End Press, 1985), and Mary Douglas, *Purity and Danger: An Analysis of the Concepts of Pollution and Taboo* (London: Ark Paperbacks, 1989).

13. Robert L. Ivie, "Literalizing the Metaphor of Soviet Savagery: President Truman's Plain Style," *Southern Speech Communication Journal*, 51 (1986), 91–105.

14. A recent, brilliant assessment of the mythical historical contributions of "real men" to American "victory" is Garry Wills, *John Wayne's America: The Politics of Celebrity* (New York: Simon & Schuster, 1997), esp. 11–27.

Containment

15. A good overview is Ernest R. May, ed., *American Cold War Strategy: Interpreting NSC 68* (Boston: Bedford Books, 1993).

16. Paul A. Chilton, *Security Metaphors: Cold War Discourse from Containment to Common House* (New York: Peter Lang, 1996), 413; Robert L. Ivie, "Cold War Motives and the Rhetorical Metaphor: A Framework of Criticism," in Martin J. Medhurst, Philip Wander, Robert L. Ivie, and Robert L. Scott, eds., *Cold War Rhetoric: Strategy, Metaphor, and Ideology* (Westport, CT: Greenwood Press, 1990), 71–79.

17. A portent of the fear of the "Other" ("enemy genes"), in this case, Japanese Americans interned in concentration camps in the Second World War, may be traced in Roger Daniels, Sandra C. Taylor, and Harry H.L. Kitano, eds., *Japanese Americans: From Relocation to Redress*, rev. ed. (Seattle: University of Washington Press, 1991).

18. Thomas G. Paterson and Les K. Adler, " 'Red Fascism': The Merger of Nazi Germany and Soviet Russia in the American Image of Totalitarianism, 1930's–1950's," *American Historical Review*, 75 (April 1970), 1046–64.

19. In the Spanish Civil War, as Franco's army advanced on Madrid in four columns, the general leading the offensive boasted of having a "fifth column," a clandestine group of fascists within the city, that would subvert the Loyalists secretly from within as his troops bridged Madrid's defenses from outside. The idea of the fifth column carried biomedical implications for the body politic and became a key part of Cold War security discourse. See John E. Haynes, *Red Scare or Red Menace: American Communism and Anticommunism in the Cold War Era* (Chicago: Ivan R. Dee, 1996), 18.

20. On disease as a metaphorical signifier, see two brilliant books by Susan Sontag, *Illness as Metaphor* (New York: Farrar, Straus and Giroux, 1978) and *AIDS and Its Metaphors* (New York: Farrar, Straus and Giroux, 1989). Sontag's focus, primarily on fiction and other literary sources, restricts the applicability of her generalizations. For suggestive analysis of the "AIDS theory of ideas," see Terry Heinrichs, "Free Speech and the Zundel Trial," *Queen's Quarterly*, 95 (1988), 837–54.

21. William E. Connolly, *Identity/Difference: Democratic Negotiations of Political Paradox* (Ithaca, NY: Cornell University Press, 1991), chaps. 1, 7; Benedict Anderson, *Imagined Communities: Reflections on the Origin and Spread of Nationalism*, rev. ed. (London: Verso, 1991); David Campbell, *Writing Security* (Minneapolis: University of Minneapolis Press, 1992), 9. Judith Butler argues (in the specific case of the body) that boundaries are "tenuously maintained by transformation of elements originally part of identity into a 'defiling otherness.' " See Butler, *Gender Trouble: Feminism and the Subversion of Identity* (New York: Routledge, 1990), 133. And Murray B. Levin, providing insight into the folklore of "otherness" during the Red Scare of 1919–1920, writes that those "Red conspirators" were "variously depicted as aliens, foreigners, Jews, vermin, lice, feces, disease, plague, epidemic, mad geniuses, scum, filth, rats, rodents, termites, snakes, criminals, idiots, anti-Christs, devils, sexually licentious, sadistic, perverse, and brutal." Levin, *Political Hysteria in America: The Democratic Capacity for Repression* (New York: Basic Books, 1971), 151.

22. Ivie, "Cold War Motives," 71; Campbell, *Writing Security*, 2.

23. Quoted in Edward Pessen, *Losing Our Souls: The American Experience in the Cold War* (Chicago: Ivan R. Dee, 1993), 146.

24. Campbell, *Writing Security*, passim.

25. One such movement, the "Rational Citizenship" movement in 1947, spearheaded by social scientists, sought to educate the public to support Cold War foreign policy in the same way that highly educated liberal elites did. But the movement, which accompanied the emergence of the anticommunist "vital center" and also sought to deter populist anticommunism, did not succeed. For one, the ideal of an informed, responsible, and involved public clashed with "realist" approaches that sought to limit public participation on foreign policy. For another, it was difficult to educate the public when so much of foreign policy was formulated privately. Charles Young, Rutgers University, H-DIPLO network, www2.h-net.msu.edu/logsearch, accessed April 9, 1996.

26. Alan Nadel, *Containment Culture: American Narratives, Postmodernism, and the Atomic Age* (Durham, NC: Duke University Press, 1995), xi; Geoffrey S. Smith, "National Security and Personal Isolation: Sex, Gender, and Disease in the Cold-War United States," *International History Review*, 14 (May 1992), 307–37.

27. Rachel S.M. Yates, "Images of Dissent, Persistence of an Ideal: Gender in Television Sitcoms in the 1950s" (master's thesis, Queen's University, 1997); Nina Leibman, *Living Room Lecture: The Fifties Family in Film and Television* (Austin: University of Texas Press, 1995); Lynn Spigel, *Make Room for TV: Television and the Family Ideal in Postwar America* (Chicago: University of Chicago Press, 1992); Ella Taylor, *Prime-Time Families: Television Culture in Postwar America* (Berkeley: University of California Press, 1989).

28. Although scholars identify the phrase "the personal is the political" with the second wave of feminism in the late 1960s, and the term *political correctness* with the late 1980s and 1990s, both concepts were central to religiopolitical and corporate patriotism after the Second World War. Du Pont's promise of "better things through chemistry" differed little from the oft-repeated media assurance that "more things are wrought by prayer than this world dreams *of* [sic]."

29. In the view of William Chaloupka, nuclear weaponry generated a symbolism of such power

> that other concerns would arise within the context of nuclear technology, sometimes even when explicit connections are absent. . . . in short, nuclearism organizes public life and thought so thoroughly that, in another era of political theory, we would analyze it as an ideology.

See Chaloupka, *Knowing Nukes: The Politics and Culture of the Atom* (Minneapolis: University of Minnesota Press, 1993), 1. For the view from the critics' side, see Lawrence S. Wittner, *One World or None: A History of the World Nuclear Disarmament Movement through 1953* (Stanford, CA: Stanford University Press, 1993).

30. Denis W. Brogan, "The Illusion of American Omnipotence," *Harper's Magazine*, 205 (December 1952), 21–28.

31. See Paul Boyer, *By the Bomb's Early Light: American Thought and Culture at the Dawn of the Atomic Age* (New York: Pantheon, 1989); and Robert W. Malcolmson, *Nuclear Fallacies: How We Have Been Misguided since Hiroshima* (Kingston and Montreal: McGill-Queen's University Press, 1985). The shameful history of official nuclear coverups is traced in Clifford Honicker, "The Hidden Files," *New*

York Times Magazine, November 18, 1989, 39ff. See also Spencer Weart, *Nuclear Fear: A History of Images* (Cambridge: Harvard University Press, 1988). The popularity of nuclear testing through the 1950s and sluggishness of dissent are noteworthy, respectively, in the Gaither Committee report and in congressional hearings sponsored by Congressman Chet Holifield in 1957 and 1958. See Dee Garrison, "Our Skirts Gave Them Courage: The Civil Defense Protest Movement in New York City, 1955–1961," in Joanne Meyerowitz, ed., *Not June Cleaver: Women and Gender in Postwar America* (Philadelphia: Temple University Press, 1994), 209; Richard Wayne Dyke, *Mr. Atomic Energy: Congressman Chet Holifield and Atomic Energy Affairs, 1945–1974* (New York: Greenwood Press, 1989).

Triumphal/fearful nuclear discourse after Hiroshima had its antecedent in attitudes toward insects and the use of pesticides. Before and during the Second World War, Edmund P. Russell III writes that

wars on human and insect enemies both focussed . . . especially on enemies that did not respect *boundaries*. Once erected, international borders, fence-rows, and the walls of homes created the rights of citizens, farmers, and homeowners to protect their land and homes against "invading" enemies—including, ironically, some longtime residents.

Italics are the author's. See Russell, " 'Speaking of Annihilation': Mobilizing for War against Human and Insect Enemies, 1914–1945," *Journal of American History*, 82 (March 1996), 1505–29. When Rachel Carson condemned insecticides in *Silent Spring* (Boston: Houghton Mifflin, 1962), corporations involved in pesticide production attacked her as a subversive, impugned her femininity, and treated her as an "insect" herself. See Carson, *Always, Rachel: The Letters of Rachel Carson and Dorothy Freeman, 1952–1954* (Boston: Beacon Press, 1995), xxviii; Mary A. McCay, *Rachel Carson* (New York: Twayne, 1993), 79–83; and Linda J. Lear, *Rachel Carson: Witness for Nature* (New York: Henry Holt, 1997).

32. On the historical and historiographical controversies, see Geoffrey S. Smith, "Beware, the Historian! Hiroshima, the *Enola Gay*, and the Dangers of History," *Diplomatic History*, 22 (Winter 1998), 121–30.

33. Paterson and Adler, " 'Red Fascism,' " passim; Sherry, *In the Shadow of War*.

34. "X" [George Kennan], "The Sources of Soviet Conduct," *Foreign Affairs*, 25 (July 1947), 566–82.

35. Nadel, *Containment Culture*, 5. For a thoughtful discussion of the background of Kennan's article and views, see John Lewis Gaddis, *The United States and the Origins of the Cold War, 1941–1947* (New York: Columbia University Press, 1973), 302–4, 321–23.

36. Frank Costigliola, " 'Unceasing Pressure for Penetration': Gender, Pathology, and Emotion in George Kennan's Formulation of the Cold War," *Journal of American History*, 83 (March 1997), 1309–39; idem, "The Nuclear Family: Tropes of Gender and Pathology in the Western Alliance," *Diplomatic History*, 21 (Spring 1997), 163–84.

37. Nadel, *Containment Culture*, 16.

38. [Kennan], "Sources of Soviet Conduct," 575.

39. Ibid., 581–82.

40. George F. Kennan, *Memoirs, 1925–1950* (Boston: Little, Brown, 1967), 302–3.

41. The author's analysis has been influenced here by Joel Kovel, *Red Hunting in the Promised Land: Anticommunism and the Making of America* (New York: Basic Books, 1994), esp. "George Kennan: Anticommunism from the Mountaintop," 39–63.

42. Costigliola, " 'Unceasing Pressure,' " 1313–23.

43. George F. Kennan, *Sketches from a Life* (New York: Pantheon Books, 1989), 37, 42–43.

44. Costigliola, " 'Unceasing Pressure,' " 1324–27.

45. See Michael Kazin, *The Populist Persuasion: An American History* (New York: Basic Books, 1995), 165–93.

46. Kennan, *Memoirs, 1925–1950*, 301.

47. William F. Buckley noted that Professor Owen Lattimore, called before the McCarthy committee in 1952 as "the architect of the China tragedy," had replaced Alger Hiss as "the first lady among American witches." The pointed comment suggested that men like Hiss and Lattimore were simply not red-blooded enough to stand up to communism. See Nicholas von Hoffman, *Citizen Cohn* (New York: Doubleday, 1988), 136.

48. Republican claims to masculinity would return with the campaign of Arizona Senator Barry M. Goldwater in 1964. The victory of Richard M. Nixon in 1968, the toughest hombre of them all (after Lyndon Johnson failed to prove his mettle), reestablished Republicanism and masculinity as synonymous. Nixon had unwitting help from Democrats Ed Muskie and George McGovern, both of whose candidacies ended with the loss of the masculine main ground.

49. Robert J. Corber, *In the Name of National Security: Hitchcock, Homophobia, and the Political Construction of Gender in Postwar America* (Durham, NC: Duke University Press, 1993), 7–8.

50. Nadel, *Containment Culture*, xi; Kazin, *Populist Persuasion*, 167.

51. Thomas Hine, *Populuxe* (New York: Alfred A. Knopf, 1987), 3.

52. The author's analysis borrows from Eve Kosofsky Sedgwick, *Epistemology of the Closet* (Berkeley: University of California Press, 1990). See also Nadel, *Containment Culture*, 29, 34.

53. The postwar nuclear family may in fact be seen as a miniature state bureaucracy, fitting well the emerging bureaucratic emphasis upon the danger—and power—of secrets within the home. In this scenario, dad (as president) and mom (as secretary of state) and the children (as patriotic citizens) guarded their families' secrets as sedulously as the government did theirs. "Closets" for "normal" white, middle-class American families were no less important than "closets" for gay and lesbian Americans. This Victorian convention of keeping private salaciousness hidden from public view converged neatly with the country's post-1945 victory narrative, which necessitated keeping an optimistic face to the world. This requirement also fit well with the values of the security state, and—interestingly—made it increasingly difficult for gays and lesbians to seek, or establish, communities of their own. My understanding of the power of secrecy and its dubious impact upon both elite and popular life is influenced by Edward Shils, *The Torment of Secrecy: The Background and Consequences of American Security Policies*, rev. ed. (Chicago: Ivan R. Dee, 1996), especially the new introduction by Daniel Patrick Moynihan at vii–xxiii; and Robert Fulford, "American Demons of the 1950s," *Queen's Quarterly*, 102 (Fall 1995), 525–45. The travails of gay and

lesbian Americans are described in John D'Emilio, *Sexual Politics, Sexual Communities: The Making of a Homosexual Minority in the United States, 1940–1970* (Chicago: University of Chicago Press, 1983), 24–31; and Lillian Faderman, *Odd Girls and Twilight Lovers: A History of Lesbian Life in Twentieth-Century America* (New York: Columbia University Press, 1991), 139–58.

54. Quoted in Kenneth Jackson, *Crabgrass Frontier: The Suburbanization of the United States* (New York: Oxford University Press, 1985), 231. For the bias against African Americans and other minorities, except as domestic servants, see Bruce Lambert, "At 50, Levittown Contends with Its Legacy of Bias," *New York Times*, December 28, 1997, 23.

55. For overviews, see Richard M. Fried, *Nightmare in Red: The McCarthy Era in Perspective* (New York: Oxford University Press, 1990); M.J. Heale, *American Anticommunism: Combating the Enemy Within, 1830–1970* (Baltimore: Johns Hopkins University Press, 1990), 122–90; Stephen J. Whitfield, *The Culture of the Cold War* (Baltimore, MD: Johns Hopkins University Press, 1991), esp. 1–25; and David Caute, *The Great Fear: The Anti-Communist Purge under Truman and Eisenhower* (New York: Simon & Schuster, 1978). For memories of red-diaper babies, see Marc Lapin, *Pledge of Allegiance* (New York: Dutton, 1991), and Ann Kimmage, *An Un-American Childhood* (Athens: University of Georgia Press, 1996).

56. Karl Baarslag, "Slick Tricks of the Commies," *American Legion Magazine*, (February 1947), 19, quoted in Kazin, *Populist Persuasion*, 181.

57. Nadel, *Containment Culture*, 76.

58. Ibid., 75–76.

59. See Stanley I. Kutler, *The American Inquisition: Justice and Injustice in the Cold War* (New York: Hill and Wang, 1982).

60. Nora Sayre, *Running Time: Films of the Cold War* (New York: Dial Press, 1979), 57–62, described *Mission to Moscow* as a "gigantic mashnote to our ally." For an overview of Hollywood's rendition of friendly Russians, see Clayton R. Koppes and Gregory D. Black, *Hollywood Goes to War: How Politics, Profits, and Propaganda Shaped World War II Movies* (Berkeley: University of California Press, 1990), 185–221.

61. On Cvetic, see Matt Cvetic (ed. Pete Martin), "I Posed as a Communist for the FBI," *Saturday Evening Post*, 223 (July 15, 22, 29, 1950), 17–19+, 34–35+, 30+. On Philbrick, see Herbert A. Philbrick, *I Led Three Lives: Citizen, "Communist," Counterspy* (New York: McGraw-Hill, 1952).

62. In 1951, the Bowman Gum Company of Philadelphia, known for its baseball cards, issued a set of cards titled "Children's Crusade against Communism," a mix of good guys (ours) and bad guys (theirs). Card #35 featured a "Visit by Red Police" to a Russian family that "may" have been listening to the radio "Voice of America." Card #2 extolled General Douglas MacArthur, head of UN forces in Korea, who "pitched in to help the South Koreans, like your dad would help the folks next door if some men were beating them up." Card #47 pictured Mao Zedung, simply, as "War-Maker." For the subsequent hearings into comic books featuring horror and violence, see James B. Gilbert's perceptive, *A Cycle of Outrage: America's Reaction to the Juvenile Delinquent in the 1950s* (New York: Oxford University Press, 1986), 91–108 and passim, and William W. Savage, Jr., *Comic Books and America, 1945–1954* (Norman: University of Oklahoma Press, 1990). On questions of delinquency generally, see Benjamin Fine's lurid *1,000,000*

Delinquents (Cleveland, OH: World, 1955); Dale Kramer and Madeleine Kerr, *Teen-Age Gangs* (New York: Henry Holt, 1953); and Harrison E. Salisbury, *The Shook-Up Generation* (New York: Harper & Row, 1958).

63. Richard Gid Powers, *Secrecy and Power: The Life of J. Edgar Hoover* (New York: Free Press, 1987), 275–311; Athan Theoharis, *J. Edgar Hoover, Sex, and Crime: An Historical Antidote* (Chicago: Ivan R. Dee, 1995), 145. On Hoover's preoccupation with the personal/private lives of the wealthy and powerful, as a means to give himself and the Bureau leverage in high-level politics, see *From the Secret Files of J. Edgar Hoover*, Athan Theoharis, ed. (Chicago: Ivan R. Dee, 1991).

64. Rebecca L. Walkowitz, "Secret Agents," in Marjorie Garber and Rebecca L. Walkowitz, eds., *Secret Agents: The Rosenberg Case, McCarthyism, and Fifties America* (New York: Routledge, 1995), 1–8; Virginia Carmichael, *Framing History: The Rosenberg Story and the Cold War* (Minneapolis: University of Minnesota Press, 1993); Ross, *No Respect*, 15–41; Ilene Philipson, *Ethel Rosenberg: Beyond the Myths* (New Brunswick, NJ: Rutgers University Press, 1988).

65. Released by the National Security Agency (NSA) in 1995–1996, intercepts of Soviet message traffic collected under the code-named VENONA project include cables sent by Soviet intelligence services from the United States between 1942 and 1946, which were intercepted and deciphered by NSA's predecessor organizations. The documents also show that Manhattan Project physicist Alvin Hall allegedly leaked information on the project to Moscow during the Second World War. Eduard Mark, "More VENONA Released," HDIPLO [E-mail], February 25, 1996; John Gaddis, "VENONA Release," HDIPLO, February 26, 1996. Also see Ronald Radosh and Joyce Milton, *The Rosenberg File: The Search for the Truth*, rev. ed. (New York: Vintage, 1984); Harvey Klehr, John Earl Haynes, and Fridrikh Igorevich Firsov, eds., *The Secret World of American Communism* (New Haven, CT: Yale University Press, 1995), 259–321.

66. Gina Luria Walker, "Cold War Casualties," *Women's Review of Books*, 11 (November 1993), 22.

67. Michael Rogin, *"Ronald Reagan, the Movie" and Other Episodes in Political Demonology* (Berkeley: University of California Press, 1987), 250. Richard M. Nixon argued as much in his 1950 Senate campaign against Helen Gahagan Douglas—whom he characterized as "the lady in pink, right down to her underwear"—thus connecting the career woman with the dreaded Other. See Ingrid Winther Scobie, *Center Stage: Helen Gahagan Douglas: A Life* (New York: Oxford University Press, 1992).

68. Whitfield, *Culture*, p. 137. On the family as bulwark against communism, and problems stemming from the weight of this responsibility, see Elaine Tyler May, *Homeward Bound: American Families in the Cold War Era* (New York: Basic Books, 1988), esp. 92–113; and Laura McEnaney, "Civil Defense Begins at Home: Gender and Family Politics in Cold War Defense Agencies" (paper presented at the annual meeting of the Organization of American Historians, Atlanta, GA, 1994).

69. Rogin, "Reagan," 251.

70. Philip Wylie, *Generation of Vipers: A Survey of Moral Want, a Philosophical Discourse Suitable Only for the Strong* (New York: Rinehart, 1946). Wylie, who first wrote of the dangers posed by mothers in the nuclear family in 1942, also blamed

the Soviets for the cholera he acquired while in Russia, as well as his stepbrother's death in a fall from a window. He also wrote *Smoke across the Moon*, an obscure novel, in which a libertine, radical woman destroys men and facilitates communist infiltration. After the war, Wylie felt that "momism" had debilitated Americans who did not take the communist threat seriously enough. But like the later John Birch Society, which attributed every ill turn in U.S. foreign policy to internal "communists," Wylie also attributed to "mom" responsibility for McCarthyism. Nonetheless, in 1950 the American Library Association named *Generation of Vipers* one of the most important nonfiction books of the past half century. Four years later, in *Tomorrow*, Wylie advanced civil defense as an antidote to momism, and he also served as special consultant to the federal civil defense administration.

On "moms" and the psychiatric profession, see Jennifer Terry, "Momism and the Making of the Treasonous Lesbian" (paper presented at the Canadian Historical Association, Montreal, 1995).

71. Quoted in Whitfield, *Culture*, 138.

72. The parallel with the Victorian admonition to young women after the industrial revolution in America to avoid too much study, lest neurasthenia and a damaged uterus result, suggests how "family values" in the 1950s proceeded with strict gender guidelines. For the earlier period, and warnings to women, see Barbara Ehrenreich and Deirdre English, *"For Her Own Good": 150 Years of the Experts' Advice to Women* (Garden City, NY: Anchor, 1989); Sheila Rothman, *Women's Proper Place: A History of Changing Ideals and Practices, 1870 to the Present* (New York: Basic Books, 1978); and John S. Haller, Jr., and Robin M. Haller, *The Physician and Sexuality in Victorian America* (Urbana: University of Illinois Press, 1974).

In 1956, after much soul-searching caused by the experiences of American prisoners of war in Korea, especially "brainwashing," the U.S. Air Force instituted an "extreme" program—including torture—to develop mental and emotional toughness among American servicemen. See Donald J. Mrozek, "The Cult and Ritual of Toughness in Cold War America," in Ray B. Browne, ed., *Rituals and Ceremonies in Popular Culture* (Bowling Green, OH: Bowling Green University Press, 1980), 178–92.

73. Whitfield, *Culture*, 139. On the postwar relationship in film between women and returning soldiers, see Sonya Michel, "Danger on the Home Front: Motherhood, Sexuality, and Disabled Veterans in American Postwar Films," *Journal of the History of Sexuality*, 3 (1992), cited in John C. Fout and Maura Shaw Tantillo, eds., *American Sexual Politics: Sex, Gender, and Race since the Civil War*, (Chicago: University of Chicago Press, 1993), 247–66.

74. Quoted in "Bad Moms of 1949," *Globe and Mail* (Toronto), May 10, 1996, 20.

75. On this activism, which historians are now assessing, see the essays in Meyerowitz, *Not June Cleaver*. See also Joanne Meyerowitz, "Beyond the Feminine Mystique: A Reassessment of Postwar Mass Culture, 1946–1958," *Journal of American History*, 79 (March 1993), 1455–82; idem, "Gender, Sex, and the Cold War Language of Reform," chapter in this volume; Susan Lynn, *Progressive Women in Conservative Times: Racial Justice, Peace, and Feminism, 1945 to the 1960s* (New Brunswick, NJ: Rutgers University Press, 1992); R. Allen Smith, "The New Jersey

Committee for a Sane Nuclear Policy, 1956–1960" (paper presented to annual conference of the Society for Historians of American Foreign Relations, Charlottesville, VA, 1993); Glen Jeansonne, *Women of the Far Right: The Mothers' Movement and World War II* (Chicago: University of Chicago Press, 1996), 165–78; Rhodri Jeffreys-Jones, *Changing Differences: Women and the Shaping of American Foreign Policy, 1917–1994* (New Brunswick, NJ: Rutgers University Press, 1995), 105–30; Wini Breines, "The 'Other' Fifties: Beats and Bad Girls," in Breines, *White and Miserable: Growing Up Female in the Fifties* (Boston: Beacon Press, 1992); Ruth Rosen, "The Female Generation Gap: Daughters of the Fifties and the Origins of Contemporary American Feminism," in Linda K. Kerber, Alice Kessler-Harris, and Kathryn Kish Sklar, eds., *U.S. History as Women's History: New Feminist Essays* (Chapel Hill: University of North Carolina Press, 1991), 313–34; David Halberstam, *The Fifties* (New York: Villard, 1993), 577–85; Harriet Hyman Alonso, *Peace as a Women's Issue: A History of the U.S. Movement for World Peace and Women's Rights* (Syracuse: Syracuse University Press, 1993), 157–92; Daniel Horowitz, "Rethinking Betty Friedan and 'The Feminine Mystique': Labor Union Radicalism and Feminism in Cold War America," *American Quarterly*, 48 (March 1996), 1–42; and Robert J. Corber, *Homosexuality in Cold War America: Resistance and the Crisis of Masculinity* (Durham, NC: Duke University Press, 1997).

76. See Breines, *Young, White and Miserable*; Susan Douglas, *Where the Girls Are: Growing Up Female with the Mass Media* (New York: Times Books, 1994); Leila J. Rupp and Verta Taylor, *Survival in the Doldrums: The American Women's Rights Movement, 1945 to the 1960s* (Columbus: Ohio State University Press, 1990); Allan Berube and John D'Emilio, "Archives: The Military and Lesbians during the McCarthy Years," *Signs*, 9 (Summer 1984), 759–75; and Kate Weigand, "The Red Menace, the Feminine Mystique, and the Ohio Un-American Activities Commission: Gender and Anti-Communism in Ohio, 1951–1954," *Journal of Women's History*, 3 (Winter 1992), 70–94.

77. In their influential *Modern Woman: The Lost Sex* (New York: Harper and Bros., 1947), Ferdinand Lundberg and Marynia Farnham railed (in Freudian terms) at would-be career women as "neurotic" females driven by the "shadow of the phallus." Reporting that half of American women were "frigid," they advised that for the female "her role is passive. It is not as easy as rolling off a log for her. It is easier. It is as easy as being the log itself" (at 275).

During the early 1950s even "logs" could be dangerous, as the horror film, *From Hell It Came* indicated. In these years, Hollywood featured an array of scifi/horror "B" films, and numerous radioactive monsters, blobs, psychopaths, body snatchers, and giant ants roamed the landscape, reflecting anxiety about the bomb, communism, and domestic arrangements. See Michael J. Strada, "The Cinematic Bogy Man Comes Home: American Popular Perceptions of External Threat," *Midwest Quarterly*, 28 (Winter 1987), 248–70, and Thomas Doherty, *Teenagers and Teenpics: The Juvenilization of American Movies in the 1950s* (Boston: Unwin Hyman, 1988). Also see Barbara Ehrenreich, Elizabeth Hess, and Gloria Jacobs, *Re-Making Love: The Feminization of Sex* (New York: Doubleday, 1986), 39–73.

78. Lesley Ring, "Ladies, Don't Forget to Burp It! Tupperware—An 'Other' Strategy of Containment in Cold War America" (unpublished paper, Norman Paterson School of International Affairs, Ottawa, Canada, December 1995).

79. Craig Thompson, "Here's Where Our Young Commies Are Trained," *Look*, March 12, 1949, cited in Barson *"Better Dead Than Red!"* (New York: Hyperion, 1992).

80. Curt Gentry, *J. Edgar Hoover: The Man and the Secrets* (New York: Norton, 1991), suggests that Hoover had an "increasingly neurotic fear of germs." The major domo of Hoover's FBI office, "Mr. Sam" Noisette, wielded a mean fly swatter whenever one appeared, while Hoover washed his hands incessantly and equipped his home with an air-filter system that allegedly "electrocuted" baneful particles. Hoover's office was similarly appointed with a "wavering, purple light" that, years later, Nixon assistant John Ehrlichmann discovered, was directed at killing germs (see 280, 462, 618). Hoover's alacrity at describing communism as a variant of bacteria, virus, or disease (and his similar public attitude toward gays, lesbians, and other sex "perverts") makes his personal abstemiousness a matter of great importance in the elite anticommunist culture as well as American attitudes toward what the director termed "sexual perversion." See Estelle Freedman, " 'Uncontrolled Desires': The Response to the Sexual Psychopath, 1920–1960," *Journal of American History*, 74 (June 1987), 83–106.

81. Suellen Hoy, *Chasing Dirt* (New York: Oxford University Press, 1995), 170.

82. See Laura A. Belmonte, "Mr. and Mrs. America: Images of Gender and the Family in Cold War Propaganda" (paper presented at the Tenth Berkshire Conference on the History of Women, Chapel Hill, NC, 1996).

83. "Iron Curtain Look Is Here," *Life*, March 10, 1952, 119.

84. Julie Whitney, "Women: Russia's Second-Class Citizens," *Look*, November 30, 1954, in Barson, *"Better Dead Than Red!"* np.

85. Lois W. Banner, *American Beauty* (Chicago: University of Chicago Press, 1983), 269–70.

86. Patrizia Gentile, "Defending Gender in the Security State: Beauty Contests and Fruit Machines, 1950–1972" (paper presented at the Learned Societies Conference, Montreal, Quebec, June 1995).

87. Carl Belz, *The Story of Rock*, 2nd ed. (New York: Harper Torchbooks, 1972), 32. On the "high culture" critique of rock, and its separation from folk tradition and blurring of boundaries between the real and the unreal, see S.I. Hayakawa, "Popular Songs vs. the Facts of Life," in Bernard Rosenberg and David Manning White, eds., *Mass Culture: The Popular Arts in America* (London: Free Press, 1964), 393–403. This critique, also the ironic staple of criticism of 1950s music by devotees of "serious" 1960s rock, misses the importance of early rock 'n' roll.

88. Yet as many black artists shifted to a white, middle-class audience, black music jettisoned its focus on such life problems as alcoholism, gambling, and drug addiction. Only jazz maintained its "vital libidinal impulses ... precisely the id drives that the superego of the bourgeois culture sought to repress." Quoted in James W. Fernandez, "Persuasions and Performances: Of the Beast in Every Body ... and the Metaphors of Everyman," *Daedalus*, 101 (Winter 1972), 45. See also Lawrence W. Levine, *Black Culture and Black Consciousness: Afro-American Folk Thought from Slavery to Freedom* (New York: Oxford University Press, 1977), 290–97; and for insights on traditional blues as an outlet for black women, Ann Ducille, "Blues Notes on Black Sexuality: Sex and the Texts of Jessie

Fauset and Nella Larsen," *Journal of the History of Sexuality*, 3 (1993), cited in Fout and Tantillo, *American Sexual Politics*, 192–219.

89. See Arnold Shaw, *The Rock Revolution* (New York: Paperback Library, 1971), 7.

90. Quoted in Jerry Hopkins, *The Rock Story* (New York: New American Library, 1970), 37.

91. Paul Ackerman, "Tin Pan Alley Days Fade on Pop Music Broader Horizons," *Billboard*, October 15, 1955, 1, 16.

92. "Crying in the Chapel," recorded in 1953 by Sonny Till and the Orioles, was itself a cover for a country and western predecessor.

93. Jonathan Eisen, ed., *The Age of Rock* (New York: Vintage Books, 1969), xi. On the Midwest phenomenon of doo wop, see Robert Pruter, *Doowop: The Chicago Scene* (Champaign: University of Illinois Press, 1996).

94. Stewart Kessler, "Chuck Berry Brings You the Free Speech Movement," in Greil Marcus, ed., *Rock and Roll Will Stand* (Boston: Beacon Press, 1969), 70; Anthony O. Edmonds, "America in the 1950s: The Roots of Our Discontent," in *Silhouettes on the Shade: A Symposium at the Carmichael Project* (Muncie, IN: Ball State University, 1973), 7.

95. "Get a Job," in Bruce Chipman, ed., *Hardening Rock* (Boston: Little, Brown, 1972), 133.

96. Dave Marsh, *The Heart of Rock & Soul: The 1001 Greatest Singles Ever Made* (New York: New American Library/Plume Books, 1989), 62, 276–77.

97. This view differs from Barbara Ehrenreich's assertion that "rock was a critique of the middle class, bubbling up from America's invisible 'others.'" See Ehrenreich, *Fear of Falling: The Inner Life of the Middle Class* (New York: HarperCollins, 1989), 95. On the role of Ricardo Valenzuela (Richie Valens) in bringing the folk traditions of Mexican music to a mass audience, and blending those traditions with numerous other musical influences as Valenzuela sought middle-class respectability, see George Lipsitz, "Land of a Thousand Dances: Youth, Minorities, and the Rise of Rock 'n' Roll," in Lary May, ed., *Recasting America: Culture and Politics in the Age of the Cold War* (Chicago: University of Chicago Press, 1989), 267–84.

98. George Lipsitz, *Rainbow at Midnight: Labor and Culture in the 1940s* (Urbana: University of Illinois Press, 1994), 56.

99. The author's experience as a teenager in San Francisco bears this out. Radio KSAN (1450AM) featured a wonderful DJ named John Hardy, who hosted late-night *Hardy's Party*. Only later did I learn that this amazing spinner of black records was white. Oakland's KWBR (1310AM, now KDIA) also employed white DJs who "sounded black." Misrepresentation of this sort (a double-agency congenial with the Cold War need to lead two or more lives) reached its height in the case of Los Angeles DJ Johnny Otis. Otis brought mixed audiences together and advanced the careers of black and Chicano performers, much as Alan Freed did in New York. Otis, who worked primarily with black musicians, married a black woman and considered himself "black by persuasion," was in fact the son of a Greek immigrant born in northern California. One of his early stars, "L'il Julian Herrera," Los Angeles' first successful Chicano performer, was born a Hungarian Jew and became "a Chicano by persuasion." See George Lipsitz, "Land of a Thousand Dances," in May, *Recasting America*, 273–74.

100. For one such riot, see *New York Times*, February 12, 1957, 1, 12. Barry Hansen calls Freed the "pusher" of rock 'n' roll—a clear connection between the music and heroin. See Hanson, "Doo Wop," in Jim Miller, ed., *The Rolling Stone Illustrated History of Rock & Roll* (New York: Random House, 1976), 82–91. On Freed's local TV dance show, after the camera caught Frankie Lyman dancing with a white girl, the show was canceled. TV DJ Dick Clark noted that "in the early days of TV, if a black performer and a white performer appeared on a show, and the white MC gave the black girl singer a friendly kiss on the cheek, there'd be an agency conference and a network blackout; at the very least, station affiliates would drop off the line." See Dick Clark and Richard Robinson, *Rock, Roll & Remember* (New York: Thomas Crowell, 1976), 82.

101. By far the best assessment of Presley as a conduit of black culture and blurred masculinity for young white Americans is Peter Guralnick, *Last Train to Memphis: The Rise of Elvis Presley* (Boston: Little, Brown, 1994). Presley's outfits were just a tad more subdued than those of gay pianist Liberace, who did smile, unceasingly, as he lived a public life very different from his closeted private existence. On Presley's influence in the music culture, and beyond, see Greil Marcus, *Mystery Train*, 3rd rev. ed. (New York: Dutton, 1990).

102. David Halberstam, *The Fifties* (New York: Random House, 1996), 457.

103. Ibid., 473.

104. Jerry Hopkins, *Elvis: A Biography* (New York: Simon & Schuster, 1971), 397–412.

105. For the development of "celebrity" see Richard Schickel, *Common Fame: The Culture of Celebrity* (London: Pavilion, 1985); for media voracity, see Suzanne Garment, *Scandal: The Culture of Mistrust in American Politics* (updated to include new material on Clarence Thomas, Anita Hill, and Bill Clinton) (New York: Anchor Books, 1992).

106. His first recorded song for Sam Phillips's Sun label was, aptly, "It's Alright Mama." See Guralnick, *Last Train*, 94–96.

107. See Hilary Radner, *Shopping Around: Feminine Culture and the Pursuit of Pleasure* (New York: Routledge, 1995).

CHAPTER 5

Presidential Decision Making and the National Security Council in Four Crises, 1950–1990

Gary R. Hess

Policymakers frequently draw upon the "lessons of the past." The origins of the Second World War provided an especially important learning experience for the American foreign policy elite. Two "mistakes" of the 1930s seemed clear. The most compelling lesson, and one referred to by American presidents in virtually every crisis over the last half century, was the "lesson of Munich," which taught the futility of attempting to appease aggressors and thus the importance of stopping expansionism in its early stages. Less well known, but also important, was the "national security lesson," which was drawn from America's lack of preparedness for war. It taught that an outdated, incoherent, bureaucratically driven system contributed to prewar planning that lacked integration between the army and navy, the coordination of political and military objectives, and the effective gathering and interpretation of intelligence. America's war, of course, began with a monumental failure of military intelligence and political analysis. The challenge of waging a global war magnified these shortcomings and led to some organizational innovations during the war, most importantly the establishment of the Joint Chiefs of Staff and later the State-War-Navy Coordinating Committee.

This "national security lesson" took on urgency as the United States waged the Cold War. Facing an adversary that seemed especially resourceful and confronting problems throughout the world, U.S. policymakers, it was generally accepted, needed a system that would coordinate the nation's military, political, intelligence, and resource capabilities. The National Security Act of 1947 addressed the need for organizational reform by establishing the National Security Council (NSC), the Central Intelligence Agency (CIA), the National Security Resources Board, and the National Military Establishment headed by a secretary of defense. In this new system that created what has been described as the "national security state," the NSC was to be the key coordinating agency. The act specified that the NSC was to advise the president "with respect to the integration of domestic, foreign, and military policies relating to the national security so as to enable the military services and other departments and agencies of the government to cooperate more effectively in matters involving the national security." The NSC was also authorized to "assess and appraise the objectives, commitments, and risks of the United States in relation to our actual and potential military power" and to make recommendations to the president on such matters. With a glance at Franklin Roosevelt's highly personalized style of decision making, the authors of the National Security Act saw the NSC as forcing the president to pay attention to his principal diplomatic and military advisers. The NSC's initial membership included the president, the secretaries of state, defense, army, navy, and air force, and the chairman of the National Security Resources Board. The president was also authorized to include certain other specified officials in NSC meetings.[1]

Since the establishment of the national security state, presidents have confronted numerous crises. In three cases, their decisions led to war: Harry Truman in Korea, Lyndon Johnson in Vietnam, and George Bush in the Persian Gulf. A decade before Johnson took the country to war, Dwight Eisenhower nearly did so as he faced a crisis in Indochina. These four cases provide perspectives on the different ways that presidents have used the instruments of decision making at their disposal. Like all presidents, Truman, Eisenhower, Johnson, and Bush relied on formal as well as informal consultation and advice. Each had one or more "close advisers," whose views held special importance. Among the formal groups at their disposal, the presidents had, above all, the NSC, which had been established to provide consideration of options and military-diplomatic coordination that are essential in crisis situations. The following analysis of these four presidents' responses to crisis will center on related questions: (1) How did each president reach national security policy decisions? (2) How did his decision-making system function in the crisis? (3) To what extent did he make use of the National Security Council? (4) Did the system allow for full exploration and discussion of policy options?

The NSC was still a relatively new agency when Truman confronted the Korean crisis during the last week of June 1950. By that time Truman had developed his own style of conducting foreign policy. This had not been an easy task. Upon becoming president, Truman established a formalistic model of management that delegated much responsibility to cabinet members, an approach that anticipated the emergence of a strong secretary of state. For most of his first two years in the White House, however, Truman was saddled with two secretaries of state (one inherited and one of his choosing) with whom he could not work effectively. Truman sought a secretary of state in whom he had confidence and the kind of policy coordination promised by the National Security Act. He supported that measure, but he found the desired coordination a few months earlier when he named General George Marshall as secretary of state. Truman had enormous respect for Marshall, whom he described as "the great one of our age" and relied heavily upon him. Marshall, with Truman's blessing, established the Policy Planning Staff, which, under the leadership of George Kennan, enjoyed greater prominence than the early NSC. In fact, Policy Planning Staff documents often were the basis of subsequent NSC studies.

Truman rarely met with the NSC and made little direct use of it. This resulted not just from Truman's preference for dealing with Marshall and, after January 1949, his successor Dean Acheson. Truman claimed that his absence fostered more open discussion. More important, Truman's studied indifference to the NSC reflected his apprehension that the NSC's powers would expand beyond advisory to policymaking functions. Keeping some distance from the NSC was a means of assuring White House control. The initial membership of the NSC, with its heavy military representation, also disturbed Truman. Accordingly, he pressed for the congressional action in 1949 that removed the three service secretaries—a step that also enhanced the stature of the secretary of defense—and added the vice president to the NSC membership. Even that modification did not make Truman feel more comfortable with the NSC, for he saw it as a cumbersome body. Members established early the practice of bringing various second-level officials to the council's meetings, which, in Truman's judgment, reduced its effectiveness.

Truman's instinctive impulse when facing a foreign policy crisis was to seek the counsel of his trusted secretary of state. Like his predecessor, Acheson enjoyed Truman's full confidence. By the time of the Korean crisis, an effective Truman-Acheson working relationship, based on profound mutual respect, was well established. They met regularly, Acheson presenting recommendations that Truman discussed and then almost invariably approved—a process, one suspects, that added to Acheson's admiration of Truman.

Unlike many subsequent secretaries of state, Acheson's authority was not challenged by the secretary of defense, which was still a new office and one that was held in 1950 by the politically ambitious and temperamental Louis B. Johnson. Acheson loathed Johnson with whom he clashed over several issues. Their most notable difference was over NSC 68's call for a drastic increase in defense spending. In passing, it might be observed that that monumental project, in which Acheson played an instrumental role, illustrated the potential for the NSC to take on the kinds of authority that Truman so feared; while NSC 68 was officially a recommendation to him, it came with the backing of virtually all major officials and agencies involved in the formulation of national security policy. In any event, Johnson believed that his opposition to NSC 68's call for increasing military expenditures reflected Truman's fiscal conservatism, but regardless of any particular issue, Truman simply did not hold him in high regard. Truman had appointed Johnson to the defense department as reward for his important role in Truman's 1948 presidential campaign but never considered him to be in the same class as Acheson. So Acheson, while never forgetting that ultimate authority rested with the president, enjoyed wide discretion, a power that he used shrewdly.[2]

Thus as word reached Washington on Sunday, June 25 of the North Korean aggression, it was Acheson who took the important initiatives. It was Acheson who informed Truman, vacationing at his Independence, Missouri, home, of the attack. It was Acheson who suggested taking the issue immediately to the UN Security Council and who helped to frame the initial resolution condemning the North Korean attack. It was Acheson who, during the first hectic hours of the crisis, grasped both the strategic importance of responding to the North Korean invasion by force if necessary and the imperative of trying to avoid conflict with the Soviet Union. It was Acheson who then framed the agenda and advanced recommendations for consideration at the Blair House meeting held on the evening of June 25, following Truman's return to Washington. It was, however, Truman who decided who should be present at that meeting. Rather than designating any specific group, such as the NSC, Truman instructed Acheson to assemble "the available people from State and Defense."

It was the Blair House group, composed of fourteen officials meeting on the evenings of June 25 and 26, that provided the advice and support to guide the most critical of Truman's decisions, such as the initial military assistance to the South Koreans, the commitment to the defense of Taiwan, and the pursuit of a second UN Security Council resolution requesting multilateral support of South Korea. At both Blair House meetings, discussion lacked direction until Acheson's recommendations were presented, briefly considered, and then accepted by Truman.

Having ignored the NSC during the first three days of the crisis, Truman convened and met with it on June 28 and 29. Truman used these occasions principally to inform the council of developments and to direct the preparation of reports on important aspects of the unfolding situation. The only issue discussed at length was the issuance of orders to General Douglas MacArthur. These two sessions reinforced one of Truman's annoyances with the NSC and help to account for its relative insignificance during the crisis, that is, the large number of nonmembers in attendance: twenty-two at the first and fourteen at the second.

In Truman's decision-making system, the formal meetings—whether with the Blair House group, NSC, or congressional leaders—were secondary to his reliance on Acheson. Throughout the critical week when the United States went to war, the secretary of state continued to dominate the process. For instance, when Jiang Jieshi offered to send some 30,000 Chinese Nationalist troops to fight in Korea, Truman instinctively wanted to accept since it would provide dramatic evidence of international support and far surpassed what other UN members were prepared to send, but it was Acheson who finally convinced Truman that the introduction of Nationalist forces would risk broadening the war.

While Acheson's role was central, the objectives and measures that he presented reflected the thinking of Truman and all of his principal advisers. Truman's steps toward intervention in Korea won wide support from both political parties and in newspaper editorials from across the land. In sum, Acheson's initiatives took hold within the context of virtual unanimity both within and outside the administration about the importance of taking a strong stand in Korea. Significantly, in the three other crises, there were sharp differences of opinion over the appropriate means and, at times, the goals of U.S. policy.[3]

If Truman distrusted the NSC as a policymaking body, his successor, Dwight Eisenhower, compensated with a vengeance. Eisenhower revisionists, led by Fred Greenstein, have clearly established that contrary to popular perceptions during the 1950s and early scholarship on the Eisenhower presidency, Eisenhower was very much at the center of policymaking. In national security policy, Eisenhower, taking advantage of his military background, effectively functioned as his own secretary of defense. Eisenhower allowed Secretary of State John Foster Dulles to play a highly visible role, but the secretary articulated a policy that grew out of consultation with and deference to the president. Eisenhower's frequent conversations with Dulles constituted a principal informal aspect of his policymaking. Depending on the issue, he would consult with other advisers as well. Eisenhower wanted subordinates, whenever possible, to reach consensus on policy recommendations, and at times, he met with small groups of advisers to debate issues informally. Under Eisenhower, the NSC became the center of the formal policymaking process. It normally met weekly and with Eisenhower almost always presiding. During the eight years of the Eisenhower administration, the NSC was convened some 360 times, an average of 45 times a year. It approved

187 serially numbered policy documents. Eisenhower sharpened NSC procedures by establishing a Planning Board, which was responsible for the preparation of papers for the council's consideration, and an Operations Coordinating Board, which was charged with implementing the council's decisions. He also established the position of special assistant to the president for national security affairs. Robert Cutler, whom Eisenhower appointed to that office in 1953, was important not only in integrating the work of the NSC but also as one of Eisenhower's close advisers.[4]

Eisenhower's system was in place by the time of the Dien Bien Phu crisis. From mid-March 1954 when the Viet Minh surrounded the French garrison until May 7 when the outpost fell to the Viet Minh, the Eisenhower administration considered the feasibility and terms of responding to France's request for U.S. military intervention. Throughout this period, Eisenhower consulted informally with a wide range of officials but principally with Dulles, Cutler, and Admiral Arthur Radford, chairman of the Joint Chiefs of Staff. Eisenhower also relied heavily on the NSC as the principal consultative and decision-making body. While the NSC apparatus later came under criticism for being too cumbersome to deal with crises, in this instance it adapted reasonably well. It established a Special Committee to address the problems connected with establishing a regional alliance. The Planning Board, when instructed by the NSC on March 29 to formulate plans for U.S. military action under various contingencies, resurrected earlier studies on the matter and presented an updated recommendation in time for the next NSC meeting.

During the seven-week Dien Bien Phu crisis, Eisenhower convened the NSC seven times, including an emergency session the day after the French surrender. The situation in Indochina dominated the agenda for several of these meetings, the most important one taking place on April 6. That extended session had an unusually wide-ranging discussion of American alternatives, resulting in a consensus that helped to guide U.S. policy during the remainder of the crisis. The outcome was consistent with the objectives that Eisenhower had evidently formulated beforehand; in the previous few days he had quietly abandoned the alternative of unilateral U.S. intervention, although that was not clear to the other members of the NSC prior to the April 6 meeting. As the NSC considered the Planning Board's report on the terms of U.S. intervention and the Special Committee's recommendation for a Southeast Asian regional defense system, Eisenhower interjected his own strong positions at some points. He did not, however, stifle debate. Secretary of the Treasury George Humphrey challenged the assumption that all contested areas, like Indochina, had to be held regardless of cost, while Harold Stassen, director of the Foreign Operations Administration, suggested a scheme for abandoning the northern half of Indochina and retaining influence in the south (which was not yet considered an acceptable outcome). Vice President Richard Nixon, Dulles, Cutler, and others entered fully into a spirited and, to a large extent, focused discussion. At its conclusion, the NSC concurred that priority should be given to organizing a regional alliance, fostering cooperation with the British, and pressing the French to accelerate plans for independence.

Having hammered out the essential priorities of U.S. policy, the NSC played a relatively insignificant role during the remainder of the crisis. In most subsequent NSC meetings, the time devoted to Indochina was mostly for informational purposes. The exception was the meeting of April 29 where Eisenhower reiterated that military intervention had to be multilateral, a conclusion largely driven by congressional reluctance to act otherwise. He was challenged by Stassen who pressed vigorously for unilateral intervention, saying Congress and the public would respond favorably to presidential leadership.[5]

Eisenhower and Dulles were able to implement the policy that they formulated early in the crisis and that the NSC had sanctioned. Through public pronouncements and consultations with congressional leaders and foreign officials, they pursued a cautious diplomacy that not only averted war but also enabled the United States to avoid the dreaded loss of all of Indochina. After the fall of Dien Bien Phu and the Geneva Conference began its deliberations on Indochina, the Eisenhower administration used the threat of intervention and its plans for a regional alliance to help induce a settlement that salvaged the southern half of Vietnam. Despite the conservative criticism of the Geneva settlement as a "sellout" to the communists, it was, in fact, as favorable an outcome as the United States had any reason to expect.

However clever the diplomacy of 1954 and the short-term gains, it presented future presidents with new and more intractable problems in Indochina. Ultimately, it was Lyndon Johnson who confronted the choice between abandoning Vietnam altogether or intervening militarily to prevent the collapse of South Vietnam. As he slowly took the United States to war, Johnson's policymaking style underlined his lack of confidence in formal processes, particularly those of the NSC. To some extent, Johnson's style reflected his inheritance from the Kennedy administration. As part of his stress on continuity with his slain predecessor, Johnson kept the Kennedy team of foreign policy advisers, notably Secretary of State Dean Rusk, Secretary of Defense Robert McNamara, and Special Assistant for National Security Affairs McGeorge Bundy. Johnson had a natural affinity with fellow southerner Rusk; Johnson's description of Rusk underlined what he sought in advisers: "He's a damned good man, hardworking, bright and loyal as a beagle. You'll never catch him working at cross purposes with his president." McNamara quickly ingratiated himself with Johnson, who came to rely on him as his principal adviser on Vietnam and allowed him to remain the most visible proponent of escalation. Bundy, the kind of intellectual whom Johnson instinctively distrusted, likewise earned the president's respect and strongly influenced Vietnam policy. From their experiences in the Kennedy administration, Johnson himself as well as Rusk, McNamara, and Bundy had been part of a "collegial" model of decision making, which was notably less formal than that of Eisenhower. Indeed Bundy's very presence at the center of policymaking underlined the growing significance of the NSC staff as a source of policy recommendations. This resulted from Kennedy's skepticism whether the bureaucratic-ridden Department of State could provide imaginative direction to the nation's foreign policy.[6]

This dependence on the NSC adviser and staff, however, did not lead to involving the formal NSC fully in the policymaking process. Kennedy believed that Eisenhower's reliance on the NSC had contributed to foreign policy inertia. To deal with crises, Kennedy created the Executive Committee of the NSC, but its deliberations were tightly controlled by the White House. In any case, the NSC was no longer at the center of policymaking. During his presidency, Kennedy convened the NSC a total of forty-three times, or about fourteen times per year. Initially, Johnson gave the NSC greater prominence, convening it twenty-four times in 1964, but afterward he rarely summoned it. Moreover, the council when it did meet under Kennedy and Johnson was a less deliberative and policy-formulating body than it had been under Eisenhower. Kennedy and Johnson used it mostly to formalize decisions that had already been reached. Under Secretary of State George Ball later reflected that the purposes of the NSC meetings were to inform members of presidential decisions and to provide "at least the illusion of participation."

Besides continuing Kennedy's practices, Johnson also brought some of his distinctive style into the policymaking process. In particular, he relied to a greater extent than Kennedy on informal advice and from a wider range of officials, notably former colleagues in Congress. A number of senators who were close to Johnson took advantage of their access to the White House to communicate their views directly to him.

Johnson's two most important steps in taking the United States to war in Vietnam were decisions made in February 1965 to begin the systematic bombing of North Vietnam and in July 1965 to make an open-ended commitment of U.S. ground forces. In each case, Johnson compressed a series of meetings into a few days to reach his decision.

The Viet Cong attack on the U.S. base at Pleiku on February 7 (Vietnam time) led Johnson to launch retaliatory air raids against North Vietnam and to consider Bundy's recommendation for a bombing program of "graduated and continuing reprisal"—an option that the military leadership had been advocating for several months. In considering this important step of escalation, Johnson appeared to rely on the NSC, which he convened four times between February 6 and 10. Its influence, however, was marginal. The meetings were not framed in ways that encouraged discussion of policy alternatives. Two of the meetings merged into joint sessions with congressional leaders whose relationship with the president was fundamentally different from that of the NSC. By the time of the first meeting, Johnson had already decided on retaliatory attacks and engaged in one of his most favored tactics: asking participants individually whether they concurred. This, of course, had an intimidating effect and only Senator Mike Mansfield openly challenged Johnson's military course and urged negotiating a way out of Vietnam. Johnson snappishly dismissed Mansfield's position. After four NSC meetings, it was still unclear whether Johnson would authorize the sustained bombing of North Vietnam. When the NSC next met on February 18, it was for a policy briefing, not discussion. Johnson reached his decision to launch Operation Rolling Thunder with scant use of formal procedures.

The spate of meetings of the NSC in the aftermath of Pleiku, as insignificant as they were in influencing policy, were, in retrospect, its high point during the Johnson presidency. In March 1965, Johnson reinstituted the Tuesday Lunch meetings with Rusk, McNamara, and Bundy, and these became the principal forum for discussing Vietnam policy. Johnson looked upon the Tuesday Lunch as an ideal vehicle for providing candid advice, free from formal agendas and policy papers, and without worry about "leaks" (which was part of his annoyance with the NSC). Still the Tuesday Lunch group was not designed to debate the essentials of U.S. policy, for all of its participants accepted without question the imperative of holding South Vietnam at any cost.

As the situation in Vietnam steadily worsened despite the bombing of North Vietnam, Johnson by late July faced the critical decision whether to Americanize the conflict through the introduction of a large ground combat force.[7] On the brink of war, Johnson moved deliberately. In his memoir, he wrote: "I wanted to go over this proposal [for an open-ended commitment] with the greatest care. I realized what a major undertaking it would be." Thus beginning on Wednesday, July 21, Johnson conducted in considerable secrecy a series of meetings that constituted the fullest debate within the administration over Vietnam policy. Johnson's leadership in these meetings was remarkable. On the surface, he appeared to be open-minded. He posed a number of basic questions. At a meeting with several advisers on the morning of July 21, Johnson prodded them with basic questions: "What has happened in recent past that requires this decision on my part? What are the alternatives?" At another session with McNamara and military leaders, Johnson posed other tough questions: "What will happen if we put 100,000 more men and then two, three years later you tell me you need 500,000 more? How would you expect me to respond to that? . . . and what makes you think that if we put in 100,000 men, Ho Chi Minh won't put in another 100,000?" At another point, he asked: "Can Westerners ... successfully fight Orientals in jungly rice-paddies? I want McNamara and General Wheeler to seriously ponder this question." At still another meeting, Johnson summed up his concerns: "There are two basic troublings with me. First, that westerners can even win a war in Asia. Second, I don't see how you can fight a war under direction of other people whose government changes every month." Johnson thus asked the right questions. He did not, however, insist that they be addressed.

Johnson's failure to pursue these questions betrayed, as did his other actions and comments, his predilection toward what he evidently regarded as the inevitable acceptance of the military solution. While urging advisers that they "consider carefully all our options," he effectively ruled out a negotiated settlement as making the United States look weak. As advisers lined up in support of the open-ended troop commitment, Johnson played his familiar tactic of asking: "Is anyone of the opinion we should not do what the memo says—If so, I'd like to hear from them now, in detail." When George Ball spoke out in opposition, Johnson appeared solicitous and invited Ball to present his case in greater detail. Ball subsequently presented his argument for disengagement with an appeal to Johnson as a potential statesman: "Every great captain in history is not afraid to make a tactical withdrawal if conditions are unfavourable to him." In Vietnam "the enemy cannot be seen.... He is indigenous to the country. I truly have serious doubt that an army of westerners can successfully fight orientals in an Asian jungle." Now Johnson posed rhetorical questions that revealed his underlying fear that American credibility was on the line: "Wouldn't all these countries say that Uncle Sam was a paper tiger? Wouldn't we lose credibility breaking the word of three presidents?" Ball's argument won no converts and was dismissed out of hand by McNamara, Rusk, and Bundy. And Johnson, when he met with military leaders the next day, took the occasion to express his contempt for any suggestion of "bugging out."

Johnson's hurried round of meetings did not include the convening of the NSC until after he had reached his decision for war, which, according to his memoir, came only after a weekend of continuing debate and personal agonizing at Camp David. Returning to Washington on Monday, July 26, Johnson met with the NSC (its first session in six weeks) and later with the congressional leadership. In both instances, Johnson presented what was essentially a fait accompli under the guise of involving the groups in his decision. Before both groups, he presented five alternatives in such a way as to preclude all but the last. The first, "bring[ing] the enemy to his knees" by massive bombing, was, Johnson claimed, not favored by most Americans. Neither was the second alternative: "pack up and go home." He added that "Ike, Kennedy, and I have given [our] commitment." The third alternative—"stay out there as we are...continue to lose territory and casualties"—was dismissed: "You wouldn't want your boy to be out there and crying for help and not get it." The fourth alternative was to "go to Congress and ask for great sums of money, call up reserves and increase draft" and going on a "war footing" including a state of national emergency, which was seen as too provocative, forcing the Soviet Union and China into greater support of North Vietnam. Thus, by a process of elimination, Johnson arrived at a fifth alternative, one that seemed a modest but necessary step: a troop increase—"give the commanders...[the] men they say they need" but without going before Congress and mobilizing the public.

Through this convoluted process, Johnson took the country to war. His informal system assured that critics of intervention were heard, perhaps more so than would have been the case had Johnson relied more consistently on the NSC. Not only Ball but also Clark Clifford as well as several senators, most notably Mansfield, had the opportunity to state their case for disengagement. Their arguments, however, were always within a framework that kept them isolated and outnumbered. Beyond his refusal to insist on answers to the tough questions, the most troubling aspect of the Johnson meetings of July 21–27 was the lack of coherent policy alternatives—the sort of operation that the NSC under Eisenhower thrived upon. Significantly, the five alternatives that Johnson presented to the NSC and congressional leaders on July 26 had never been considered as such by any group in the previous five days, and the military option that he presented as the fait accompli was one to which the military leaders, had they discussed it per se, would have had serious reservations.

Finally and briefly, a quarter century after Johnson took the country into a long and frustrating war in Vietnam, George Bush faced a crisis in the Persian Gulf that led to a short and decisive war. While the documents for this period remain classified, a number of early histories of the Persian Gulf crisis and war and the joint memoir of Bush and Scowcroft, together with those of Powell and Baker, tell a great deal about the inner workings of the Bush administration. By the time of Iraq's invasion of Kuwait on August 1, 1990, Bush had established a policy making system that was similar to that of Eisenhower. Bush combined frequent meetings of the NSC with reliance on informal counsel from his most trusted advisers. Closest to the president were three longtime associates: Brent Scowcroft, assistant to the president for National Security Affairs who was sometimes referred to as "Mr. Bush's Shadow"; James Baker, secretary of state; and Richard Cheney, secretary of defense. Bush also relied on four other advisers, who—together with Bush, Scowcroft,

Baker, and Cheney—were commonly referred to as the Big Eight. They included: Dan Quayle, vice president; General Colin Powell, chairman of the Joint Chiefs of Staff; Robert Gates, deputy national security adviser; John Sununu, White House chief of staff. At times, William Webster, director of the Central Intelligence Agency, also was part of the inner circle. Gates, as Scowcroft's deputy, formed a link between Bush's inner circle and an ongoing "crisis management team" representing several agencies (the so-called Deputies Committee) that he chaired.

From the outset of the crisis, Bush, with Scowcroft as his principal confidante, assumed that the United States had to provide international leadership in responding to Iraq's aggression. Bush immediately instructed Ambassador Thomas Pickering to draft a resolution for the UN Security Council, which was summoned into an emergency session at 2:00 in the morning of August 2 and four hours later passed the first in a series of resolutions that underlined Iraq's international isolation. The first week of the crisis was the most significant phase of Bush's decision making, for during that hectic period, the United States established the political, economic, and military base of opposition to Iraq that presented Saddam Hussein with the choice of defying an American-led international coalition or undertaking a humiliating retreat from Kuwait.

Bush relied upon the NSC as his principal means of formal policy-making. It met on each of the first four days of the crisis. Meeting with the NSC at 8:00 A.M. on August 2, Bush found the members of the council uncertain whether the United States could or should reverse Iraqi aggression. Any use of force seemed unpromising on both strategic and political grounds. The Central Command had planned only for the defense of Saudi Arabia, which led to Powell's suggestion that it was time to "draw the line in the sand" or accept the takeover of Kuwait while preparing to defend Saudi Arabia.

After fulfilling an obligation to speak at the Aspen Institute where he denounced the Iraqi invasion, Bush returned to Washington and immediately began to force consideration of exerting economic and military pressure. Both he and Scowcroft had been disturbed by hand-wringing at the August 2 NSC meeting; in Scowcroft's words,

I was frankly appalled at the undertone of the discussion, which suggested resignation to the invasion and even adaptation for a *fait accompli*. There was a huge gap between those who saw what was happening as the major crisis of our time and those who treated it as the crisis *du jour*.

So before the NSC met again on the morning of August 3, Bush and Scowcroft planned to take the initiative. They agreed that Scowcroft,

Cheney, and Under Secretary of State Lawrence Eagleburger would be the first speakers at the meeting. Scowcroft also arranged for the preparation of a policy paper outlining the strategic significance of the Persian Gulf crisis and setting forth the various means, including armed conflict, of forcing Iraq's withdrawal. The remarks of Scowcroft, Cheney, and Eagleburger—all stressing the importance of a firm response to the realization of a stable post-Cold War world—had the desired effect. While Powell doubted the feasibility of the military option, the consensus that Bush sought emerged: that U.S. power had to be exerted through the imposition of economic sanctions and, pending the approval of the Saudi government, the movement of a U.S. force to Saudi Arabia.

Bush convened the NSC again on August 4 at Camp David where he spent the first weekend of the crisis and the next day at the White House. By this time, the military option dominated the discussion. Powell and H. Norman Schwarzkopf outlined plans to dispatch a sufficiently large ground force that would deter Iraq from attacking, but military and civilian advisers at this early stage disagreed over whether the United States had the military capability, as well as sufficient domestic and international support, to liberate Kuwait. Powell said that the United States should be ready to "do more than simply show the flag," which led a member of the NSC staff to envision "something along the lines of the Korean War model of a US-led multinational force." While the full dimensions of the military option remained unclear at this stage, the NSC discussions of August 4 and 5 underlined how quickly the Bush administration had accepted the necessity of employing force at least as a deterrent and potentially as the agent of liberating Kuwait.

Within the next few days, the objectives outlined in the NSC meetings were realized, as the UN Security Council imposed economic sanctions and Saudi Arabia approved the deployment of U.S. forces. This provided the background for Bush's first formal statement to the American public on August 8 that demanded the "immediate, unconditional, and complete withdrawal of all Iraqi forces from Kuwait" and concluded with a reference to the "lessons" of the 1930s: "[If] history teaches us anything, it is that we must resist aggression or it will destroy our freedoms."[8]

This overview of four presidents' crisis management suggests distinctive approaches to decision making. It is difficult to assess the significance of the various systems in terms of the resulting decisions. Acheson's central role in the Korean decision was possible not only because he enjoyed Truman's confidence but also because his recommendations reflected the unanimous thinking of the administration, members of Congress, and the public. The similarities of Eisenhower's and Bush's decision-making processes (at least to the extent that we can understand the latter), with the combination of reliance on informal advice and the

NSC, indicate what would appear to be the value of full consideration of policy options and a give-and-take involving the president. As the studies of Eisenhower and Bush both illustrate, however, the president ultimately dominates the NSC and can easily manipulate it in ways that ensure the outcomes that he sought beforehand. Whatever the deficiencies of the NSC model, it appears clearly superior to the system employed by Johnson, which studiously avoided difficult questions and consideration of policy options. Some scholars have suggested that there was no way that Johnson could have rationalized an exit from Vietnam in 1965. When one considers that Johnson faced more serious questioning of U.S. objectives than did the other three presidents in their crisis, it does seem plausible that a more open decision-making process might have yielded a different outcome. If not different, the option at least would have been subjected to more serious scrutiny, and diplomatic and military leaders would have been part of it. While no one policymaking system is necessarily superior, it does seem evident that the means by which a president seeks advice does influence the efficacy of his decisions.

NOTES

1. On the development of the national security state, see Thomas H. Etzhold, "American Organization for National Security, 1945–1950," in Thomas H. Etzhold and John Lewis Gaddis, eds., *Containment: Documents on American Policy and Strategy, 1945–1950* (New York: Columbia University Press, 1978), 1–24; Melvyn P. Leffler, *A Preponderance of Power: National Security, the Truman Administration, and the Cold War* (Stanford, CA: Stanford University Press, 1992), 174–79; Carnes Lord, *The Presidency and the Management of National Security* (New York: Free Press, 1988), 61–69; John Prados, *Keepers of the Keys: A History of the National Security Council from Truman to Bush* (New York: Morrow, 1991).

2. On Truman's leadership and management style, see Alonzo L. Hamby, *Man of the People: A Life of Harry S. Truman* (New York: Oxford University Press, 1995), 298–311, 510–14; Leffler, *A Preponderance of Power*, 26–30, 268–72; Cecil V. Crabb, Jr., and Kevin Mulcahy, *Presidents and Foreign Policy Making: From FDR to Reagan* (Baton Rouge: Louisiana State University Press, 1986), 122–55; Alexander L. George and Juliette L. George, *Presidential Personality and Performance* (Boulder, CO: Westview Press, 1998), 206–7; Lord, *The Presidency and the Management of National Security*, 69–70.

3. This summary of the Korean decision-making process is drawn from Department of State, *Foreign Relations of the United States 1950* (Washington, DC: Government Printing Office, 1976), 7: 128–271; Dennis Merrill, ed., *Documentary History of the Truman Presidency* (Washington, DC: University Publications of America, 1995), 18: 1–176; Dean Acheson, *President at the Creation: My Years at the State Department* (New York: Norton, 1969), 402–25; Harry S. Truman, *Memoirs*, vol. 2: *Years of Trial and Hope, 1946–1952* (New York: Doubleday, 1956), 377–

96; D. Clayton James with Anne Sharp Wells, *Refighting the Last War: Command and Crisis in Korea, 1950–1953* (New York: Free Press, 1993), 14–16, 140–45.

4. On Eisenhower's policymaking style, see Kenneth W. Thompson, "The Strengths and Weaknesses of Eisenhower's Leadership," in Richard Melanson and David Mayers, eds., *Reevaluating Eisenhower: American Foreign Policy in the Fifties* (Urbana: University of Illinois Press, 1987), 13–30; Richard A. Melanson, "The Foundations of Eisenhower's Foreign Policy: Continuity, Community, and Consensus," in ibid., 31–66; H.W. Brands, *Cold Warriors: Eisenhower's Generation and American Foreign Policy* (New York: Columbia University Press, 1988), 3–26, 185–211; Richard H. Immerman, "Eisenhower and Dulles: Who Made the Decision?" *Political Psychology*, 1 (1979), 13–20; Fred L. Greenstein, *The Hidden-Hand Presidency: Eisenhower as Leader* (New York: Basic Books, 1982); Anna Nelson, "The 'Top of Policy Hill': President Eisenhower and the National Security Council," *Diplomatic History*, 7 (1983), 307–26; I.M. Destler, "The Presidency and National Security Organization," in Norman A. Graebner, ed., *The National Security: Its Theory and Practice, 1945–1960* (New York: Oxford University Press, 1986), 226–42; George and George, *Presidential Personality and Performance*, 207–10; Lord, *The Presidency and the Management of National Security*, 70–71.

5. John H. Burke and Fred I. Greenstein, *How Presidents Test Reality: Decisions on Vietnam 1954 and 1965* (New York: Russell Sage Foundation, 1989), 28–115; Richard Immerman, "Between the Unattainable and the Unacceptable: Eisenhower and Dienbienphu," in Melanson and Mayers, *Reevaluating Eisenhower*, 120–54; George C. Herring and Richard H. Immerman, "Eisenhower, Dulles, and Dienbienphu: 'The Day We Didn't Go to War' Revisited," *Journal of American History*, 71 (1984), 343–63; Department of State, *Foreign Relations of the United States 1954* (Washington, DC: Government Printing Office, 1982), 1163–68, 1250–66, 1323–26.

6. This discussion of and citations on policymaking under Kennedy and Johnson draws on Burke and Greenstein, *How Presidents Test Reality*, 134–46; Crabb and Mulcahy, *Presidents and Foreign Policy Making*, 198–220; David M. Barrett, *Uncertain Warriors: Lyndon Johnson and His Vietnam Advisers* (Lawrence: University Press of Kansas, 1993), 1–12; George W. Ball, *Diplomacy for a Crowded World: An American Foreign Policy* (Boston: Little, Brown, 1976), p. 199; George and George, *Presidential Personality and Performance*, 210–12; Lord, *Presidency and the Management of National Security*, 71–72.

7. This account of Johnson's decision making in 1965 is drawn from the following sources, as are all citations: Department of State, *Foreign Relations of the United States 1965* (Washington, DC: Government Printing Office, 1996), 2: 240–413, 3: 188–273; Larry Berman, *Planning a Tragedy: The Americanization of the War in Vietnam* (New York: Norton, 1982), 31–153; Brian Van De Mark, *Into the Quagmire: Lyndon Johnson and the Escalation of the Vietnam War* (New York: Oxford University Press, 1991), 61–91, 153–83; Barrett, *Uncertain Warriors*, 13–61; Burke and Greenstein, *How Presidents Test Reality*, 118–255.

8. This discussion of Bush's decision-making process and handling of the early stages of the Persian Gulf crisis is based on George Bush and Brent Scowcroft, *A World Transformed* (New York: Knopf, 1988), 302–41 et passim; Lawrence Freedman and Efraim Karsh, *The Gulf Conflict 1990–1991: Diplomacy and War in the New*

World Order (Princeton, NJ: Princeton University Press, 1993), 65–128; Herbert Parmet, *George Bush: The Life of a Lone Star Yankee* (New York: Scribner, 1997), 442–63; Colin Powell, *My American Journey* (New York: Random House, 1995), 459–76; James A. Baker, *The Politics of Diplomacy: Revolution, War, and Peace, 1989–1992* (New York: Putnam's, 1995), 275–91 et passim.

CHAPTER 6

Peacekeeping: Canada's Inevitable Role

Norman Hillmer

From the perspective of fifty years, Canadian peacekeeping has acquired a certain inevitability. Since the country's first mission to Kashmir in 1949, tens after tens of thousands of Canadian peacekeepers have served in UN and other peace support operations. The common claim, both in the country and outside, is that the practice was a Canadian invention, manufactured by Foreign Minister Lester B. Pearson in the hurly-burly of the Suez Crisis.[1] His 1957 Nobel Peace Prize became a national talisman, contributing to a peacekeeping momentum that no politician could or wanted to ignore. Peacekeeping was impossible to resist, fitting the government's internationalist objectives and appealing to a public anxious to believe that Canada could be the world's conscience, untainted by power politics and considerations of narrow or selfish interests. In 1999, commenting on the possibility of a peace force to Kosovo after the North Atlantic Treaty Organization's (NATO) military action against Yugoslav President Slobodon Milosevic, Prime Minister Jean Chrétien told the media that peacekeeping had become automatic, the instinctive Canadian response to international crisis.[2]

Suez has a prehistory. Peacekeeping was not part of the UN Charter, which focused on the deterrence and, if necessary, the destruction of aggression. The new international organization, with fresh memories of the abject failure of the League of Nations, was designed to collect for security and in defense of the peace. But the Military Staff Committee and military forces envisioned in the Charter never took root. With each of the five permanent members of the Security Council possessing a veto, the United Nations waged war only once, in Korea during the early 1950s, and that under accidental circumstances.

Thus a UN activity in the middle ground emerged between the clarity of war making and the murky mediation and negotiation of peacemaking. Peacekeeping was conflict management, requiring impartial peace supervision in the field, at the locus of the problem; analyst Alan James calls it "hand-dirtying work," far from the comfortable rooms of diplomacy.[3] The United Nations made a straightforward proffer of assistance, which could be rejected without recrimination or retribution. The final decision on a peacekeeping force was for the parties to the conflict, not the international community as a whole. Against the background of Cold War politics, and encouraging the maximum possible disengagement of the Great Powers from the region of conflict, the United Nations turned to those of its members willing and able to serve as peacekeeping agents, the middle powers such as Canada.[4]

Impressive as the national peacekeeping record became, in the beginning it fell far short of the widely held Canadian self-image of "the young Lochinvar who came out of the North . . . to put the world right."[5] Stern caution governed the country's reactions to international peace initiatives in the early Cold War. With the world-weary Prime Minister Mackenzie King clinging to power in 1948, his distrust of international organizations as keen as ever, the government did not contribute to the United Nations Truce Supervisory Organization (UNTSO) in the Middle East. The next year, Canada agreed to dispatch four army officers to the United Nations Military Observer Group in India and Pakistan (UNMOGIP), but without any joy. The postwar, pre-Korea Canadian Army was a puny thing, uninterested in an overseas commitment, and the government, now under Louis St. Laurent, was wary of alienating India or Pakistan, the parties contesting the territory of Kashmir and Canada's partners in the newly multiracial British Commonwealth. The cabinet was characterized by a top public servant as "allergic" to Kashmir,[6] but Foreign Minister Pearson was an enthusiast. He prevailed.[7]

Ottawa did exhibit considerable interest in various schemes aimed at the establishment of a permanent contingent that could be placed at the disposal of UN headquarters and missions. Canadian Brigadier H.H. Angle, UNMOGIP's first commander (a grand word for the leader of only a few observers), participated in the planning for a UN Field Service, a concept agreed to by the General Assembly in November 1949. Yet the Field Service would be tiny, barely 300 men who could provide transport, security, and communications services. That was a long way from the original design of the United Nations' founders, who had imagined "a body prepared to wage war in defence of peace."[8] Even Mackenzie

King, arguing that a weak United Nations "was doing more to draw us into war than to keep us out," had believed that the "sooner it got to work creating an international force, that would give meaning to its words . . . the better."⁹

With the outbreak of war in Korea, Canada (with Foreign Minister Pearson in the lead) and six other countries put forward the "Uniting for Peace" Resolution, calling for member states to keep forces in a state of readiness for UN duty. An international army was not a realistic possibility, but Canada took the initiative in proposing the earmarking of national contingents; indeed, the Canadian infantry brigade in Korea was designated as a standby force for UN or NATO service. The truth was, however, that Canada's military was consistently setting up roadblocks in the way of contributions to UN units of any size or shape, pleading the case that the armed forces had no personnel to spare or share. In April 1951, responding to a request from the United Nations to list the people who could be made available, Ottawa stated it did not "at present" contemplate the recruitment and organization of further military units specifically for the use of the United Nations. The government would cooperate with other UN members in collective action against breaches of the peace and acts of aggression "to the extent that its military resources and its existing defence obligations permit."¹⁰

"Qualified and hedged," the leading historian of Canadian peacekeeping characterized the Canadian response, "yet apparently one of the very few affirmative answers" to the UN canvass of peace force possibilities.¹¹ Canada did not have the indelible attachment to peacekeeping that later came with Suez, the Nobel Prize, and years of successful practice in the art. Nevertheless, it valued its position as a solid, stable, and realistic partner both in the United Nations and the Western alliance system—reliable if unspectacular.¹²

In precisely this spirit of Good International Citizen, the Canadian government in 1954 sent peacekeepers to UNTSO and to the International Control Commissions (ICCs) in Vietnam, Laos, and Cambodia. The ICCs were carried out under the authority of the 1954 Geneva Conference, not the United Nations. Pearson expressed the motivation in a letter to one of the commissioners: "Canada's acceptance of the invitation to participate in the supervision of the cease-fire agreements was dictated simply by the Government's desire to contribute by this kind of service to the establishment of peace and security in Southeast Asia." The country had no particular axe to grind, no special regional interests in Indochina, no history of unpopular policies or attitudes there.¹³ Soon enough, however, Canadians began to take the ICCs very personally. They were a powerful breeder of anticommunism in the foreign affairs and military personnel who served on the commissions, as Canada shifted more and more to Western positions in tilts with Indian and Polish colleagues.

The four observers despatched to UNTSO in 1954 were joined later in the year by General E.L.M. Burns, who was appointed the mission's Chief of Staff. The decision to participate was taken in the context of growing concerns about peace and stability in the Middle East and after representations from the British and American delegations at the United Nations. Pearson's Department of External Affairs clearly interpreted the call to find a commander for UNTSO as a direct request for Canadian involvement: The secretary general of the United Nations was "in effect appealing to the Canadian Government to help prevent a breakdown of United Nations authority in a fresh and very difficult test to which it is being subjected." Burns was a UN employee, but his role increased official Ottawa's sense that it had a stake in Middle East peacefulness. His rock-solid, unsmiling impartiality became an asset of Canadian diplomacy and was seen as such.[14]

Burns was nearby when the Suez Crisis erupted, and he was a natural to lead the United Nations Emergency Force (UNEF), which Pearson concocted after the British and French (in collusion with the Israelis) attacked Egypt in an attempt to wrest back the Suez Canal, seized earlier in 1956 by Egyptian president Nasser. In an episode laden with irony, the foreign minister had to battle hard to get Canadian soldiers (Burns apart) into UNEF because of Egyptian doubts that a former British colony, sporting British-looking uniforms and British-sounding unit names, was an appropriate peacekeeper in the wake of a British invasion. When the Egyptian foreign minister went out of his way to keep Canada out of UNEF, Pearson reacted angrily: "The Canadian Government could not give one inch." In view of Canada's central part in the UN emergency session on Suez and the independence of its policy, he told the Egyptians their position was "outrageous." If it was allowed to stand, the public's reaction would be violent and very damaging to the United Nations' reputation among Canadians. The argument concerning uniforms was pure nonsense, since all UN soldiers wore distinctive headgear and armbands. "Under no circumstances would we accept the Egyptian request."[15]

The glow of the Nobel Prize Pearson won for his Middle Eastern initiative has tended to obscure his ideas about the way peacekeeping must operate if it was to be successful. Pearson was only able to mastermind the first of the large multinational UN peace forces by compromising on firmly held convictions. He got a truce, the withdrawal of British and French soldiers, and an emergency force of interposition with the power to defend itself. He wanted, however, a much tougher mandate for UNEF, as well as a direct link to negotiations for a political settlement. Unless peacemaking accompanied peacekeeping, "we'll go through all this again if we do not take advantage of the crisis to pluck something out—how was it Hotspur put it: 'Out of this nettle, danger, we pluck this flower, safety.' " Peacekeeping over the long haul in support of an unsatisfactory status quo had little interest for him. He also thought it a tragic miscalculation to give Nasser the power to jettison UNEF at any time he might decide it in the future.[16]

Pearson consistently argued over the next many years that the United Nations must develop its own peacekeeping capability through a pooling of available national resources. In 1957, just before the government changed its stripe from Liberal to Conservative, he called for a permanent contingent of UN peacekeepers. "Are we," he asked, "to go on from crisis to crisis improvising in haste? Or can we now pool our experience and our resources, so that the next time we, the governments and peoples whom the United Nations represents, will be ready and prepared to act?"[17] The John Diefenbaker government, led by a man who believed *he* had invented peacekeeping, put a battalion on standby for UN duty and formally integrated the dispatch of peace forces into its 1959 White Paper on Defence.

The apparent success of UNEF created zeal for another big peacekeeping operation. This time it was inside the Congo, after forces from ex-colonial master Belgium intervened in the chaotic early days of independence following the mutiny of the Congolese military in the summer of 1960.[18] Initially, the Diefenbaker government was hesitant to make blanket commitments for Canadian participation in Opération des Nations Unies au Congo (ONUC), concerned as it was that the request might be for the combat troops that had been put on standby for UN operations. Commenting on ONUC's mandate to assist in the maintenance of law and order, Under Secretary of State for External Affairs Norman Robertson remarked, "It is difficult to see any United Nations force in this role because in effect the United Nations would have taken up arms against citizens of a state in what was essentially a domestic situation."[19] Moreover, given the legacy of Belgian rule, it seemed particularly unwise to place white Canadians, especially those who spoke French, in a position where they might be called on to fire on the Congolese. Canada's ambassador to the United Nations was repeatedly instructed to advise Secretary General Dag Hammarskjöld not to expect such a force from Canada. Diefenbaker was particularly concerned about Hammarskjold's vague and speculative references to possible participation by a "trans-Atlantic French-speaking country."

It is unlikely that Hammarskjold ever contemplated the use of Canadian combat forces. Canada was the sole available source of trained signalers and communications units that could work in both English and French, and that was the basis of the request when it came after the ONUC commander reached the capital of Leopoldville safely. With the

United Nations' critical need for technical personnel and a favorable public on its mind, the government agreed to a maximum of 500 peacekeepers. Army signalers, the bulk of the Canadian offering, established secure and reliable links between UN headquarters in Leopoldville and the various ONUC detachments deployed throughout the Congo. There was a strong Canadian presence in the capital throughout the mission's four-year mandate, and members of the 57th Canadian Signals Unit were among the last peacekeepers to leave the Congo in 1964.

The military was characteristically unhappy about losing a concentration of valued expertise, but External Affairs took a loftier view. Norman Robertson wrote soberly:

Success for the United Nations in the Congo and in Africa might establish the Organization firmly as the strongest influence for peace in the world. Undoubtedly, success in the Congo will rally public support but with that public support must come the material support, as distinct from lip service from member states. Failure, on the other hand, in the Congo might mean the final failure of the United Nations.[20]

After Pearson returned to government in 1963 as prime minister, he traveled to the UN General Assembly to stress the need for a sharing of practical experience and technical information on the way to urging "the development in a co-ordinated way of trained and equipped collective forces for UN service to meet possible future demands for action under the blue flag of the United Nations."[21] In May 1964, Pearson returned to the theme for *Maclean's* magazine, advocating a major reform in the way the international community did business. "If," he wrote,

the United Nations Assembly as such refuses to take that initiative—if it is unable to agree on permanent arrangements for a stand-by force—then why should a group of members who feel that this should be done, not do something about it themselves? Why should they not discharge their own responsibilities individually and collectively, by organizing a force for this purpose, one formally outside the United Nations but ready to act on its request? To do so would require a number of middle powers whose credentials and whose motives are above reproach, to work out stand-by arrangements among themselves consistent with the United Nations Charter. What is needed, in fact, is an entirely new arrangement by which these nations would establish an international peace force, its contingents trained and equipped for the purpose, and operating under principles agreed in advance.[22]

The *Maclean's* article was doubtless written with Cyprus in mind. Earlier in 1964, communal violence between the Greek-Cypriot majority and the Turkish minority had threatened to rip the island asunder and bring intervention from the two mother countries, both Canada's allies in

NATO. A frantic search ensued to cobble together enough countries and enough men to make yet another peacekeeping improvisation possible. Sweden, Finland, and Ireland hung back, and so did Canada, all setting conditions and waiting for someone else to take the lead. Pearson was skeptical that Greeks and Turks on Cyprus would ever find common ground, and his government did not wish to appear too close to the British, a guarantor of the Cypriot constitution with a peace force already in place there. But concerns quickly took hold in Ottawa that the government had set the bar too high. Canadian reluctance might be fatal to the whole project of a United Nations Force in Cyprus (UNFICYP). External Affairs worried that "our friends and allies" would not understand an unwillingness to assist in the solution of a serious threat to the peace involving NATO, the Commonwealth, and the United Nations. The United States, fearful of a split in NATO, and Britain poured the pressure on Ottawa, which was now saying that it was "simply asking for the answers to certain questions which would enable us to serve the United Nations responsibly." Foreign Minister Paul Martin set off on a round of diplomacy, and the logjam was broken—with the considerable assistance of Finland and Sweden.[23]

Assiduously cultivated by Martin himself, the legend grew that he had "authored" UNFICYP and saved the day.[24] And with it the notion of peacekeeping as uniquely, peculiarly Canadian was taking firm hold. With UNEF and the Cyprus force on the ground, and ONUC in its final days, there were 2,600 Canadian Armed Forces peacekeepers in 1964. The Defence White Paper of that year stated the case for peacekeeping with a strength of language not seen before in a Canadian public policy document. It was "essential that a nation's diplomacy be backed up by adequate and flexible military forces to permit participation in collective security and peacekeeping, and to be ready for crises should they arise."[25]

The notion that peace had become a Canadian profession was challenged by a series of developments in the middle 1960s. The United Nations was reeling from an accumulation of disappointment and controversy, not least over the Congo, which had been costly, violent, and divisive. In 1967 UNEF was ordered out of Egypt by Colonel Nasser, causing a veteran UN hand to exclaim that Pearson had been right all along about the need for a tougher peacekeeping regimen; the eleven-year tab had been $64 million, two-thirds of which would never be recovered for the Canadian taxpayer.[26] The Vietnam War, assassinations, and race riots were souring the Canadian public on American leadership at the United Nations and elsewhere; since there had always been close Canada–United States cooperation in peacekeeping, this was a matter of crucial importance. Quebec nationalism made Canadians turn inward, wondering about the survival of their own country. Canada, too, mattered less on the international scene than it had in the golden Suez days: Japan and western Europe had recovered from the 1939–1945 war, knocking Canada several pegs down in the world rankings.

Inevitably, doubts crept in about whether Pearsonian internationalism, with its Canada-as-global-busybody persona, had served the country well. Criticisms of peacekeeping became commonplace, and government statements began to reflect a new emphasis on settling international disputes rather than simply tinkering with the symptoms: "[U]nlike peacekeeping," one official pronouncement read, "the peaceful settlement of disputes has been neglected too long by us. It is easy to pay lip service, of course, to the concept of peaceful settlement, and more difficult to suggest how in practice it might be implemented."[27]

A "self-proclaimed contrarian"[28] seized the moment. Succeeding Pearson as prime minister in 1968, Pierre Trudeau argued that foreign policy must begin at home and be carried out in the interests of domestic harmony and national prosperity. Pearson and his "helpful fixing" of world problems was the implicit target of the criticisms, and he was not amused. "If we withdraw into a foreign policy of narrow nationalism with economic growth as its main objective," he protested, "Canada's voice might be heard but it would not impress."[29] Trudeau long afterward claimed that Pearson, "that most decent of Canadians," was his mentor in international relations. The intention was not to challenge Pearson's concept of Canada as a middle power but, "with the greatest of respect to him," "to explore opportunities that would ensure that Canada would function as an 'effective power.'" Whatever that meant, it was clear that peacekeeping had little role or significance for Trudeau, or for his closest adviser on such questions, Ivan Head. The Trudeau–Head foreign policy memoir on the years 1968–1984 scarcely considers peacekeeping.[30]

The 1971 White Paper on Defence put the dissatisfaction of the period in stark terms. Peacekeeping all too often had been frustrating and discouraging. Terms of reference had been inadequate. There had been a lack of coordination among peacekeeping countries, while some of the big powers had failed to give political support and the international community had not provided sufficient logistical and financial resources. Operations, moreover, could easily slide into open-ended commitments in the absence of a political settlement between the disputing parties. In the future, the government would look to "the promise of success" and the "existence of realistic terms of reference."[31] If the 1964 White Paper "represented a peak," wrote the respected defense expert Rod Byers, "then 1971 represented official disillusionment over the utility and future prospects for peacekeeping."[32]

The government griped about peacekeeping but did not rule it out.

Canada had been part of an international control commission in Vietnam since 1954, an involvement described as a farce by Trudeau's foreign minister, Mitchell Sharp. Thus, when the issue arose in late 1972, there was little enthusiasm in the government or bureaucracy for yet another commission to supervise yet another cease-fire. Sharp "recognized the risks, but I also wanted to help the United States extricate itself from Vietnam and I didn't want Canada to be blamed for complicating the cease-fire negotiations."[33] Conditions were laid down, but a crucial one, an independent oversight of the commission's work, was never met. Canada agreed to membership anyway, to the delight of critics who thought that Canada was again tripping all over itself to please the United States and keep the peace, no matter what.

Service on the International Commission for Control and Supervision (ICCS) was even more short-lived than the continued existence of South Vietnam. Sharp and Parliament having roundly condemned U.S. policy in Vietnam in the course of negotiations to set up the commission, Canada regularly made its doubts known about the whole exercise throughout its six-month tenure on the ICCS. The media and public on the whole supported the government, but Canada's uncharacteristically "open-mouth diplomacy" won few friends in the international community.[34] Trudeau and Sharp wanted it both ways: participation without the pain of ever having to admit to full-throated commitment; criticism of the Americans while remaining their faithful ally.

The importance of Canada's position as an international peacekeeper, even in Trudeau's Ottawa, was demonstrated much more forcefully when another UNEF force was assembled in the aftermath of the brief 1973 Arab-Israeli Yom Kippur War. Citing long experience with peacekeeping in Indo-China, Sharp announced the government's willingness to serve on four conditions: a clear mandate for the force, including freedom of movement; the existence of a responsible political authority with the power to supervise the mandate; Canada's acceptability to all parties; and equitable financing arrangements. But there were objections from the Soviets and the Egyptians, and Sharp's team had to kick their diplomacy into high gear to find an acceptable compromise in the form of a Canadian-Polish deployment agreement for the sharing of UNEF's logistics.

For several commentators, Canada had shown itself willing to go to any length to keep its record of perfect attendance at every peacekeeping operation in tact. The opposition Conservatives said that Sharp was begging, nothing less. The Toronto *Globe and Mail*'s Hugh Winsor wrote that the government,

after being quick to offer assistance, was disturbed when the call didn't come and enormously pleased when it did. One only had to observe the air of relief displayed by Canadian diplomats in New York or the enthusiasm of the armed forces officers in their preparations to appreciate this.

Whatever the government might protest, the "legacy of Lester Pearson is still felt."[35]

Winsor was reflecting the by then widely held notion that Pearson had created a peacekeeping itch that every government was compelled to scratch. But the former foreign secretary and prime minister never wanted a policy of "my peacekeeping, right or wrong." In a sense, Canadian thinking and international circumstances had caught up with him. From the beginning, he had wanted the clearly understood mandates Sharp championed, and he emphasized the tie to conflict resolution long before it was a gleam in the eye of the authors of the 1971 White Paper.

The Trudeau government continued to embrace peacekeeping, including a 1978 venture in Lebanon, and often for the most apparently Pearsonian of reasons. As Byers put it, after a close questioning of decision makers in the mid-1970s, "Canada participates in peacekeeping out of a sense of responsibility to the international community, and actions in this policy sphere constitute an 'ought' for the policymaker." Yet the Trudeauites were skeptical, and they were ambivalent. They tried to lay down standards. They questioned peacekeeping-without-end, particularly in Cyprus, which had begun as a three-month commitment and was now in its second decade.[36]

Although there were no new UN missions for most of the 1980s, peacekeeping had become established international practice: steady, bland, dull even—but a recognized symbol of stability and the collective will of a fractious world community to act together for peace. In 1988, UN peacekeeping forces were awarded a Nobel Peace Prize. Canadians accepted the award as if it were their own. The Montreal *Gazette* recalled that Pearson had been "the key figure who made peacekeeping forces what they are today: an almost standard device to give combatants a face-saving out." He had persuaded the United Nations to do the right thing at a crucial and dangerous time. "He won the Nobel Peace Prize for that; now his child has grown up and won the prize itself."[37] A correspondent for the Toronto *Globe and Mail* declared that peacekeeping was "the proudest peacetime tradition of the Canadian military."[38]

The winding down of the Cold War ignited an explosion of expectations. East-West cooperation in the Security Council during the Persian Gulf crisis in 1990–1991 heralded a rebirth of confidence in the UN Charter, while discussions of global peace enforcement migrated from the fringes of academic debate to the political mainstream. Chunks of the Berlin Wall appeared on mantles around the world as mute testimony to a world order that would never return. The nature of warfare, indeed the international system itself, had changed, the experts claimed; traditional diplomatic and military methods would be insufficient to handle the "new" security challenges.

Peacekeeping was suddenly every country's preoccupation and support for a UN rapid reaction force built quickly. Even a UN army, for decades a polite fiction, was now much discussed, especially as blue berets went in their thousands to zones of conflict from Central America to Asia, from the Balkans to southern Africa. A United Nations determined to be energetic by the outbreak of peace was suddenly intolerant of half-measures. The number of missions (and missionaries) mushroomed. The mandates grew more complex, the rhetoric more assertive.

Prime Minister Brian Mulroney, in power from 1984 to 1993 and an influential player in fora such as the G7 and the Commonwealth, believed fervently in the United Nations as a place where a "mid-level power" could make its mark independent of the United States. He was disinclined to pass up any opportunities to have the military carry out its role as the world's peacekeeper sans pareil. His foreign minister from 1991 was Barbara McDougall, another self-confessed international enthusiast, succeeding Joe Clark, who believed passionately that Canada defined its interests more broadly and less selfishly than other nations.[39]

The circumstances of the very early 1990s made such influential Canadians almost giddy with anticipation. The end of the Cold War caused a hardened veteran, General Romeo Dallaire, "trained for war as a member of NATO," to dream of "the entry into the new world order with its promise of peace, disarmament and prosperity."[40] The Gulf War also had a powerful impact on Ottawa, making it seem as if cooperation to good ends between large coalitions of nations was not simply desirable but possible.

For a moment, though, Canada seemed to pull back. After a four-decade stint with NATO in Europe, the government announced that it would bring most of its forces home. Almost immediately, some became all, to the howls of Canada's European allies. Long-standing reservations had also been expressed about the peacekeeping mission in Cyprus, and this commitment was wound down. The NATO role was viewed as a "presence mission." So was Cyprus, where Canada had helped keep Atlantic alliance members Greece and Turkey from each other's throats for almost thirty years; the peacekeepers, many argued, had frozen the conflict and made a political settlement even more elusive.[41]

These were places where Canadians stood and waited upon events, rather than acted to alter them. In light of the revised circumstances of the international environment that seemed to favor Pearsonian skills and methodologies, and the paring of expenditures that necessarily went with the early post–Cold War mentality, it made sense to put forces where they would, to use a favorite Clark phrase, "make a difference." The United Nations mattered in a way it had not before, as the essential framework of a global cooperative security dialogue; it was a place where Canada—and Canadian troops, money, and knowledge—could count. With Canadians in a leading role, the United Nations would become a true international actor, not simply a talk shop, to fight the new regional battles and seize the new opportunities thrown up by a more equitable global environment.

Mulroney himself led the way. At California's Stanford University in September 1991, he proclaimed that borders meant nothing if they got in the way of simple notions of right and wrong. "Invocations of the principle of national sovereignty are as out of date and as offensive to me as the police declining to stop family violence simply because a man's home is his castle."[42] The foreign minister, warming to the theme, vigorously argued the case for interventionism in pursuit of humanitarian good works. "How many men, women and children have become victims of all manner of brutality, racism and discrimination," McDougall asked on behalf of a "new internationalism," "because the shield of national sovereignty was raised before the international community? Now that the Iron Curtain and the Berlin Wall have fallen, is it not time to respect human dignity as much as, if not more than national sovereignty?"[43] The government fully took on board Boutros Boutros-Ghali's 1992 *Agenda for Peace*, with its expansive peacekeeping menu, and indeed took credit for pushing the UN secretary general to his muscular stance.

In March 1992, Canada's involvement with the United Nations Protection Force in the former Yugoslavia (UNPROFOR) was initiated. With General Lewis MacKenzie as chief of staff and an initial injection of 1,200 military and 45 members of the Royal Canadian Mounted Police, this was the largest UN peacekeeping force since that sent to the Congo in the early 1960s. By August a worsening Bosnian situation occasioned a second UNPROFOR, a humanitarian mission, with another 1,200 Canadians. That same month, a substantial contribution to the United Nations Operation in Somalia (UNISOM I) was authorized. At year's end, with Canada's Airborne Regiment only days away from departure and hopes for UNISOM I fading, the United States announced that it would lead an intervention into Somalia. By January 1993, a multinational coalition of 38,000, including more than 25,000 U.S. Marines, were on the ground. The Airborne joined the American force, called the Unified Task Force (UNITAF), or sometimes Operation Restore Hope.

The new conflicts proved no more amenable to well-intentioned ministrations than the old and may even have been less so. National finances exercised a powerful restraint on international activism. Messy intrastate conflicts left no borders to watch or cease-fire lines to police. In the absence of clear political objectives, potential troop contributors balked at open-ended commitments. The American experience in Somalia[44] highlighted the domestic repercussions of incurring casualties on UN missions where national interests were poorly defined, while the brutal death of a Somali teenager at the hands of Canadian soldiers left a permanent scar on a proud peacekeeping heritage. In the Balkans, UN troops seemed stranded, unable to fulfill their vast, ever-changing mandate, yet equally unable to withdraw for fear of precipitating wider carnage. Instead, the polyglot force watched helplessly as ethnic hatred led to mass butchery. Canadian troops were underequipped, widely scattered, and enormously vulnerable. Increasingly, the United Nations subcontracted its task to NATO; alliance air strikes made Canadians attractive targets for Serb hostage-taking.[45]

McDougall lamented "the rapid and widespread descent into instability that followed the end of the Cold War." But that only made Canada more indispensable in the search for "what we thought we had achieved then—a new level of stability, harmony and hope." The "situation Canada happily finds itself in is that our expressed perspective, our skills, and our steadfastness to our own ideals may be what the world needs in the face of these dauntingly complex challenges.... We will continue to be activists when it comes to peace and security, especially through the UN."[46] Appetizing domestic advantages added to the appeal of these arguments. Internationalism was a popular stance for an unpopular government. The independence movement in Quebec, moreover, was attracting adherents at an alarming pace. Foreign policy had been a potent instrument of national unity since the Second World War and remained so.

As McDougall spoke, in February 1993, there were more than 4,700 Canadian Forces personnel on peacekeeping duties around the world, the government's ceiling of 2,000 having been long ago breached.[47] The country's expenditures on peace support—a term then coming into vogue to describe the myriad new tasks under the peacekeeping umbrella—went from $10 to $12 million in 1991–1992 to roughly $130 million in 1993–1994. The defense budget meanwhile was falling by hundreds of millions of dollars.

Terminology was becoming a struggle, and confusion abounded. Suez-style operations, where large forces interposed themselves between two parties who had agreed to a cease-fire, were called "traditional" or "classical" peacekeeping, in order to distinguish them from the new "second generation" or "wider" missions, which could include the monitoring or administration of elections; preventive deployments; implementation of peace settlements; humanitarian, human rights, and information functions; nation-building mandates such as the training of police; and enforcement of Security Council resolutions. Boutros-Ghali's *Agenda for Peace* removed the consent of all concerned parties, a bedrock of Cold

War peace operations, from the list of peacekeeping prerequisites. To this was added a recommendation that "peace-enforcement units" be made part of the mix, in order inter alia to secure elusive cease-fire lines and ensure the delivery of humanitarian assistance. Boutros-Ghali also spoke of preconflict preventive peacekeeping to resolve disputes before they got out of hand and postconflict peace-building to identify and support structures that would diminish the chances of further confrontation.[48]

After a Liberal government took power in the fall of 1993, it produced a Defence White Paper that placed traditional peacekeeping and the use of force on a continuum. Small observer actions were at one end and operations to enforce the will of the international community at the other, with humanitarian assistance and the rebuilding of infrastructures as possibilities along the way. The document used peacekeeping and enforcement almost interchangeably, mentioning, for example, the Gulf War and UNPROFOR in ex-Yugoslavia in the same breath and suggesting (as did the Boutros-Ghali paper) that the lines between quite different endeavors had become blurred.[49]

Politicians and professors were growing wary about a "much broader, riskier, tougher, more expensive"[50] peacekeeping, and the public was too. Testifying to a special joint foreign policy committee of the House of Commons and the Senate in 1994, academic Dan Middlemiss warned that Canada must not continue to be the automatic peacekeeper, "the 911 of the international community." His Dalhousie University colleague, Denis Stairs, observed that "the demand is too high, the expectations are too high, and our capacity to deliver is too low."[51] While demonstrating overall support for peacekeeping, polls reflected the uneasiness of Canadians about missions that placed their soldiers in peril.[52]

The joint committee added its voice to a Senate study of the year before, recommending greater discernment in choosing when to keep the peace and when not. Both reports demanded a clearer sense and definition of the national interests involved, as did members of the Reform Party, who broke the long tradition of bipartisanship on the peacekeeping issue. There were also calls for reforms in the way the United Nations did their end of the business and thus for improved coordination at headquarters in New York and quicker response times to international emergencies.[53]

Officials in the departments of national defence and foreign affairs began to advocate a more carefully thought out and selective national peacekeeping strategy. The 1994 Defence White Paper established "certain key principles" for the design of all future missions: a clear and enforceable mandate; an identifiable and commonly accepted reporting authority; a mixture of national contributions appropriate to the mission; effective consultation between mission partners; a recognized focus of authority; a clear and efficient division of responsibilities and agreed operating procedures for operations involving (as missions increasingly did) both military and civilian resources; and acceptance of Canadian participation by all parties to the conflict, except in enforcement of NATO actions. In addition, there had to be a real prospect of success. Multilateral operations, whether they threatened international peace and security or addressed humanitarian tragedy, "must not become ends in themselves; they must be part of a comprehensive strategy to secure long-term, realistic, and achievable solutions."[54]

The Nobel medal did not lose its luster. In a January 1994 debate in the House of Commons, speaking as Canadian soldiers were pinned down in Srebrenica in the former Yugoslavia, leader of the Opposition Lucien Bouchard acknowledged that peace operations had become a "thorn in the flesh of our diplomacy and our foreign commitments." But there was no question of withdrawal. Peacekeeping was a source of enormous pride to Canadians.

The disinterested and humanitarian nature of our international interventions was hailed again and again. And did not the architect of Canada's peacekeeping role win the Nobel Prize? Indeed, more than anybody, Lester B. Pearson symbolizes the necessary assuming of a democratic country's moral obligations.

It would be easy "to throw our hands up, pack our bags and leave but this is not the way Canada earned its well-deserved reputation abroad as a steady peacemaker willing to walk the extra mile in the name of peace."[55]

The Liberals of Jean Chrétien, in power since 1993 and the direct descendants of the Pearsonian tradition, were unlikely to disagree. Against a background of a one-quarter cut in the defense budget in the last half of the 1990s, the tempo of Canadian peacekeeping operations has accelerated. The Department of National Defence's Directorate of Peacekeeping Policy listed a staggering thirty-nine separate Canadian contributions to peace support missions under the Chrétien government to the end of March 1999—in Bosnia and Somalia, of course, but also places as varied as Haiti, the Dominican Republic, El Salvador, Honduras, and Guatemala; the Western Sahara, Arabian Gulf, and Turkey; and Mozambique, Rwanda, Zaire, the Central African Republic, and Kenya. A good sprinkling of these were not UN operations, from the high-end NATO Implementation Force (IFOR) in the former Yugoslavia to a 1994 humanitarian outreach of medical assistance and water purification to refugees in Rwanda.[56]

Improvisation had marked forty years of peace missions. The Chrétien government pushed hard for a "UN peace operation system" [57] and in particular for a more responsive headquarters and a better design and quicker delivery of missions. Speaking to the UN General Assembly in

September 1995, Foreign Minister André Ouellet unveiled an ambitious scheme to build a rapid reaction capability for peace operations. The study contained a number of recommendations aimed at ensuring early warning of crises-in-the-making, contingency planning, timely decision making, transport and logistical support, accessible financing, and properly trained and equipped people. At the heart of this effort to formulate a coherent peacekeeping methodology was the Vanguard Concept, designed to get command-and-control facilities into place within seven days and deploy a multidisciplinary group of 5,000 military and civilian personnel in another five weeks at the maximum.[58]

The most promising and practical development in the direction of Vanguard was the Multinational United Nations Stand-by Forces High Readiness Brigade (SHIRBRIG), which Canada has been hatching with Austria, Denmark, the Netherlands, Norway, Poland, and Sweden after 1996. Planning for SHIRBRIG was well advanced, and a Canadian deputy commander has been designated. The defense department's move to obtain improved air and sea lift capacity was consistent with the desire for fast action and effective deployments.

The report of the 2000 Brahimi Panel on United Nations Operations, recommending tight coordination, rigorous mandates, standby forces, and brisk mobility, was yet another attempt to put peacekeeping on a firm organizational and operational basis. But it went a good deal further than that. Brahimi's fundamental premise is that the United Nations has signally failed to meet the peace challenge of the post–Cold War era. The panel views peacekeeping as having evolved from a traditional, primarily military, model of observing cease-fires and force separations after interstate wars to a complex military-civilian endeavor to build peace in the dangerous aftermath of civil wars. Traditional peacekeeping, with its bedrock principles of impartiality, consent, and the use of force only for self-defense, was and is fine as far as it goes, although it is "difficult to justify unless accompanied by serious and sustained peacemaking efforts that seek to transform a ceasefire accord into a durable and lasting peace settlement." Modern peacekeeping in the context of intrastate/transnational conflicts, however, has less room for maneuver. It does not deploy into postconflict situations so much as it deploys to create such situations.

Brahimi wants, therefore, a robust force posture and a sound peacebuilding strategy to offer peacekeepers a ready exit. The United Nations must be willing to choose sides. When "one party to a peace agreement clearly and incontrovertibly is violating its terms, continued equal treatment of all parties by the United Nations can in the best case result in ineffectiveness and in the worst may amount to complicity with evil." Operations ought to have the authority to use force. That "means bigger forces, better equipped and more costly, but able to pose a credible deterrent threat, in contrast to the symbolic and non-threatening presence that characterizes traditional peacekeeping." When the United Nations dispatches its forces in the cause of peace, they should be prepared to confront war and violence "with the ability and determination to defeat them." Otherwise, it would be best not to go at all.[59]

Much of this was in direct line with Pearsonian thinking. As a way station on the road to a permanent UN peace force, Pearson championed the concept of coherent, multinational standby forces formed by member states to ensure rapid and effective peace deployments. Peacekeepers alone, he declared, cannot create peace; they can only carve out the space in which peace may be constructed. He also consistently sought an explicit link between the peacekeeping function and measures that bear in directly on conflict resolution and reassembling the foundations of harmony. Nor would he have had any hesitation in supporting the fundamental Brahimi notion that peacekeepers must have the ability to project credible force if certain operations are to succeed. Pearson, indeed, was the last prime minister of Canada to take the country's armed forces seriously.

The Canadian government immediately embraced the Brahimi report,[60] with all its implications for a more intrusive, pervasive, and expensive peacekeeping, but without discussing the country's very considerably diminished resources "to perform the task, with reasonable safety, reasonably well."[61] Over the last five years of the century, calling inter alia for an integrated Brahimi-style approach to peace support operations as part of an overall concern for human security,[62] Canadian foreign policy took the form of a rhetorical Lochinvar, making a comprehensive assertion of international moral leadership to "shape the world of the next century for the better."[63] Public support of peacekeeping was broad and deep, and showed no signs of abating.[64] As the prime minister put it, when the military was being scoured for 600 personnel to send to East Timor in September 1999, Canadians love their peacekeepers. "They think it is a nice way for Canadians to be present around the world." "We are always there," Jean Chrétien enthused, "like the Boy Scouts."[65] Almost a half century after the Suez Crisis, the will to "put the world right" remained vibrant.[66]

NOTES

1. See, for example, Graham Evans and Jeffrey Newnham, *The Penguin Dictionary of International Relations* (London, 1998), 426.

2. Canadian Broadcasting Corporation, national radio news broadcast, May 15, 1999.

3. Alan James, "The History of Peacekeeping: An Analytical Perspective," *Canadian Defence Quarterly* (September 1993), 11.

4. Ibid.; Alastair Taylor, David Cox, and J.L. Granatstein, *Peacekeeping: International Challenge and Canadian Response* (Toronto, 1968), 4.

5. The phrase is that of John W. Holmes, the most influential commentator on and historian of Canada's post–Second World War foreign policy. See John English, " 'A Fine Romance': Canada and the United Nations, 1943–1957," in Greg Donaghy, ed., *Canada and the Early Cold War, 1943–1957* (Ottawa, 1998), 75.

6. Memorandum from Acting Under Secretary of State for External Affairs Escott Reid to Pearson, January 15, 1949, in Hector M. Mackenzie, ed., *Documents on Canadian External Relations*, vol. 15: *1949* (Ottawa, 1995), 302–3.

7. Taylor, Cox, and Granatstein, *Peacekeeping*, 101–2; D. Colwyn Williams, "International Peacekeeping: Canada's Role," in R. St J. Macdonald, Gerald L. Morris, and Douglas M. Johnson, eds., *Canadian Perspectives on International Law and Organization* (Toronto, 1974), 651.

8. James, "History," 11.

9. David A. Lenarcic, "Postwar Portents: The Origins of Canadian Thinking on United Nations Forces, 1948–1951" (unpublished manuscript, courtesy of the author), 4.

10. Ibid., 22–24, passim.

11. J.L. Granatstein, in Taylor, Cox, and Granatstein, *Peacekeeping*, 106–7.

12. English, "Romance," 80–81.

13. Secretary of State for External Affairs to Commissioner, International Supervisory Commission for Vietnam, August 24, 1954, in Greg Donaghy, ed., *Documents on Canadian External Relations*, vol. 20: *1954* (Ottawa, 1997), 1717.

14. On impartiality, see memorandum from Acting Under Secretary of State for External Affairs Jules Léger to Pearson, November 12, 1954, in ibid., 1614–17; for the paragraph more generally, consult Lisa Y. Dillon, "Prelude to Suez: Canadian Relations in the Middle East, 1953–55" (master's thesis, Carleton University, 1991), 28–32.

15. Memorandum of A.D.P. Heeney, "Middle East Crisis; U.N. Emergency Force," November 12, 1956, National Archives of Canada, Records of the Department of External Affairs, 50, 366–40.

16. Norman Hillmer, "Peacekeeping: Canadian Invention, Canadian Myth," in Sune Åkerman and J.L. Granatstein, eds., *Welfare States in Trouble: Historical Perspectives on Canada and Sweden* (Uppsala, Sweden, 1995), 163.

17. Government of Canada, *Towards a Rapid Reaction Capability for the United Nations* (Ottawa, 1995), 1.

18. Alan James, "Reluctant Heroes: Assembling the United Nations Cyprus Force, 1964," *International Journal*, 53.4 (Autumn 1998), 733–34. The account of ONUC that follows is based closely on Kevin A. Spooner, "The Origins of Canadian Participation in the United Nations Operation in the Congo, 1960" (master's thesis, Carleton University, 1995).

19. Spooner, "The Origins of Canadian Participation," 49.

20. Ibid., 79. On the "fundamental differences of opinion" and "basic incompatibility of views" between the military and the Department of External Affairs in these years, see David A. Lenarcic, "A Case of Double Vision: Canadian Peacekeeping Policy in the 1960s" (unpublished manuscript, courtesy of the author).

21. Williams, "International Peacekeeping," 660, 665–6. See also "Before the

Eighteenth Session of the United Nations," September 19, 1963, in L. B. Pearson, *Words and Occasions* (Toronto 1970), 216.

22. Taylor, Cox, and Granatstein, *Peacekeeping*, 48.

23. This paragraph is based on James, "Heroes," 734–46.

24. Ibid., 743–45.

25. Rod B. Byers, "Peacekeeping and Canadian Defence Policy: Ambivalence and Uncertainty," in B.D. Hunt and R.G. Haycock, eds., *Canada's Defence* (Toronto, 1993), 183.

26. John English, *The Worldly Years: The Life of Lester B. Pearson*, vol. 2: *1949–1972* (Toronto, 1992), 141, quoting Brian Urquhart; on UNEF financing, Williams, "International Peacekeeping," 658.

27. Quoted in Williams, "International Peacekeeping," 688. See also 670.

28. English, "Romance," 74.

29. Lester B. Pearson, *Mike: The Memoirs of the Right Honourable Lester B. Pearson*, Vol. 2: *1948–1957* (Toronto, 1973), 29–32.

30. Ivan L. Head and Pierre Elliott Trudeau, *The Canadian Way: Shaping Canada's Foreign Policy 1968–1984* (Toronto, 1995), x, 7, 345–61.

31. Minister of National Defence, *Defence in the 1970s: White Paper on Defence* (Ottawa, 1971), 39–40.

32. Byers, "Peacekeeping and Defence,"183–84.

33. Mitchell Sharp, *Which Reminds Me . . . A Memoir* (Toronto, 1994), 212.

34. R.B. Byers, "External Affairs and Defence," in John Saywell, ed., *Canadian Annual Review of Politics and Public Affairs 1973* (Toronto, 1974), 284–89.

35. Hillmer, "Invention," 165; Byers, "External Affairs," 251–57.

36. Byers, "Peacekeeping and Defence," 184–85, 189–90.

37. "Pearson's Baby Grows Up," *The Gazette* (Montreal), September 30, 1988, B-2.

38. Paul Koring, "Role as Peacekeepers Now Proudest Tradition of Canadian Military," *Globe and Mail* (Toronto), September 30, 1988, A3.

39. Joe Clark, " 'The First International Country,' " *International Journal*, 52.4 (Autumn 1997), 541.

40. Romeo Dallaire, "Rwanda—Operations Other Than War" (unpublished manuscript, courtesy of the author).

41. Interview with Hon. Barbara McDougall, March 19, 1999.

42. "Notes for an Address by Prime Minister Brian Mulroney on the Occasion of the Centennial Anniversary Convocation, Stanford University, California, USA," September 29, 1991.

43. Quoted in Norman Hillmer, "Canadian Peacekeeping and the Road Back to 1945," in Fabrizio Ghilardi, ed., *Canada E Italia: Prospettive di Co-operazione* (Pisa, 1994), 156.

44. See Mark Bowden, *Black Hawk Down: A Study of Modern War* (New York, 1998).

45. Norman Hillmer and Dean Oliver, "The NATO–United Nations Link: Canada and the Balkans, 1991–1995," in Gustav Schmidt, ed., *A History of NATO: The First Fifty Years* (London, 2001).

46. "An Address by the Honourable Barbara McDougall . . . to a Seminar on Canada's Agenda for International Peace and Security," February 8, 1993, Department of External Affairs, Statement 93/7.

47. Chief of the Defence Staff, "Current Peacekeeping Operations," February 16, 1993.

48. Report of the Secretary-General on the Work of the Organization, "An Agenda for Peace: Preventive Diplomacy, Peacemaking and Peacekeeping," A/47/277, June 17, 1992.

49. *1994 Defence White Paper* (Ottawa, 1994), chap 6; Daniel Livermore, "Peacekeeping: Between Hope and Despair," (a paper presented to the Ninth Asia-Pacific Round Table, Kuala Lumpur, June 1995).

50. Lloyd Axworthy, in Minutes of the Standing Committee on External Affairs and International Trade, February 17, 1993.

51. Quoted in Special Joint Committee of the Senate and the House of Commons Reviewing Foreign Policy, *Canada's Foreign Policy: Principles and Priorities for the Future* (Ottawa, November 1994), 18.

52. Norman Hillmer, "Canadian Peacekeeping: Old and New," in *Peacekeeping 1815 to Today. Proceedings of the XXIst Colloquium of the International Commission of Military History* (Quebec City, Quebec, 1995), 543; Andrew F. Cooper, *Canadian Foreign Policy: Old Habits and New Directions* (Scarborough, Ontario, 1997), 194.

53. *Canada's Foreign Policy*; Senate of Canada, Standing Committee on Security and National Defence, *Meeting New Challenges: Canada's Response to a New Generation of Peacekeeping* (February 1993).

54. *1994 Defence White Paper*, 28–9; Hillmer, "Canadian Peacekeeping," 542–3; confidential interviews carried out in Ottawa, Summer 1995.

55. Cooper, *Canadian Foreign Policy*, 198.

56. National Defence, "Past Canadian Commitments to Peace Support Operations (as of March 31, 1999)."

57. Maxime Faille, "Towards a UN Rapid Reaction Capability: A Canadian Initiative," *Canadian Defence Quarterly* (December 1995), 14–15.

58. Ibid.; Government of Canada, *Towards a Rapid Reaction Capability for the United Nations*.

59. *Report of the Panel on United Nations Peace Operations*, United Nations A/55/305-S2000/809, August 2000. Quotations from viii, ix, 3, and 9.

60. Minister of Foreign Affairs and Minister of National Defence Press Release, "Canada Welcomes Recommendations of Peacekeeping Review," August 23, 2000.

61. Denis Stairs, "Canada and the New World Order," in Michael J. Tucker, Raymond B. Blake and P.E. Bryden, eds., *Canada and the New World Order: Facing the New Millennium* (Toronto, 2000), 4.

62. Lloyd Axworthy, "Foreword," in Gregory Wirick and Robert Miller, eds., *Canada and Missions for Peace: Lessons from Nicaragua, Cambodia and Somalia* (Ottawa, 1998), x–xi.

63. Lloyd Axworthy and Sarah Taylor, "A Ban for All Seasons: The Landmines Convention and Its Implications for Canadian Diplomacy," *International Journal*, 53.2 (Spring 1998), 203; Norman Hillmer and Adam Chapnick, "The Axworthy Revolution," in Fen Osler Hampson, Norman Hillmer, and Maureen Molot, eds, *Canada among Nations 2001: The Axworthy Legacy* (Don Mills, Ontario, 2001).

64. Goldfarb Poll, June 1999, cited in Lieutenant General Romeo Dallaire and Major Robert Near, "Securing the Army's Future—Enhancing the Conflict Res-

olution Capability of the Canadian Army for the 21st Century" (unpublished manuscript, note 8).

65. Quoted in "Peacekeepers: Military Budget Puts Constraints on Canadians," *Washington Post*, September 26, 1999, A25.

66. I am grateful to the Lester B. Pearson Canadian International Peacekeeping Training Centre and the Social Sciences and Humanities Research Council of Canada for support of the research carried out for this chapter, which was completed at the end of 2000. Part of the foregoing was written as a briefing for the Pearson Centre, and the author is indebted to Anne Hillmer, Dean Oliver, Alex Morrison, Kevin Spooner, and Grant Dawson for their assistance.

CHAPTER 7

Three Degrees of Separation: The Evolving Convergence of Human Rights Law, Humanitarian Law, and Refugee Law

Donna E. Arzt

We have recently passed the fiftieth anniversary of a three-year series of events: first, the adoption by the United Nations General Assembly on December 9, 1948, of the Convention on the Prevention and Punishment of the Crime of Genocide, followed one day later by the Universal Declaration of Human Rights; second, the diplomatic conference held in Geneva in 1949 that produced four treaties concerning the protection of victims of war, including the entirely new Geneva Convention IV Relative to the Protection of Civilian Persons in Time of War, and third, in the following year, 1950, the creation by the United Nations of the office of the High Commissioner for Refugees (UNHCR), whose mandate would become coextensive with the 1951 Convention Relating to the Status of Refugees. It was also in 1950 that the Council of Europe adopted the European Convention for the Protection of Human Rights and Fundamental Freedoms, which predated by sixteen years the promulgation of the binding international human rights Covenants intended by the United Nations to implement the Universal Declaration.[1]

While all of these closely timed developments had at their core the promotion of the same fundamental objective, namely, individual human dignity, they were originally conceived as discrete endeavors in three separate fields of public international law: (1) the law of war, which is as old as public international law itself; (2) human rights law, which could readily be dated to the eighteenth century but which was not identifiable as a subject of international treaty making until two words, *human* and *rights*, were inserted in the Preamble of the UN Charter; and (3) refugee law, the subject of which only began to appear with a few international instruments concluded through the League of Nations.[2] How it is that they have come to converge into one area of international law—by no means a single field, yet assuredly closer than even the veritable "six degrees of separation"[3]—is the subject of this chapter.

Before explaining how the "six degrees" have been reduced to three, I will briefly sketch the modern origins and major characteristics of human rights law, humanitarian law, and refugee law, summarizing how over the past half century they have increasingly come to intersect. I will then explore the influence of post–Cold War trends; highlight some conceptual deviations between the three fields of law; survey their converging features; report recent trends toward internalization and demilitarization; and finally, suggest what gaps must be filled on the path to further convergence.

THE HUMAN RIGHTS IDEA: A NONVIOLENT REVOLUTION

It's helpful to recall that the phrase "promoting and encouraging respect for human rights and fundamental freedoms for all" almost failed to be included in article 1 of the UN Charter. The United States, the United Kingdom, and the Soviet Union initially wanted the Charter to be purely formalistic and for an elaborate bill of rights to be drafted later. Fortunately, because of the last-minute insertion of that phrase, the Universal Declaration of Human Rights can be considered an authoritative interpretation of the Charter phrase, such that member states—from China to Chile to Cameroon to the Czech Republic—are required by the Charter's Supremacy Clause to treat the promotion of human rights as superior to any other international obligation except that other fundamental principle of the Charter itself, the avoidance of threats to international peace and security.[4]

More important, the insertion into the Charter of that phrase about human rights epitomized one of international law's two most revolutionary conceptual breakthroughs in the twentieth century: from 1945 onward, international human rights law would regulate the conduct of sovereign states in how they treat their *own* citizens as well as nationals of other states. This was one of the first steps in the transformation from a system of state sovereignty, in which individuals are the subjects of the state and the passive object of arbitrary governmental discretion, to the development of a global civil society in which concern for the dignity of individuals is paramount even over sovereignty. As stated in 1991 by then-UN Secretary General Javier Perez de Cuellar: "It is now increasingly felt that the principle of noninterference with the essential domestic jurisdiction of States cannot be regarded as a protective barrier behind which human rights could be massively or systematically violated with impunity."[5]

The ideology of human rights asserts that certain types of political systems—slave and apartheid societies, for instance—are illegitimate and to be universally condemned. Human rights are, in the words of my own teacher, Louis Henkin, "*the idea* of our time."[6] A corollary of this preeminence is the concept that human rights are *erga omnes*, that is, owed not simply to the victim but to the entire international community. Moreover, some rights are nonderogable, meaning that even during a national emergency or serious threat to national order or security, they can never be suspended. Among this class of fundamental rights are the right to life, the right not to be tortured or made a slave, the prohibition on ex post facto (retroactive) criminal laws, and the right to freedom of thought, conscience, and religion.[7]

FROM NUREMBERG TO GENEVA: INTERNATIONAL HUMANITARIAN LAW

I mentioned two conceptual breakthroughs, both of which happened to have taken place in the same year, 1945. The second one was not a product of the United Nations, but it similarly grew out of the end of the Second World War: the Nuremberg and Tokyo trials, in which for the first time in history, individuals were held responsible for violating international law, which until then had been thought to apply only to states. This "Nuremberg Principle," which was promoted by the United States more vigorously than by any of the other Allies, is the flip side of human rights: If individual rights are to be paramount, then individual responsibility must be enforceable.

"Geneva Law," as distinguished from the "Nuremberg branch" of international humanitarian law, was not a radical new development of mid-century but a further codification of customary international norms that had begun to emerge a century earlier. In contrast to "Nuremberg Law," which suffered a forty-some year gap before another international tribunal was established, "Geneva Law" has further evolved, so that it now includes the two additional protocols of 1977 as well as the four Conventions of 1949. Its basic rules of conduct can be summarized as follows:

Persons who are no longer taking an active part in hostilities, such as the wounded and sick, prisoners, and civilians, must be protected and spared as much as possible from the horrors of combat;

Civilians must be treated humanely: torture, cruelty, and other violence to their person, the taking of hostages, and the passing of sentences without a fair trial are all prohibited;

Armed forces must distinguish between combatants and noncombatants and between military targets and civilian objects;

Objects indispensable to the survival of the civilian population, such as foodstuffs, livestock, and water resources, cannot be attacked or destroyed, and starvation as a means of warfare is prohibited;

Hospitals, ambulances, and medical and religious personnel must be respected and protected so that the wounded and sick can be collected and cared for; and

Parties to a conflict must agree to respect and protect relief operations of a humanitarian, impartial, and nondiscriminatory nature.[8]

BATTING CLEANUP: THE UNHCR AND REFUGEE LAW

While human rights law has been criticized as too quixotic, or compared to a high-jump bar set at an unrealistic level, humanitarian law is perhaps too modest, in that it posits the inevitability of war instead of its eradication. Indeed, we do not pass laws instructing murderers on how to murder—"slay police and other criminals, not civilians; use a sharp instrument instead of a blunt one"—yet we tell warriors whom to kill and how to do it. Both the overly utopian human rights and the unpretentious humanitarian law are inherently precarious. They risk failing to constrain the worst excesses of human cruelty. Therefore, a third field of law is needed to regulate the inevitable consequence of that failure: A law of refugees must provide an escape hatch for those who must flee war, other atrocities, and persecution. However, the international refugee law that has actually emerged falls far short of this goal.

The chief reason for creating the UN High Commissioner for Refugees and adopting the Refugee Convention was to mop up the human aftermath of the Second World War by finding permanent homes for those displaced by the war and whose native countries had, in the half decade after the war ended, come under communist control. Hence, the Refugee Convention applied only to a person who,

as a result of events occurring before 1 January 1951 and owing to a well-founded fear of being persecuted for reasons of race, religion, nationality, membership of a particular social group or political opinion, is outside the country of his nationality and is unable, or owing to such fear, unwilling . . . to return.[9]

State parties had the option of applying this definition either to events occurring in Europe before the operative 1951 date or to events occurring elsewhere, but either way, the definition excluded more than it included. (In 1967 the 1951 temporal limit was lifted.) Among the unprotected were those fleeing poverty or environmental disasters (whether natural or humanly caused) and, most significantly, those fleeing war, unless they could prove a well-founded fear of individualized persecution, either in the past or future. Those simply fleeing war's violence were not to be granted the status of "Convention" ("mandate" or de jure) refugees. At best, they would be treated charitably as "humanitarian" (de facto) refugees or the deliberately vague "displaced persons."

Once officially classified as "Convention refugees," such persons would become entitled to certain standards of treatment regarding their legal status and living conditions. Most significantly, they were to be protected from *refoulement*, that is, expulsion to a territory where their life or freedom would be threatened by persecution. However, the bottom line was that asylum was up to the sovereign discretion of states. True, the Universal Declaration of Human Rights did contain the right of every person to "seek and enjoy in other countries asylum from persecution." Yet those carefully chosen words omit the right to "obtain" asylum. That sly phrase was neither repeated in the International Covenant on Civil and Political Rights, where it logically should have reappeared, nor codified in any other binding international treaty. In those regional Conventions where asylum was recognized, it was carefully worded as a sovereign right of the state, not a human right of the individual.[10]

In the Western alliance during the Cold War era, granting asylum to Convention refugees—most of whom were fleeing communist regimes—was encouraged because it constituted an ideological victory. This would change with the end of the Cold War, when refugees would become a nuisance, though it would no longer be possible to ignore the reality that displaced persons had become not just a by-product but the *chief* product of wars of ethnic nationalism. Because of this reality, refugee law has begun to expand to cover a wider array of humanitarian refugees and other displaced persons, including victims of war and those who have never crossed international frontiers ("internally displaced persons," or IDPs). However, the new refugee regime seems to prefer "containment" to actual "protection," as well as temporary arrangements and repatriation instead of what used to be called the "durable solutions" of permanent asylum and third-country resettlement.[11]

AN INCREASINGLY CLOSER INTERSECTION

To sum up this introductory discussion, Figures 7.1 and 7.2 illustrate the relationship between the three fields of international law in the post–World War II era and in the present, respectively. Figure 7.1 reflects the state of the law around 1951, when all three fields existed but none had yet evolved beyond the parameters of their prevailing texts, the Geneva

**Figure 7.1
Circa 1951**

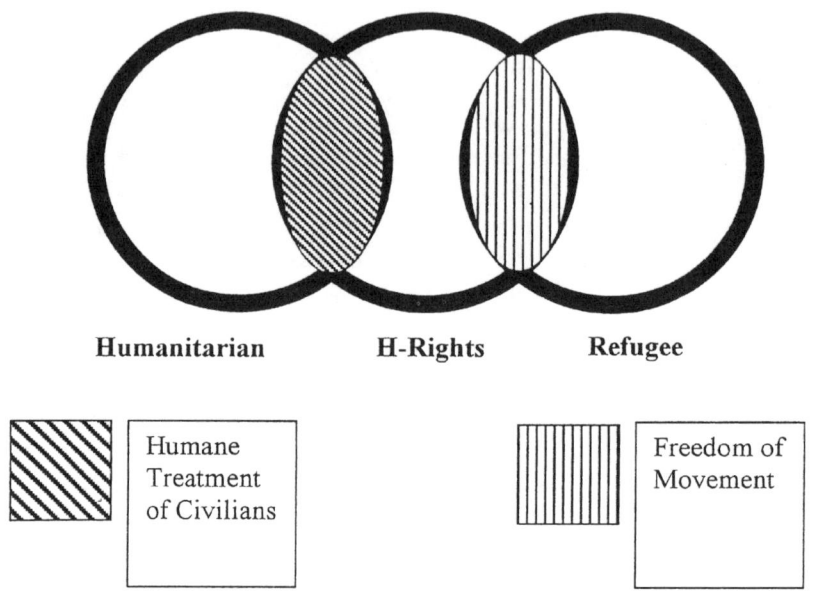

Conventions, the Universal Declaration, and the Refugee Convention. Figure 7.2 demonstrates how at the present time the three fields, through developments among intergovernmental organizations and actual state practice, have expanded and evolved to cover much more overlapping ground.

In Figure 7.1, there is some area of overlap between human rights law and humanitarian law, and some between human rights law and refugee law, but no intersection between refugee and humanitarian law. In addition to the general subject of freedom of movement, denial of food to a peacetime population on the basis of race, religion, nationality, and so on, would constitute an example of the intersection of refugee and human rights law. Denial of food to a civilian population during a wartime siege would constitute an example of inhumane treatment that fell under both humanitarian and human rights law.

In Figure 7.2, all three fields of international law intersect in the prohibition on ethnic cleansing, because forcible deportation of civilians from their homes is a violation of both humanitarian and human rights law and an increasing concern of refugee law. Other kinds of human rights violations can also cause persons to become displaced, while genocide and other crimes against humanity during wartime and postwar occupations are now prohibited by humanitarian law, as well as during peacetime by human rights law.

Figure 7.2
Circa 1999

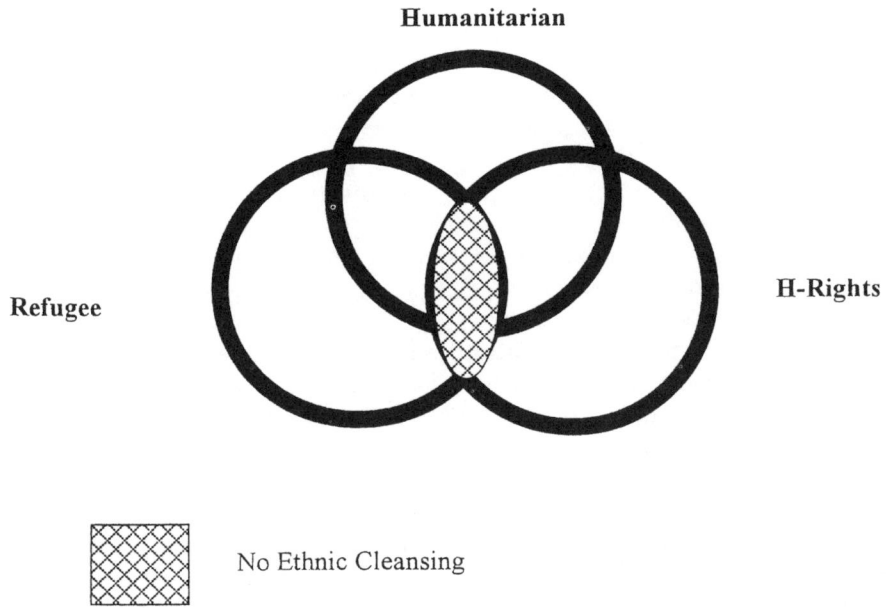

Will a future Figure 3 ever show all three circles merged or collapsed into one, the visual representation of "zero degrees of separation"? That will likely never happen, because each field of law will always, in part, perform a distinct function. But as the trends and conjunctures described in the rest of this chapter will demonstrate, the nexus between the three will continue to merge.

THE INFLUENCE OF POST–COLD WAR TRENDS

Before examining the contours of this evolving intersection, it is useful to consider the reasons for its emergence. I can identify four trends in the post–Cold War era that may account for the juridical development.

The first trend is globalization, which seems to have precipitated a decline in the power and status of the state itself—in the face of increased power, if not status, for nonstate actors, ranging from transnational corporations, intergovernmental and nongovernmental organizations (IGOs and NGOs), to national liberation and terrorist movements. Similarly, ideological empires have been replaced by a multiplicity of smaller nationalisms, for which the universalism of human rights jurisprudence (or, for that matter, Marxism) is anathema. Globalization, of course, is primarily about the free flow across borders of capital, goods, and services, as opposed to the free flow of people (unless they are specialized laborers essential to facilitating international trade and investment). While borders are loosening for trade, they are rigidifying to human migration.

But this unraveling of the sanctity of sovereign borders is not entirely a process of disintegration, because at the same time diplomacy in the post–Cold War era is also undergoing transformation, thereby constituting a second trend. Legitimacy is replacing stability as the touchstone for international diplomacy. "Sovereign equality," that mythic premise of the UN Charter that treated all states as if they were equal (irrespective of relative gross domestic product [GDP] or Security Council vetoes), is being replaced by what might be called conditional or "normative equality," a trend that is putting content back into the neutral vessel of international relations. Some states are, in fact, more equal than other states, because some such as Iraq, Iran, Libya, Burma, and Yugoslavia, to name frequent targets of multilateral economic sanctions, consistently refuse to play by the normative rules. The new content of the vessel is primarily composed of human rights standards. In a variation on the old axiom that democracies do not go to war against each other, relevant actors in the international community have adopted the thesis that systematic violation of human rights norms leads to national instability, which leads to interethnic tension, with refugee flows constituting the final tripwire before armed conflict breaks out.[12] Thus, legitimacy assures stability, not the other way around.

A third trend underlying the convergence comes from changes in geopolitics that have altered the purpose and nature of warfare. To quote Aryeh Neier, a refugee-turned-human rights activist: "Traditional objectives of war—to conquer territory or to subjugate others—were secondary, if present at all" in the wars in the former Yugoslavia and Rwanda. "Instead, in both cases, the central purpose of those behind these crimes was to eliminate entire populations: through a combination of 'ethnic purification' and murder in the former Yugoslavia; through breathtaking slaughter—800,000 killed in three months—in Rwanda" (that is, nearly three times the rate of Jewish dead during the Second War II).[13] In other words, ethnic cleansing not as a methodology of warfare but its very goal: the persecution of noncombatants so as to either turn them into refugees or eliminate them entirely.

While many commentators have observed that interethnic warfare was kept in check by the superpower standoff (or kept artificially dormant in socialist states such as Tito's Yugoslavia), a caveat is in order: It would be wrong to date the origin of ethnic cleansing to the post–Cold War conflicts in Rwanda and the former Yugoslavia, because in fact the concept of total war, involving civilians as well as combatants, had been invented—if not perfected—by Hitler. In 1944 and the early months of 1945, it was more important for the Nazi machine to kill more Jews than to try to win the war. But one difference between 1940-style ethnic cleansing and that of the 1990s is key: The Nazis went to some amount of effort to conceal the true nature of their crimes. Victims were shipped by train hundreds of miles from home, under the guise of "relocation" and other subterfuges. Once they arrived at the concentration camps, they were led to believe they were entering showers in order to be "disinfected." Camp guards were usually not recruited among local residents but brought in from other parts of the Reich.[14]

By contrast, ethnic cleansing in the former Yugoslavia was conducted neighbor upon literal neighbor, without disguise or pretense. Similarly, the slaughter of the Tutsis took place right out in the open, right on the spot, in virtually every village of Rwanda, as well as in the refugee camps pitched in neighboring states. (Because civilian targets have been singled out for persecution, literally by name and address, in the former Yugoslavia as well as in the Rwandan war, refugee law does most probably apply.) Most were hacked to death with machetes, the most rudimentary of weapons. Those who were not killed were slashed in the Achilles tendon to prevent them from fleeing. More significantly, the slaughter oftentimes occurred in the very presence of UN observers, who did nothing because their orders had been to monitor, not intervene.[15] Thus, while the purpose and nature of war have been changing for at least a half century, its horrors no longer need be concealed. International law has been forced to catch up with reality by explicitly dealing with ethnic cleansing in the ad hoc International Criminal Tribunals for Rwanda and the Former Yugoslavia.

Consequently, a fourth post–Cold War trend is not an economic, diplomatic, or military development but a jurisprudential one: the synthetic action of international criminal law, a field that barely existed even seven years ago. After an absence of almost fifty years since the Nuremberg and Tokyo Tribunals closed, international criminal law now operates in the two ad hoc tribunals and the emerging International Criminal Court to hold individuals personally responsible for the most egregious of human rights violations, including genocide and ethnic cleansing. While the defendants at Nuremberg could plausibly argue that the tribunal violated the fundamental principle of *nulla poena sine lege*, no punishment without a law, today that charge is totally without merit. International criminal law now stands for the proposition that justice is a necessary precondition to peace, required to break the cycle of revenge that impunity fuels. Criminal sanctions can potentially obviate the need for later generations to retaliate against the abusers of their parents.

Like globalization, "normative sovereignty," and interethnic conflict, this fourth trend is also a product of the end of the Cold War. Before 1989, East and West would never have agreed to let the Security Council exercise such power so as to create new institutions, however limited in temporal and geographic scope, whose reach stretched within sovereign territories. In upholding the jurisdiction of the International Criminal Tribunal for the Former Yugoslavia in the first case to be prosecuted there, the appeals chamber held that national borders

> should not be considered as a shield against the reach of the law and as a protection for those who trample underfoot the most elementary rights of humanity. ... State sovereignty must give way in cases where the nature of the offenses alleged does not affect the interests of one state alone but shocks the very conscience of mankind.[16]

Even the venerable House of Lords, when forced, however reluctantly, to address the immunity of a former head of state, Augusto Pinochet, for conspiracy to commit torture, recognized that in addition to specifically created international tribunals, "[i]ndividual states have taken jurisdiction to try some international crimes even in cases where such crimes were not committed within the geographical boundaries of such states."[17]

In sum, the economic, geopolitical, and juridical loosening of international borders has produced a substantive international law that likewise reflects a more flexible attitude toward sovereignty. Before examining the specific effect that these post–Cold War influences are having on the three fields of international law, I will first survey a few of the ways in which the three have historically and conceptually diverged. This will help explain the limits to complete unification of the fields—why the three degrees will never be reduced to none.

CONCEPTUAL DISPARITIES

When Grotius wrote his treatise *De Jure Belli Ac Pacis* (1625), not only did he conceive of a clear dichotomy between the two, but the law of war took up many more pages than did the law of peace. A comparable treatise written today would reverse that ratio. Nevertheless, the dichotomy is no longer as stark. While humanitarian law applies during wartime and to postwar military occupations, human rights law applies at all times, during peacetime and during war, as well as in the twilight zone of civil emergencies, when martial law might be declared. This broad coverage for human rights has become especially important as the dividing line between belligerent conflict and civil unrest, or between international and internal armed conflict, has become increasingly hazy in the post–Cold War era.[18] Refugee law, however, applies primarily to peacetime, except in war zones where individualized persecution is being committed—a trend that, too, seems to be increasingly more prevalent.

Over time, humanitarian law has come to encompass an ever-expanding circle of protected persons: first, only prisoners of war; then also wounded and sick soldiers and seamen; then civilians in international armed conflict, followed by civilians in noninternational armed conflict; and recently, specialized categories of persons such as journalists and medical personnel. By contrast, human rights law was launched with the premise of universal coverage, with provisions that began "everyone . . . ," "anyone . . . ," and "every human being has the right. . . ." Over time, narrow spectrum treaties have produced specialized coverage of ostensibly divergent categories of rights (civil and political versus economic, social, and cultural) and particular populations such as women, racial minorities, children, migrant workers, and the like. Ironically, humanitarian law is more consistent than human rights law because it is universal, not regional in application, so there are no variations from one continent to the next.

Always the weak cousin, refugee law has remained relatively stagnant. Other than the lifting of the 1951 temporal limit by the 1967 Protocol Relating to the Status of Refugees, the category of persons formally protected by treaty has not expanded beyond those fearing persecution for reasons of race, religion, nationality, membership in a particular social group, or political opinion. In the absence of any treaty amendments, the amorphous social group category, added to the 1951 Convention at the last moment without much floor debate, has recently (though sporadically) been used by some asylum-granting states as a catch-all covering gender, sexual orientation, and very particularized groups such as "persons fleeing China's one-child policy."[19] As previously noted, expansion of international protection has been de facto, when the UNHCR has deemed it expedient and host states have consented.

A further dichotomy resides in the type of language or drafting style found in the treaties of the three fields: Humanitarian law conventions tend to employ detailed, specific language in a multitude of provisions, because they are meant to be understood easily and implemented immediately by military personnel in the field. By contrast, human rights treaties—often the product of prolonged negotiation and compromise—usually contain general if not ambiguous language that must be further interpreted by international organs (committees for international treaties, courts, and commissions for regional ones) created in accordance with the terms of the particular treaty. Petitions for redress to these human rights organs can take three to five years before a final decision is rendered, though some bodies can issue interpretive guidelines on a less protracted basis. Refugee law is intended to be administered by each state in which refugees seek asylum; it is therefore expected that its rather vague language (more akin to human rights treaties than to humanitarian law conventions) will be subject to multiple if not conflicting interpretations.[20]

Perhaps most conspicuously, the norms of humanitarian law generally appear as duties and prohibitions imposed on combatants and commanders, whereas human rights norms are drafted as outright entitlements belonging to individuals (or in rare cases, collectives such as "peoples"), while refugee norms are described as the obligations of states that have agreed to uphold them.[21] While these technical differences can affect the justiciability of the norms, in conceptual terms the distinctions are only linguistic because legal rights do not exist without a correlative duty on the part of another (whether a person or the state itself) who is obligated to provide the right, and vice versa. This relationship is easiest to conceptualize in the area of civil and political rights, which are primarily of a "negative" character rather than affirmative. For example, freedom of thought and expression correspond to the duty not to prevent individuals from expressing their thought; similarly, the right to bodily integrity corresponds to the prohibition on torture. As seen in the next section, one person's "negative right" is another entity's duty to refrain from interfering with it.

CONVERGING COVERAGE AND QUESTS

The above-identified disjunctures between the three fields of international law are outweighed by their common features. All three emphasize nondiscrimination[22] on the basis of a nucleus of attributes that are of a substantially immutable character, such as race, religion, nationality, and political opinion.[23] All three, moreover, can easily be read as striking a balance between aspirational ideals and gritty realism; between humanitarianism and military necessity; between rights and limitations for national security, public health or public order; and between territorial asylum and the sovereign privilege to exclude the unwanted.

More substantively, humanitarian law, human rights law, and refugee law share a common core of norms that apply "at any time and in any place whatsoever" within their respective contexts.[24] The minimum norms that have applied since 1949 in noninternational armed conflicts overlap substantially with those human rights that cannot be suspended ("nonderogable rights") even in an officially declared state of emergency. Literally, *nothing* justifies the suspension of these most fundamental protections. Common article 3 of the four Geneva Conventions of 1949 was elaborated into the more detailed provisions of 1977's Protocol II, about which the International Committee of the Red Cross has commented:

"Protocol II contains virtually all the irreducible rights of the Covenant on Civil and Political Rights. . . . These rights are based on rules of universal validity to which States can be held, even in the absence of any treaty obligation or any explicit commitment on their part."[25]

Or to quote the Convention against Torture, itself an elaboration on the Covenant:

No State may permit or tolerate torture or other cruel, inhuman or degrading treatment or punishment. Exceptional circumstances such as a state of war or a threat of war, internal political instability or any other public emergency may not be invoked as a justification of torture or other cruel, inhuman or degrading treatment or punishment.[26]

In other words, virtually the same standards of conduct serve as minimum guarantees owed to individuals in the twilight zone of domestic disturbances caused by armed insurrection, natural disaster, civil unrest, or the like. Moreover, as Table 7.1 shows, both sets of minimum norms, under humanitarian and human rights law, roughly approximate the fundamental protections and standards of treatment owed to international refugees, even when states do not intend to grant them permanent asylum. Refugees are always protected by human rights law and may be protected by humanitarian law when they are in the power of a party to the armed conflict.[27]

This increasingly compressed common core is not accidental. In the past decade, international actors and institutions have been intentionally promoting the links between all three fields of international law by means of operations with parallel or integrated functions. For instance, in the Balkans, *both* the United Nations High Commissioner for Human Rights, Mary Robinson, and the office of the prosecutor for the United Nations International Criminal Tribunal for the Former Yugoslavia, Justice Louise Arbour, interviewed Kosovo refugees in order to collect evidence of summary executions, rapes, and other atrocities: acts simultaneously constituting both war crimes and gross violations of human rights. As these crimes were being committed in "real time," Robinson's and Arbour's investigators were seen to be "riding in on the shoulders" of the North Atlantic Treaty Organization (NATO) forces and courting the allies for classified surveillance data collected to assess bomb damage but that promised to provide hard evidence to use in court. Meanwhile, the UNHCR administered emergency relief to the same refugees in Albania and Macedonia.[28]

Similarly, throughout the 1990s, UN peacekeeping missions deployed to El Salvador, Cambodia, Haiti, and elsewhere with explicit mandates to monitor human rights and promote the institutional infrastructure in order to entrench human rights. For instance, the functions of the United

Table 7.1
The Overlapping Core in Humanitarian Law, Human Rights Law, and Refugee Law

Common Article 3 Duties and Prohibitions[1]	Nonderogable Human Rights[2]	Basic Refugee Rights and State Duties[3]
noncombatants treated humanely w/o any adverse distinction as to race, religion, sex, birth, or wealth, etc.		Convention provisions applied w/o discrimination as to race, religion, or country of origin; national treatment regarding certain rights[4]
	freedom of thought, conscience & religion	
no violence to life & person (murder, mutilation, cruel treatment, torture)	right to life, no arbitrary deprivation of life and rights of persons sentenced to death; no torture or cruel, inhuman, or degrading treatment	no expulsion or return ("*refoulement*") to frontiers where life or freedom threatened due to race, etc. [unless security or serious criminal danger]
no taking of hostages	no slavery, slave trade, or servitude	[slavery on basis of race, etc., implicitly covered]
no outrages upon personal dignity, esp. humiliating & degrading treatment	[repeat: no cruel, inhuman, or degrading treatment]	[degrading treatment implicitly constitutes persecution]
no sentences & executions w/o previous judgment by regularly constituted court and all judicial guarantees	no imprisonment for inability to fulfill contract; no ex post facto convictions or penalties; right to recognition as a person before the law	no expulsion for national security or public order w/o decision reached with due process of law

[1] See art. 3(1) of all four Geneva Conventions of 1949, applying to armed conflicts not of an international character. See also art. 4(2) of Protocol II of 1977, expanding Common article 3's list to prohibit, for example, collective punishments, acts of terrorism, rape, enforced prostitution, slavery, and pillage.

[2] See the 1967 International. Cov. on Civil & Pol. Rights art. 4(2), listing art. 6, 7, 8(1), 8(2), 11, 15, 16, and 18, rights that cannot be suspended even during official states of emergency.

[3] See 1951 Refugee Convention art. 3, 32 and 33.

[4] Same treatment as accorded nationals required by art. 4, 14, 16, 20, 22, 23, and 24 for religion, artistic, and industrial rights, access to courts, rationing, elementary education, welfare, labor rights, and social security.

Nations Human Rights Field Operation forces in Rwanda (HRFOR) included:

a. To carry out investigations into violations of human rights and humanitarian law, including possible acts of genocide;
b. To monitor the ongoing human rights situation, and through their presence [to] help redress existing problems and prevent possible human rights violations from occurring;
c. To cooperate with other international agencies in charge of reestablishing confidence and thus facilitate the return of refugees and displaced persons and the rebuilding of civil society;
d. To implement programs of technical cooperation, particularly in the area of the administration of justice.[29]

In such an "integrated mandate," each function is mutually reinforcing and reflexive. "Peacekeeping" is increasingly coming to mean "justice promoting" as an essential step in "peace building." As observers of HRFOR have noted:

Justice and national accounting for the genocide was essential to reconciliation; preventing or addressing current human rights violations was essential to refugee return and confidence building in local communities, as well as to ending the impunity that had prevailed in Rwanda under previous governments. Effective assistance for the administration of justice, building other essential institutions, and developing human rights training and awareness were necessary if the violations were to be prevented or addressed.[30]

In addition to the integrative work of intergovernmental units of the United Nations, international nongovernmental organizations are increasingly engaged in the collection of data and production of reports on compliance of states with international humanitarian and refugee law.[31] Human Rights Watch, Amnesty International, the Lawyers' Committee for Human Rights, and other NGOs have been active in lobbying for the establishment of the ad hoc tribunals for the former Yugoslavia and Rwanda, as well as for the permanent International Criminal Court. They were particularly helpful in articulating standards derived from international human rights treaties such as the International Covenant on Civil and Political Rights[32] for protection of the rights of detained war crime defendants and in establishing acceptable forms of criminal punishment. For instance, while the majority of Nuremberg's Major War Criminals were executed, the death penalty is no longer an available punishment in the ad hoc tribunals and future criminal court.

Other evidence of overlap appears in peace agreements such as the much-breached Dayton Accords, which recognize that "the observance of human rights and the protection of refugees and displaced persons are of vital importance in achieving a lasting peace."[33] However, the Accords contain an internal contradiction that itself illustrates how the three fields of international law must, of necessity, be treated as an integrated whole: the Accords promote the right of displaced persons to return to areas that the Accords themselves legitimize as under the control of the very persons who perpetrated ethnic cleansing against the would-be returnees. Their homecoming has thus been obstructed by police harassment, limits on their freedom of movement, and discriminatory local legislation.[34]

The earlier failure of NATO's IFOR (Implementation Force) and SFOR (Stabilization Force) units to arrest indicted Bosnian Serb leaders Radovan Karadzic and Ratko Mladic undoubtedly warmed the heart of Slobodan Milosevic. As stated by former ad hoc tribunal prosecutor Richard Goldstone: "[The atrocities in] Kosovo might well have been prevented" if Karadzic and Mladic had been arrested five years ago when their indictments were issued. "It would have shown a will to act" by the international community. "[I]t would have chilled the spine of Milosevic."[35]

NEW TRENDS: INTERNALIZATION AND DEMILITARIZATION

The evolutionary process by which international humanitarian law has become applicable to armed and even unarmed conflicts within a state's borders has been a slow one. Despite the foundation laid in 1949 by Common Article 3, and irrespective of what should have been the influence of human rights law, which since 1948 had condemned abuses committed by states against their own nationals, this development suffered from the stagnation of the Cold War, which analogously froze other aspects of public international law. A thaw occurred during the 1970s, due to the Nixon-Brezhnev and Nixon-Zhou detente, which contributed to the atmosphere allowing the adoption of the two Geneva Protocols in 1977. But Protocol II, which applies to noninternational armed conflicts, did not attract most of its ratifications until 1988 and thereafter.[36]

Even with the end of the Cold War, some anomalies remain. For instance, grave breaches of the Geneva Conventions of 1949, a special category of explicitly enumerated war crimes, only cover victims who are in the hands of a party to the armed conflict or occupying power of which they are *not* nationals—in other words, international conflicts. It took a major leap in 1995 to surmount this hurdle. In holding that the International Criminal Tribunal for the Former Yugoslavia's (ICTFY) jurisdiction over war crimes applied to internal as well as international armed conflicts, the Tribunal's appeals chamber identified a trend in international law in which "the distinction between interstate wars and civil wars is losing its value as far as human beings are concerned."[37] This was admittedly a deliberate effort to push the envelope of customary international law, given that the Security Council had explicitly limited the Tribunal's subject matter jurisdiction over grave breaches to their scope within the Geneva Conventions and given that its territorial jurisdiction was explicitly identified as "the Territory of the Former Yugoslavia," which includes five separate and independent states.[38] Even the International Committee of the Red Cross had taken the position that as of the date of the ICTFY's creation in 1993, international humanitarian law limited the applicability of war crimes to situations of international armed conflict.[39]

The International Criminal Tribunal for Rwanda, which in most ways is modeled after the ICTFY, explicitly diverges on this very point: In addition to grave breaches, war crimes, genocide, and crimes against humanity, its subject matter jurisdiction also covers violations of Common Article 3 to the Geneva Conventions of 1949 and Protocol II of 1977, while its territorial jurisdiction covers one state, Rwanda (supplemented by nationality jurisdiction for those crimes that were committed by Rwandan nationals outside the state).[40] Thus, within the course of the eighteen months between the creation of the two ad hoc tribunals in May 1993 and November 1994, the Security Council had itself taken the leap of applying international criminal law to internal armed conflicts. If we add to the trajectory the recent ICTFY indictment of Milosevic and the House of Lords's decision in the Pinochet extradition, the pattern shown in Table 7.2 emerges: over time, and with increasing rapidity since 1993, the concept of crimes against humanity is in the process of being extended not only to internal armed conflict, and not only to soldiers, but also to civilians and heads of police states during conflicts short of outright war.

The ad hoc Tribunal's May 1999 indictment for crimes against humanity of a standing head of state—Milosevic himself—will probably turn out to be epoch making for international law. The United Kingdom's effort at extraditing the former head of state Augusto Pinochet for similar crimes was less epoch making. Nevertheless, both of these cases are notable for at least three reasons, even beyond their application to noninternational settings. First, their application to civilian leaders. (Granted, Pinochet was also a general, but his extraditable actions were taken as president.) Human rights law was always intended to cover acts by civil authorities against nationals. With these two new, prominent cases, international humanitarian law is now swiftly moving in that direction as well. In fact, the ad hoc tribunal for Rwanda has already indicted and/or convicted a businessman, the editor in chief of a journal, the director

Table 7.2
The Evolution of Crimes against Humanity

Phases:	1	2	3	4
Context:	internat'l armed conflict	internal armed conflict with spillover	internal armed conflict	police states
Who Held Responsible:	military and civil leaders	plus paramilitary	plus civilians	former/present heads of state
Watershed Case(s):	Nuremberg 1945–1949	Bosnia 1993 (1995)–present	Rwanda 1994–present	Pinochet, Milosevic 1999

Notes: Crimes against humanity have been selected for this example because of the particularly daunting standard of proof: crimes against humanity, which include murder, extermination, deportation, rape, torture, and persecutions on political, racial, and religious grounds, must be committed systematically against a population—in contrast to war crimes that can be committed by one soldier operating on his own, against a single victim.

Sources: See M. Cherif Bassiouni, *Crimes against Humanity in International Law* (New York: Transnational Publishers, 1992). The Nuremberg trial did not extend crimes against humanity to the Nazis' treatment of their own nationals because the Tribunal's jurisiction over such crimes was limited to those committed in connection with aggressive war. See Telford Taylor, *Final Report to the Secretary of the Army on the Nuernberg [sic] War Crimes Trials under Control Council Law No. 10* (1949), reprinted in Jordan J. Paust et al., *International Criminal Law: Cases and Materials* (Durham, NC: 1996), Carolina Academic Press, 1031–33.

of a tea factory, a university lecturer, and a student—all civilians without formal connection with either the military or the civil government.[41]

Second, their application of crimes against humanity to contexts short of armed conflict. (Genocide, a specific type of crime against humanity defined by the 1948 Genocide Convention, has always been applicable to peacetime as well as wartime. But genocide is especially hard to prove.) The Milosevic indictment covers acts of persecution against Kosovo civilians committed on and after January 1, 1999, in other words, before the NATO bombing campaign began in mid-March. Pinochet's extradition was approved only for his crimes after 1988: an awkwardly reasoned if not artificial temporal limitation imposed by the Lords but one that demonstrates this point because it was long after the end of the Chilean "Dirty War" that followed the coup against Salvador Allende in 1973.[42]

Finally, their application to a head of state and a former head of state demonstrates once and for all that sovereignty provides no insulation for these most egregious abuses of power. The House of Lords held that Pinochet could claim no immunity, direct or derivative, while Milosevic cannot even raise an official immunity claim because the international community explicitly excluded it when creating the ICTFY. "The official position of any accused person, whether as *head of State* or Government or as a responsible Government official, shall not relieve such person of criminal responsibility nor mitigate punishment."[43] The emphasized language demonstrates that the Tribunal's statute was indeed drafted back in 1993 with this specific *head of state*'s indictment in mind.

TOWARD UNIFICATION: FILLING THE GAPS

Before concluding, I would like to touch on a few lacunae that need to be filled in order to facilitate the further merger of humanitarian, human rights, and refugee law. Four points in particular seem most pressing, not merely for aesthetic reasons, to collapse the three circles into one, but for the sake of juristic consistency, pragmatic coherency, and true implementation of the principle that human rights are *erga omnes*, the obligation of all to all. These "missing links" involve the roles of intergovernmental institutions, nongovernmental institutions, legal education, and internally displaced persons.

First, the proliferation of UN and regional peacekeeping operations in the last decade demands that peacekeepers and other IGO field officials be held accountable to the same standards that are imposed on the governments that they are monitoring. Numerous reports have emerged of human rights and humanitarian law violations (not to mention corrupt practices) by agents of international organizations, particularly civilian police and peacekeepers. This has been a particular problem when peacekeeping has been "farmed out" to underprepared regional organizations such as the Economic Community of West African States (ECOWAS), whose agents were cited for looting property in Monrovia, as well as facilitating the delivery of weapons and ammunition to the very Liberian factions they were supposed to be policing. But the problem is not limited to such "proxy peacekeepers." In 1993, several Somalis were killed at the hands (in one case, literally) of peacekeeping troops from Canada, "the only country in the world to have turned peacekeeping into a national vocation," to quote a commissioner who investigated the embarrassing debacle and its coverup.[44]

In addition to better training and oversight for troops and personnel sent on such missions, steps must be taken to clarify that international human rights, refugee, and humanitarian law norms apply to these individuals when they are functioning as agents not of states but of intergovernmental organizations. One method would be for the UN General Assembly or Security Council to request such a clarification as an advisory opinion by the International Court of Justice. Another way would be for the United Nations itself, along with NATO, ECOWAS, and other bodies, to formally ratify humanitarian, human rights, refugee, and other relevant treaties, thereby imposing obligations of compliance on their individual agents.[45]

A second problem that has arisen in the context of recent armed conflicts and humanitarian crises is the increasing attacks on international organizational personnel and humanitarian relief workers from both IGOs and NGOs. For instance, UN military observers were taken hostage by Bosnian Serb forces and used as human shields against NATO bombing in May 1995. At least twenty-eight Red Cross workers were murdered in the Great Lakes region of Africa in 1996–1997, in many cases while transporting the wounded in official vehicles with clearly marked emblems.[46] This increase in attacks on aid workers and even ambulances and hospitals is yet another symptom of the post–Cold War change in the nature of war. The protection of the wounded, sick, and civilians is no longer considered a legitimate function of neutral and impartial parties, according to this kind of warfare. When the very purpose of war is to destroy enemy populations through ethnic cleansing and sieges, relief workers are considered belligerents. Moreover, when humanitarian crises are precipitated by the very collapse of governmental infrastructures, such as in Somalia, who can be held accountable for failing to guarantee the safety of relief workers? While interfering with the delivery of food and medical supplies to the civilian population is already prohibited by Geneva Protocol I,[47] the international community must do more to enforce this norm and to declare that its violation is intolerable.

A third gap involves the education of the professionals who are charged with implementing and enforcing international law: lawyers who will work for governments, particularly military departments, as well as NGOs and even large private law firms, which are increasingly handling international human rights and refugee cases on a pro bono basis. While I cannot speak from personal knowledge about legal education outside the United States or in military academies, as a U.S. professor of international law I have found it remarkable that most casebooks and document supplements for human rights courses do not contain the Refugee or Genocide Conventions and most such collections for public international law courses do not contain even one of the four 1949 Geneva Conventions.[48]

But perhaps this is quibbling when in fact, outside of Puerto Rico and Quebec, no U.S. or Canadian law school requires students to take even a single international law course; in Australia and the United Kingdom, they seldom do. By contrast, among law schools in twenty-eight civil law countries, 65 percent require at least one introductory course in public international law.[49] In the educational publishing business, content follows demand and so before we can complain about publishing omissions, law faculties must first demonstrate an interest in teaching courses that include all three degrees of separation.

Finally, until a treaty is adopted for the protection of internally displaced persons, until the international definition of refugee is expanded to cover, at a minimum, those displaced by war, and until existing treaties are amended to cover persecution on the basis of gender and other common targets of human bias,[50] refugee law will remain not only the weak leg of the tripod but the chief barrier to full merger of the three fields. Human rights law has long established the principle that international law protects individuals from abuses by their own governments. Humanitarian law, through Common Article 3 and Protocol II, applies basic protections to noncombatants in noninternational armed conflicts. Therefore, it is only logical that refugee law be extended to protect IDPs, whom the UNHCR identifies as those who "have fled from areas affected by the conflict and violence, have been or would be exposed to human rights abuses, including persons belonging to groups compelled to leave their homes by campaigns of ethnic and religious persecution," but who, often for purely fortuitous reasons, have not crossed an international frontier.[51] Logic—and recent history, as witnessed in Bosnia, Kosovo, and Rwanda—dictate that IDPs are even more at risk for genocide, ethnic cleansing, and other atrocities than those fortunate enough to skip across an arbitrary line known as a border.

Once these gaps are filled, it will be easier to address even broader problems such as the norms that apply to internationally created safe havens and "no fly zones"; the law applicable during widespread domestic violence that does not quite rise to the level of armed conflict; and the trigger mechanisms and rules of engagement pertaining to instances of humanitarian intervention, such as the recent NATO action regarding Kosovo.[52]

CONCLUSION

The twentieth century witnessed the development of radically new norms and subjects of international law—as well as the unleashing of vicious hatreds and violence that presaged, if not made imperative, those very norms. All three fields of international law surveyed in this chapter will continue to influence each other in the new century. As it has already done, human rights law will continue to prod the other two to improve the treatment of a country's own nationals, whether they are the victims of an internal armed conflict or displaced persons unable to escape their persecutor's own borders.

Admittedly, major lapses in the collective, political will to implement, coordinate, and enforce these bodies of law have created a culture of impunity in which, with but small exception, most war criminals and human rights violators go unpunished and states are allowed to commit *refoulement* against refugees. However, this trend may be on the verge of reversing itself. As Kofi Annan has said of the establishment of a permanent International Criminal Court:

[T]he Rome Statute was a gift of hope to future generations and a giant step forward in the march towards universal human rights and the rule of law.... It puts the world on notice that crimes against humanity, which have disfigured and disgraced this century, will not go unpunished in the next. I believe the establishment of such a Court will be a fitting way to inaugurate the new millennium.[53]

At the end of the most atrocity-ridden century, a full five decades after the international community rose to codify its abhorrence of this conduct, it is heartening to realize that at least some of those responsible for its horrors will be punished—or, at least, indicted.

NOTES

1. Convention on the Prevention and Punishment of the Crime of Genocide, G.A. Res. 2670 (1948), 78 U.N.T.S. 277, entered into force 1951; Universal Declaration of Human Rights, G.A. Res. 217 (III 1948), U.N. Doc. A/811; Geneva Convention (IV) Relative to the Protection of Civilian Persons in Time of War (1949), 75 U.N.T.S. 287, entered into force 1950; Statute of the Office of the United Nations High Commissioner for Refugees, G.A. Res. 428 (V 1950); Convention Relating to the Status of Refugees (1951), 189 U.N.T.S. 150, entered into force 1954; and European Convention for the Protection of Human Rights and Fundamental Freedoms (1950), 213 U.N.T.S. 221, entered into force 1953. The International Covenants on Civil and Political Rights, 999 U.N.T.S. 171 (ICCPR), and on Economic, Social and Cultural Rights, 993 U.N.T.S. 3, were not adopted by the UN General Assembly until 1967 and did not enter into force until 1976.

2. On the separate origins of each of these three fields, see, example, Walter Laquer and Barry Rubin, eds., *The Human Rights Reader* (New York: New American Library, 1989); Frits Kalshoven, *Constraints on the Waging of War* (Geneva: International Committee of the Red Cross, 1991); A.P.V. Rogers, *Law on the Battlefield* (Manchester: Manchester University Press, 1996); and Guy S. Goodwin-Gill, *The Refugee in International Law* (2nd ed. Oxford: Clarendon Press, 1996). Before 1945, "human rights" were usually referred to as "the rights of man."

3. *Six Degrees of Separation*, a 1990 play by John Guare, made into a 1993 movie starring Will Smith, Donald Sutherland and Stockard Channing.

4. United Nations Charter (1945), 3 Bevans 1153, entered into force 1945. On the drafting of the Charter and its relationship to the Universal Declaration, see Henry J. Steiner and Philip Alston, *International Human Rights in Context: Law, Politics, Morals* (Oxford: Clarendon Press, 1996), 118–22. The Charter's "Supremacy Clause" is article 103.

5. Javier Perez de Cuellar, *Report of the Secretary-General on the Work of the Organization*, U.N. Doc. A/46/1, September 1991.

6. Louis Henkin, *The Age of Rights* (New York: Columbia University Press, 1990), 3. See also Thomas Buergenthal, "The Human Rights Revolution," *St. Mary's Law Journal*, 23 (1991), 3. In the present chapter, unless regional systems of human rights are explicitly referred to, "human rights law" will refer to the body of international treaties and other agreements adopted under UN auspices.

7. See article 4(2) of the ICCPR, ibid. Other treaties may declare additional rights as nonderogable. For instance, article 27(2) of the American Convention on Human Rights, 9 I.L.M. 101 (1970), also treats rights of the family and the child, the right to a name and a nationality, and the right to participate in government as nonderogable. On *erga omnes* obligations, see *Barcelona Traction, Light and Power Company, Ltd. (Belg. v. Spain)*, 1970 ICJ Rep. 3; and Theodor Meron, *Human Rights and Humanitarian Norms as Customary Law* (Oxford: Clarendon Press, 1989), 188–201.

8. See Jean-Phillipe Lavoyer, "Refugees and Internationally Displaced Persons: International Humanitarian Law and the Role of the ICRC," *International Review of the Red Cross*, no. 305 (March 1, 1995), 162–80. A third branch of International Humanitarian Law, sometimes called "Hague Law," primarily concerns the kinds of weaponry permitted during armed conflicts. "Arms control" is a more contemporary designation for this third branch.

9. Article 1(A)(2). 189 U.N.T.S. 150 (1951). The definition of refugee in some regional agreements, such as the Organization of African Unity's 1969 Convention on Refugee Problems in Africa, is broader.

10. Universal Declaration, ibid., article 14. "Non-*refoulement*" is required by article 33(1) of the 1951 Refugee Convention. A UN conference, meeting in Geneva in 1977, considered a Convention on Territorial Asylum, but it was not adopted, despite the fact that its provision on Grant of Asylum, article 1, merely would have required that each contracting state, "acting in the exercise of its sovereignty, *shall endeavor in a humanitarian spirit to grant asylum* in its territory to any person eligible for the benefits of this Convention" (emphasis added). See Report of the United Nations Conference on Territorial Asylum, UN Doc. A/CONF.78/12 (21 April 1977); and Goodwin-Gill, *The Refugee in International Law*. Compare the Caracas Convention on Territorial Asylum and the Caracas Convention on Diplomatic Asylum, both adopted in 1954 by the Organization of American States (Treaty Series 34). For instance, the former provides in article 1: "Every State has the right, in the exercise of its sovereignty, to admit into its territory such persons as it deems advisable."

11. See James Hathaway, "A Reconsideration of the Underlying Premise of Refugee Law," *Harvard International Law Journal*, 31 (1990), 129; Julie Mertus, "The State and the Post–Cold War Refugee Regime: New Models, New Questions," *Michigan Journal of International Law*, 20 (1998), 59; and Bill Frelick, "Refugee Rights: The New Frontier of Human Rights Protection," *Buffalo Human Rights Law Review*, 4 (1998), 261. Frelick goes so far as to accuse the UNHCR and European governments of preventing Bosnian Muslims from seeking asylum by trapping them in "safe havens" in Bosnia. Ibid., 268–71.

12. As stated by then-UN Secretary General Boutros Boutros-Ghali:

The time of absolute and exclusive sovereignty has passed; its theory has never been matched by reality. It is the task of leaders of states today to understand this and find a balance between the needs of good international governance and the requirements of an ever more interdependent world.

An Agenda for Peace: Preventive Diplomacy, Peacemaking and Peace-Keeping, U.N. Doc. A/47/277, 1993, para. 17. See also Thomas M. Franck, *The Power of Legitimacy among Nations* (New York: Oxford University Press, 1990).

13. Aryeh Neier, *War Crimes: Brutality, Genocide, Terror and the Struggle for Justice* (New York: Times Books, 1998), xii. See also Philip Gourevitch, *We Wish to Inform You That Tomorrow We Will Be Killed with Our Families: Stories from Rwanda* (New York: Farrar, Straus & Giroux, 1998), 3.

14. See Daniel Goldhagen, *Hitler's Willing Executioners: Ordinary Germans and the Holocaust* (New York: Knopf, 1996).

15. The slaughter was in fact preceded by a warning to top UN officials that Hutu extremists were planning the extermination of Tutsis, creating weapons arsenals, and planning to kill Belgian troops so as to provoke them into withdrawing. All but a few thousand peacekeepers actually left Rwanda, during the very period that the worst slaughter was taking place. Neier, *War Crimes*, 216–25.

16. *Prosecutor v. Tadic*, Case IT-94-I-AR72 (October 2, 1995), 31–32. See Michael P. Scharf, *Balkan Justice: The Story behind the First International War Crimes Trial since Nuremberg* (Durham, NC: Carolina Academic Press, 1997), 103–7. A related trend might be the inevitable jurisprudential confluence that results from a synergy of all three streams of law operating in tandem in international institutions such as the UN Human Rights Commission, the UNHCR, the European and Inter-American Courts of Human Rights, and NGOs such as the International Committee of the Red Cross, as well as the ad hoc criminal tribunals. The Human Rights Commission, for instance, has been frequently invoking humanitarian law in support of its recommendations. See, for instance, its *Report on the Situation of Human Rights in Kuwait under Iraqi Occupation*, prepared by Mr. Walter Kalin, U.N. Doc. E/CN.4/1992/26.

17. *Regina v. Bartle and the Commissioner of Police for the Metropolis and Others, Ex Parte Pinochet* (U.K. House of Lords, March 24, 1999) (Lord Browne Wilkinson), 2. The Pinochet decision marks "the first time [that] a local domestic court has refused to afford immunity to a head of state or former head of state on the grounds that there can be no immunity against prosecution for certain international crimes." Ibid., 13.

18. In fact, only about 18 percent of all wars since 1945 have been strictly *inter*state. K.J. Holsti, *The State, War and the State of War* (New York: Cambridge University Press, 1996), 25. On the treatment of human rights in states of emergency, see Joan J. Fitzpatrick, *Human Rights in Crisis: The International System for Protecting Human Rights during States of Emergency* (Philadelphia: University of Pennsylvania Press, 1994).

19. See Karen Musalo, Jennifer Moore, and Richard Boswell, *Refugee Law and Policy* (Durham, NC: Carolina Academic Press, 1997), 549–728. The 1967 Protocol is found at 606 U.N.T.S. 267.

20. See Hurst Hannum, *Guide to International Human Rights Practice*, 2nd ed. (Philadelphia: University of Pennsylvania Press, 1992).

21. For example: "It is prohibited to make improper use of the distinctive emblem of the red cross, red crescent or red lion and sun or of other emblems, signs or signals." Protocol I Additional to the Geneva Conventions of 1949 (1977), art. 38(1). "Everyone shall have the right to freedom of association with others, including the right to form and join trade unions for the protection of his interests." International Covenant on Civil and Political Rights (1967), art. 22(1). (Note that most rights in this treaty are limited in the interests of public order, public health, etc.) "The Contracting States shall accord to refugees lawfully staying in their territory the same treatment with respect to public relief and assistance as is accorded to their nationals." Refugee Convention (1951), art. 23. But note that the International Covenant on Economic, Social and Cultural Rights is drafted in the form of obligations—albeit attenuated ones—of states. For instance: "The States Parties to the present Covenant recognize the right to work . . . and will take appropriate steps to safeguard this right" (art. 6(1)).

22. See, for instance, articles 13 and 27 of Geneva Convention IV of 1949; article 3 of the ICCPR (as well as specific human rights treaties on nondiscrimination, such as the International Convention on the Elimination of All Forms of Racial Discrimination, 66 U.N.T.S. 195 [1965], entered into force January 1969, and the Convention on the Elimination of All Forms of Discrimination against Women, 19 I.L.M. 33 [1980], entered into force September 1981); and article 3 of the Refugee Convention.

23. Conspicuously absent from the text's list of commonly protected attributes is sex or gender, because of its omission from the Refugee Convention. Yet all three fields of law have recently undergone a "gender awakening" through the discovery that women are indeed the targeted victims of war and human rights atrocities. The crimes of sexual assault and rape have been among the most frequent charges against defendants in the ad hoc tribunals for the former Yugoslavia and Rwanda. The human rights movement has recently focused on concerns such as domestic violence and female genital mutilation (FGM), which involve abusive acts by private, nonstate actors. Finally, regarding refugees, the Convention category of "membership in a social group" is now being used in Canada, France, the United Kingdom, and the United States to grant asylum to victims of gender persecution (as well as homophobic persecution) such as FGM. These developments, epoch making in themselves, are outside the scope of this chapter.

24. The quoted language is from Common Article 3 of the four Geneva Conventions of 1949.

25. Y. Sandoz, C. Swinarski, and B. Zimmerman, eds., *Commentary on the Additional Protocols of 8 June 1977 to the Geneva Conventions of 12 August 1949* (Geneva: International Committee of the Red Cross, 1987), 1340. See also *Human Rights and Humanitarian Norms as Customary Law*, 73.

26. Convention against Torture and Other Cruel, Inhuman or Degrading Treatment or Punishment, Annex G.A. Res. 46 (XXXIX 1984), 23 I.L.M. 1027), entered into force June 1987, article 3. On the nonderogation principle in the ICCPR, see Thomas Buergenthal, "To Respect and to Ensure: State Obligations and Permissible Derogations," in Louis Henkin, ed., *The International Bill of Rights: The Covenant on Civil and Political Rights* (New York: Columbia University Press, 1981).

27. See article 73 of Protocol I. The fundamental refugee norm of non-

refoulement also appears in article 45(4) of Geneva Convention IV. However, when the refugees' host country is not a party to the armed conflict, they are not under the protection of humanitarian law. See Lavoyer, "Refugees."

28. See "Robinson Report on Kosovo Crimes," *BBC News*, May 31, 1999, pub. at 21:47 GMT; Charles Trueheart, "War Crimes Panel Gathers Evidence against Milosevic," *Washington Post*, May 11, 1999, A13; "Cook Boost to War Crimes Probe: NATO Aerial Photographs of Suspected Mass Graves," *BBC World Service*, April 20, 1999; William Branigin, "U.S. Evidence Enhances Case against Milosevic," *Washington Post*, May 28, 1999.

29. See Alice Henkin, ed., *Honoring Human Rights: From Peace to Justice, Recommendations to the International Community* (Washington, DC: Aspen Institute, 1998), 101.

30. Ibid., 101–2.

31. For instance, Human Rights Watch has published reports on violations of humanitarian law in, for example, Turkey (1995), the Philippines (1990), and along the Israel-Lebanon border (1996), as well as numerous reports on the former Yugoslavia. This organization also maintains a separate division devoted to arms control. Or note the issues listed on the Web page of Advocacy Net (http://www.advocacynet.org): the International Criminal Court; Bosnian Refugees after Dayton; Human Rights Defenders; Land Mines; Violence against Women in Southeast Asia; Civil Society in Kosovo.

32. See ICCPR articles 6 through 11, and 14 and 15.

33. Article VII, General Framework Agreement for Peace in Bosnia and Herzegovina. Annex 6 of the Accords, on Human Rights, explicitly incorporates by name fifteen separate human rights treaties that are to be monitored by a Commission on Human Rights consisting of an Ombudsman and Human Rights Chamber and gives open-ended permission to local and international human rights NGOs to conduct observer missions. See also Annex 7 on Refugees and Displaced Persons.

34. Henkin, *Honoring Human Rights*, 72, 79. As of 1998 only about 250,000 of the Bosnian war's over 2 million displaced had been able to return to their former homes, if those happen to be in areas where they constitute the ethnic majority. Ibid., 79.

35. Quoted by Trueheart, "War Crimes Panel." On May 27, 1999, the International Criminal Tribunal for the Former Yugoslavia announced the indictment of and issuance of an arrest warrant against five persons, including Slobodan Milosevic, president of the Federal Republic of Yugoslavia, for murder, persecution on political, racial, or religious grounds, and deportation, all crimes against humanity. Press Release JL/PIU/403-E. On June 28, 2001, the government of Serbia turned Milosevic over to the tribunal for trial on these charges. See Ruth Wedgewood, "Former Yugoslav President Slobodan Milosevic to Be Tried in The Hague," *ASIL Insights* (July 2001).

36. Only sixty-four countries ratified Protocol II between 1977 and 1987; eighty more countries did so between 1988 and the present. Cuba, Haiti, Iran, Iraq, Israel, Myanmar, North Korea, Syria, Turkey, and the United States are among those countries that still have not become parties to it. Calculations and omissions based on March 1999 figures in the International Committee of the Red Cross (ICRC) online database at http://www.icrc.org. It should be noted that the

ICCPR and its companion Covenant on Economic, Social and Cultural Rights, did not enter into force until 1976—probably also a consequence of Cold War stagnation.

37. Geoffrey R. Watson, "The Humanitarian Law of the Yugoslavia War Crimes Tribunal: Jurisdiction in the Prosecutor v. Tadic" (unpublished manuscript, 1996), 54, quoted in Scharf, *Balkan Justice*, 107, discussing Decision on the Defence Motion for Interlocutory Appeal on Jurisdiction, 2 October 1995, IT Doc. IT-94-1-AR72, 68. One judge on the five-person panel dissented from this conclusion.

38. Article 2, Statute of the International Tribunal, Annex to UN Security Council Resolution S/RES 827 (May 25, 1993). See Part IV of the Official Summary of the Tadic verdict, reprinted in Scharf, *Balkan Justice*, 282–85. By contrast, the Statute's article 3 on war crimes makes no reference to treaty law, suggesting that it codifies customary international law, an evolving standard. Ibid, 106, 120.

Slovenia and Croatia had declared their independence from Yugoslavia in June 1991 and were recognized as such by the European Community in December of that year. Macedonia first sought international recognition of its sovereignty in September 1991. Bosnia-Hercegovina declared its independence in March 1992, while Serbia and Montenegro announced their formation of the new Federal Republic of Yugoslavia the next month. The United Nations admitted Slovenia, Croatia, and Bosnia-Hercegovina as new members in May 1992, while in April 1993, the month before the creation of the ICTFY, the United Nations determined that Serbia-Montenegro was not entitled to succeed to the membership of the Federal People's Republic of Yugoslavia and had to reapply as a new state. Scharf, *Balkan Justice*, 230–35.

39. Scharf, *Balkan Justice*, 106, describing Preliminary Remarks of the International Committee of the Red Cross, 22 February 1993, reproduced in Virginia Morris and Michael Scharf, *An Insider's Guide to the International Criminal Tribunal for the Former Yugoslavia*, vol. 2 (Irvington-on-Hudson, NY: Transnational Publishers, 1995), 391.

40. Article 4, Statute of the ICTR, established by Resolution 955 of the UN Security Council (November 8, 1994). The two ad hoc tribunals share their appeals chamber and chief prosecutor.

41. See the case summaries for the Rwandan tribunal at http://www.un.org/ictr or http://www.ictr.org.

42. The United Kingdom ratified and implemented the Torture Convention in 1988, even though torture has been held by other courts to have been a violation of customary international law before 1980. See the prominently cited *Filartiga v. Pena Irala*, 630 F.2d 876 (2nd Cir. 1980) (torture committed in Paraguay in 1976 within the subject matter jurisdiction of United States District Courts).

43. Article 7(2) of the ICTFY Statute. Though now a former head of state, Milosevic was in office when he was first indicted.

44. Peter Desbarats, *Somalia Coverup: A Commissioner's Journal* (Toronto: McClelland & Stewart, 1997), 3. See also *Honoring Human Rights: From Peace to Justice*, 133–61; and Rubin Friedman, "Racism in the Canadian Armed Forces?" *Tribune des droits humains*, 4.1 (January 1997), 24.

45. The International Court of Justice (ICJ) ruled early on that the United Nations (and by extension, other IGOs) has the capacity to bring an international

claim for reparations when one of its agents has suffered injury. *Case Concerning Reparations for Injuries Suffered in the Service of the United Nations*, 1949 I.C.J. 174. If the United Nations possesses international rights, by implication it also possesses international duties. But it would be helpful for the ICJ to clarify this as a principle of customary international law. Most of the relevant treaties are only open for ratification by states, not IGOs, so a new treaty or treaties should be drafted to bind the United Nations and other organizations to the same norms embodied in the existing humanitarian, human rights, and refugee treaties. See Julianne Peck, "The UN and the Laws of War: How Can the World's Peacekeepers Be Held Accountable?" *Syracuse Journal of International Law and Commerce*, 21 (1995), 283. In August 1999 U.S. Secretary General Kofi Annan promulgated a bulletin on "Observance" by United Nations Forces of International Humanitarian Law," ST/SGB/1999/13. A "bulletin's" status as a legal authority is less solid than other methods suggested.

46. Scharf, *Balkan Justice*, 38, 152–53; Neier, *War Crimes*, 155–71; International Federation of Red Cross and Red Crescent Societies, News Release, "Red Cross Workers Killed in Rwanda," September 15, 1997; Integrated Regional Information Network for the Great Lakes, Emergency Update No. 20, September 17, 1997.

47. See articles 54, 70, and 85(2) of Protocol I.

48. While this is not the place for a comprehensive review of the literature, I will note for commendation the one collection that does contain the leading treaties in all three fields, humanitarian law, human rights law, and refugee law: The *Basic Document Supplement to International Law: Cases and Materials*, edited by Louis Henkin, Richard Crawford Push, Oscar Schachter, and Hans Smit (St. Paul: West Publishing, 1993). Yet Henkin et al. is but one of about a half dozen public international law texts published for use in U.S. law schools.

49. John King Gamble, *Teaching International Law in the 1990's* (Washington, DC: American Society of International Law, 1992), 22, 77.

50. Not to mention persecution on the basis of disability and sexual orientation, both of which were practiced by the Nazis, though not given much scholarly or popular attention until long after the 1951 Refugee Convention was drafted to cover the Nazis' "better known" victims, those of race, religion, nationality, and political opinion. See Richard Plant, *The Pink Triangle: The Nazi War against Homosexuals* (New York: Henry Holt, 1988); G. Ally, Peter Chroust, and Christian Pross, *Cleansing the Fatherland: Nazi Medicine and Racial Hygiene* (Baltimore: Johns Hopkins University Press, 1994).

51. *UNHCR Background Note: Informal Meeting of Government Experts* (UNHCR, Geneva, March 23, 1994), 2. See also *Comprehensive Study Prepared by Francis M. Deng, Representative of the Secretary-General on the Human Rights Issues Related to Internally Displaced Persons*, U.N. Doc. E/CN.4/1993/35 (1993). Ironically, Protocol II offers more protection to IDPs than does refugee law. See Lavoyer, "Refugees."

52. A "no fly zone" in northern Iraq was established by the UN Security Council pursuant to Resolution 688 (April 5, 1991) to protect Iraqi Kurds. Six cities were designated as "safe areas" in Bosnia: Sarajevo, Bihac, Tuzla, Gorazde, Zepa, and Srebrenica. The latter two were overrun by Serbs, while in all, the resident and refugee populations were like ducks in a barrel to the snipers and bombarders. Similarly, the Bosnian "no fly zone" was violated over 465 times with

impunity because it was not enforced for the first sixteen months of its existence. Scharf, *Balkan Justice*, 33, 35–36.

The International Committee of the Red Cross defines internal disturbances as incidents

marked by serious disruption of domestic order resulting from acts of violence which do not, however, have the characteristics of armed conflict. They encompass, for example, riots by which individuals or groups of individuals openly express their opposition, their discontent of their demands, or even isolated and sporadic acts of violence. They may take the form of fighting between different factions or against the power in place.

Cornelio Sommaruga, "Humanitarian Law and Human Rights in the Legal Arsenal of the ICRC" (speech delivered on March 16, 1995, at the Graduate Institute of International Studies, Geneva).

On humanitarian intervention, see Peter Malanczuk, *Humanitarian Intervention and the Legitimacy of the Use of Force* (Boston: M. Nijhoff International, 1994); and Sean D. Murphy, *Humanitarian Intervention: The United Nations in an Evolving World* (Philadelphia: University of Pennsylvania Press, 1996).

53. United Nations, Press Release SG/SN/6895 L/2908, February 16, 1999.

CHAPTER 8

A View from Above: Watersheds in the Evolution of War and Military Institutions during the Twentieth Century

John A. Lynn

As we face the new millennium, time takes the head seat at the intellectual table, and civilization discusses its future and its past. As father and citizen, I am much concerned with things to come, but as a historian I concentrate on what has already been. Of course, time not only changes history but the life of the historian as well. Because I am now beginning my seventh decade of life, well-meaning people expect different things of me than when I was a younger scholar still trying to prove myself. They ask me to muse broadly instead of speaking only on my particular specialty, *ancien régime* and Revolutionary France. A noted French scholar—I think it was Leroy Ladurie—divided historians into trufflegrubbers and parachutists; truffle-grubbers stay close to the ground— and the dust of the archives—sensing the most minute detail but only within a restricted range, while parachutists view the work from a great height where one can see much further; however, from their vantage, nothing but the major features of the terrain stand out. To be sure, I have dug up my share of truffles, but more and more I find myself being handed a parachute and invited to jump. Such an invitation led me to write this chapter.[1]

I intend to survey two critical watersheds in the nature of war and military institutions in the twentieth century. First, the contours viewed from this altitude reveal a transition from the Clausewitzian War of Annihilation to a more complex form of conflict that I will call "War of

Legitimacy." Second, the forces mustered to contend in the great struggles, 1914–1945, followed a mass-reserve form inherited from the nineteenth century, but these have been reshaped into a smaller, more professional, and more deadly pattern, in what I call the "volunteer-technical" style.

A WORD ABOUT TECHNOLOGY

Before sharing with you my survey, let me comment concerning an issue that I will *not* stress, although nearly everyone else does: technology. When someone rises to discuss watersheds in military history in the twentieth century, it is expected that they talk about weaponry. That is really not the task that I have set for myself here, but let me briefly say something about it. The three technologies that most transformed warfare in the twentieth century have been the internal combustion engine, the atomic bomb, and electronics. The four-cycle gasoline engine was a nineteenth-century advance; the first practical one came out in 1876 and soon found its way into early automobiles. From this technology derived the truck, which transformed mobility and logistics, the airplane with its variety of purposes, and the tank so central to combat. Certainly rocket and jet technologies surpass the internal combustion engine for aerospace applications, but they still do not surpass its impact, and it could be argued that they are both simply different kinds of internal combustion engines. The atomic bomb and its thermonuclear child have unleashed the possibility of mass destruction on the world and by doing so redefined the very nature, or should I say "natures," of war. I will have more to say about this transformation soon. Electronics, which grew modestly from telephone and radio to the solid-state components that made modern personal computers (PCs) possible, has revolutionized communications, blest us with computers, and armed us with precision-guided munitions. No one can deny the importance of these technologies.

Yet my views toward the role of technology in shaping warfare are self-consciously counterrevolutionary in this age of the Military Technical Revolution, or Revolution in Military Affairs, or whatever the current defense lexicon calls it. For one thing, I do not see technology as dictating military practices and warfare but as offering menus, and the most interesting questions have to do with the choices that are made, choices that flow from conception and doctrine rather than from the hardware itself. My favorite example of this fact is the contrast between the way the Germans and the French opted for different applications of the tank during the interwar period. For another thing, I regard technology as much more stable than generally believed. This conclusion is reinforced by my belief that the most revolutionary war of our century came very early, the First World War. The fact that the most radical changes came *then* implies a relative stability *later*. On land, the First World War saw the use of so much that is still with us today: small arms technology is still very much what it was; indirect-fire artillery comes in at this time, although fire control has improved markedly; modern armor is certainly greatly improved, but it is surprising how fast things were moving by the end of the First World War, and had the war gone on into 1919 we might very well have seen armored divisions. With one important exception, the aircraft carrier, all the major surface combat ship-types were already in place by 1900, while the U.S. Navy commissioned the first modern submarine, the *Holland*, that year. The *Dreadnought*, representing the culmination of nineteenth-century naval technology, came down the ways in 1906. Of course the airplane, powered by that internal combustion engine, transformed naval warfare in our century, but it is also interesting to note that the first aircraft carrier hit the waves in 1916, so it is another First World War innovation. It can be argued that all the major functions of airpower were already in place, at least in embryonic form, by the end of the First World War, with the exception of airborne and air-mobile troops. Of course the helicopter came after the Second World War, but perhaps that too can best be seen as a refinement of the airplane, albeit an immensely important one.

I do not want to make too much of this; certainly the twentieth century has been transformed by technology, but I simply question the extent to which technology alone has transformed the *nature* of war, which I see as responding to other forces.

THE NATURE OF WAR

In some ways the nature of war has remained unchanged over the course of our century; fear, pain, and death have always been present, as have courage and sacrifice. Yet in other ways, war has changed in character, with conflicts fought by different kinds of adversaries, for different reasons, and at different levels of intensity. Great world clashes have given way to bitter tribal struggles.

Clausewitz and Theory

Karl von Clausewitz (1780–1831), the Prussian staff officer and intellectual who wrote *On War*, recognized two kinds of warfare, total and limited, but after 1945 a third variety of conflict emerged to dominate the second half of the century, before terrorism emerged as a seemingly more pressing threat in 2001. I do not want to turn this into an analysis of Clausewitz as applied to the twentieth century, but he has framed so much of our discussion of war and supplied so much of our conceptual framework that it seems impossible to avoid him, at least as a touchstone.

Let me borrow a few concepts from him to make my point: (1) the Clausewitzian trinity, (2) the tendency for war to escalate, and (3) his dualistic typology of war. Clausewitz argued that war was a "paradoxical trinity."[2] This trinity can be defined roughly as the people, the military, and the government, and each had its "principle." That which compels the people is passion and primordial violence; that which involves the military is capability and chance; that which directs the government is policy and reason. The great transformation of warfare brought by the French Revolution and Napoleon resulted from the addition of the first element, the people, into the arena of conflict as active participants whose commitment drove the national warfare of the Revolutionary and Napoleonic era to new levels of mobilization and violence.

War, he theorizes, drives to extremes. The involvement of the people, the competition between adversaries in war, and the play of measure and countermeasure push violence toward excess. So strong are the forces that strip away limitations that "to introduce the principle of moderation into the theory of war itself would always lead to logical absurdity."[3] The tendency toward extremes compels Clausewitz to theorize that in a "perfect" situation war would achieve a theoretical ideal of absolute war—that is, war without any constraint. But reality imposes obstacles and limitations that keep war from reaching this theoretical absolute, although escalation toward it is very real, indeed.

Actual war, as opposed to the theoretical possibility of absolute war, falls into two categories, which he saw as "quite different" and separated by "points of irreconcilability."[4] These categories refer to the *political character* of these wars, above all, although they seem to differentiate the harshness of military means as well. (The contrast between the political and military characters of conflicts is central to the analysis of war presented here.) The first type of war strives "to overthrow the enemy" and "render him politically helpless" so that the foe must accept any kind of peace, including one that meant the extinction of the regime or the state itself. Hans Delbrück (1848–1929), the noted German military historian and analyst, discussed such war aims as the strategy of annihilation. And nowadays we use Delbrück's terminology to label such a total war as a War of Annihilation. The second type of war aims at much less; for example, one could fight simply to seize a piece of territory or to impose some particular concession. It is a war fought for discrete, but not complete, advantage and can be termed limited war, or War of Attrition, fought in accord with what Delbrück called a strategy of exhaustion. The goal, in a War of Attrition, is simply to make continuing a war more unacceptable that conceding to an opponent's demands.

The World Wars as Wars of Annihilation

Few would doubt that the two world wars both qualify as Wars of Annihilation in their political context. They were near-absolute tests of states and their forces, fought in an unlimited military fashion and ending in imposed settlements and the destruction of entire regimes. Governments mobilized military manpower, productive labor, and material resources to the extent of their abilities, holding little back. War leaders played to and played with the passions of the citizenry, and those passions escalated over the course of the conflicts, eventually not only accepting but demanding strikes against enemy populations as well as against their armed forces. Thus, adversaries pursued these struggles with a full utilization of their state, or societal, assets and a near-complete dedication of the will of the people to the war effort. The latter entailed both a tolerance for acts that inflicted great and cruel losses on the foe, military and civil, as well as a willingness to accept whatever casualties were necessary to defeat the enemy.

Alliances fought both world wars, and the major partners in each alliance engaged fully in the conflict. During the First World War, France, Britain, and Russia (before it was driven from the war) mobilized to the extreme, as did Germany and Austria-Hungary on the other side of no-man's land. The Allies and the Axis mobilized even more completely in the Second World War, although the Third Republic fell early in the struggle. Each side sought the total defeat of its enemy's will. With the exception of Japan's more limited war aims vis-à-vis the United States and Great Britain, the goal of contending parties was not to gain limited concessions or territories from their enemies. With such total goals came extreme acts of violence; belligerents practiced genocide and mass destruction—the Holocaust and the atomic bomb.

The Changing Military Character of Warfare after 1945

A number of factors changed the *military character* of warfare, amounting to a true watershed, after 1945, none more so than the addition of nuclear weapons to Great Power arsenals (Figure 8.1). Nuclear weaponry threatened humanity with extinction and brought Clausewitz's nightmare ideal of absolute war within the realm of the possible and altered forever the spectrum of warfare. Conflicts now divided into three distinct military levels defined by weaponry and intensity. Warfare could now be nuclear, conventional, or low intensity. Nuclear warfare, obviously, threatened the use of nuclear warheads, first delivered by aircraft and later by missiles. Theorists tried to construct a notion of limited nuclear warfare but discovered this to be an oxymoron, because the Clausewitzian mechanisms of escalation would quickly drive the employment of

Figure 8.1.
Nature(s) of War Since 1945

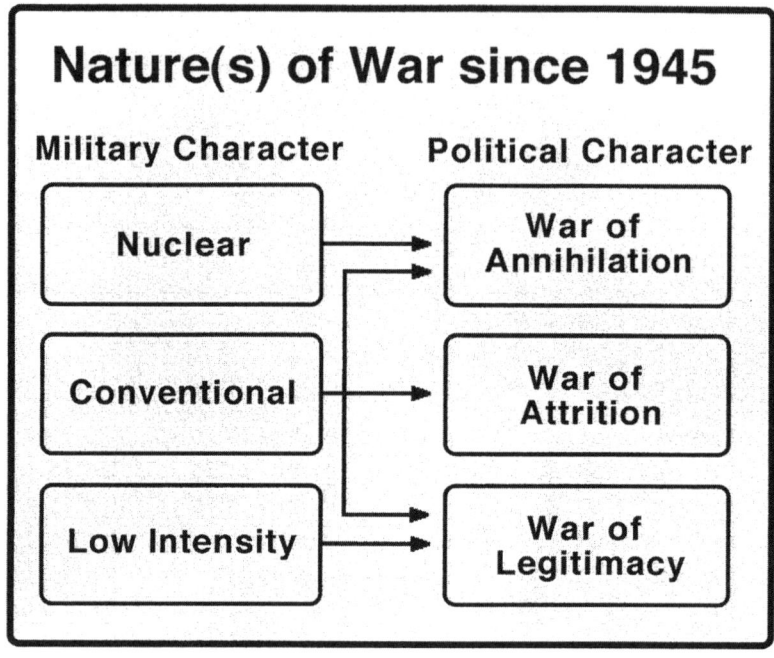

weapons from partial to full, which by the late 1960s meant the utter devastation of entire states.

This awful weaponry not only set the terms of nuclear war, but it also imposed the limits of conventional war. By the term *conventional* I do not simply mean "nonnuclear," as is the common usage today, but rather I mean warfare fought within the constraints of conventions, either agreed upon by the parties explicitly or forced upon them by their allies. Of course the most common convention was the choice to avoid the use of nuclear weapons or actions that might risk escalation to nuclear holocaust. In this sense, conventional war was defined by the existence of nuclear weaponry. The Korean War provided the first example of this new level of warfare, when the same weapons that had been used to achieve total victory in the Second World War were employed with restraint to keep the war from growing beyond an extent acceptable to the parties involved. During that conflict, U.S. forces did not strike into China, although Chinese troops fought against the United States below the Yalu and enemy fighter aircraft flew from bases in China. During the Vietnam conflict, the U.S. Navy enjoyed command of the seas around North Vietnam but decided not to impede Soviet ships for fear of precipitating a wider, potentially nuclear war. Likewise, American forces did not invade North Vietnam for fear of bringing China into the conflict. The Falklands War of 1982 was almost eighteenth-century in its limited nature, which restricted the war to a zone around the islands.

Low-intensity conflicts go by several names, guerrilla or brushfire wars, insurgencies, wars of national liberation, and so on. Low-intensity conflict is usually asymmetrical; that is, one side employs guerrilla methods out of necessity, while the other calls in a fuller range of modern tactics and methods. Guerrillas primarily use the arms of the infantry company, supplemented by mines and booby traps. The weapon of choice is the AK-47, not the tank. Low-intensity conflict has a small entry price, as it were; weaponry is cheap and numbers are few. Before the Second World War, military technology greatly favored the developed states when they employed forces in Third World settings, but the mass availability of simple but effective modern weapons since then has robbed status quo forces of their previous advantage. The stakes increase when guerrillas coordinate with main force units capable of heavier firepower.[5] Experience has demonstrated that guerrillas and insurgent main force units are best dealt with by an opponent able to adopt many of their methods.

New Political Elements in War

In regard to political shifts in warfare, a key characteristic of warfare during the Cold War was the bipolar nature of international power. The Second World War left two superpowers at center stage, the Soviet Union and the United States, each with a supporting cast but clearly playing the lead. So great was the power of these two that they ultimately chose not to fight one another but to invest in surrogates fighting proxy wars. The fact that both superpowers were willing to arm and support their allies meant that guns were always primed to fire.

The bipolar power struggle grew out of the rival geopolitical and economic interests of the contending parties and out of their roles as champions of different ideologies. Marxism-Leninism in its Russian or Chinese Maoist variants seemed to enjoy more victories in the short run but ultimately fell victim to both the expense of Great Power confrontation and the rising tide of ethnic and religious identification. Smaller states found it advantageous to join one side or the other, since alignment promised a cornucopia of aid and arms. Even India, that great champion of nonalignment under Nehru, turned to the Soviet Union under his daughter, Indira Gandhi.

Decolonization also defined warfare after 1945. Peoples fought to expel their old masters in Asia and Africa. The Vietminh drove the French from Vietnam, and later the Front National de Libération (FLN) succeeded in liberating Algeria. The British left their colonies with better grace but still fought in Malaya and Kenya. Portugal lost Goa and later Angola through force of arms and internal revolt. As opposed to such wars against nineteenth-century imperialists, other anticolonial struggles were self-declared battles against the "neocolonial" powers of the later twentieth century, the United States and the Soviet Union, and the regimes they sponsored.

The bipolar, ideological, and anticolonial aspects of war encouraged the intervention of third parties in ostensibly intrastate conflicts; so the United States fought in Vietnam and the Soviets in Afghanistan. However, another, more positive development also has encouraged intervention in intrastate wars since the Second World War. This is the growth of an international system which seeks concert and joint action rather than promoting unilateral belligerence. International pressure and consultation have moderated conflicts, or at least labored to do so. Military forces of many nations have taken part in peacekeeping and peacemaking operations under the international auspices of the United Nations, the North Atlantic Treaty Organization (NATO), the Organization of American States, or other regional combinations.

The collapse of the Cold War may have ended bipolar power struggles and ideological clashes between communists and anticommunists, but new or altered *causae belli* have stepped forward to take their places. Factors that modernization theorists once declared would wane, notably ethnic identification and religious fundamentalism, waxed instead and now fuel conflict. Ethnic identification is usually defined in terms of peoples with relatively small numbers and limited geographical extent; therefore, ethnic wars are most likely to be intrastate in character. Religious identification more easily crosses state boundaries, as in the case of Islamic fundamentalism. Often ethnic and religious issues combine in potent and cruel alliance, from Kosovo to Sri Lanka.

Moreover, as the old colonial masters no longer occupy lands they once held, borders they drew and institutions they established still inspire conflict. Tribes thrown together or split up for the geographical convenience of imperial powers now battle in Africa. Also the dissolution of still one more vast empire, the Soviet Union, has left a whole new legacy of postcolonial disputes among once-subject peoples. It is to be feared that time and blood alone will sort out the troubles of Soviet successor states.

The Rise of War of Legitimacy since 1945

This quick survey suggests that something very new has happened since 1945, something that does not fit neatly into the Clausewitzian typology. Without doubt the military character of nuclear war matches the political character of War of Annihilation in its most brutal extremes. Certain conventional wars also fit the category of War of Annihilation, for example, the opening phase of the Korean War, as North Korea tried to eliminate South Korea with a full-scale invasion, or the final stage of the Vietnam War, when the North Vietnamese Army utterly obliterated the state of South Vietnam, after the United States had abandoned the conflict.[6] Certainly, from an Arab point of view, Arab-Israeli wars of 1948 and 1967 meet this criteria as well. Other conflicts with more modest aims, such as the Korean War, the Falklands War, and the Gulf War, come under the heading of War of Attrition within the new constraints of conventional warfare. However, the great rush of low-intensity wars that followed the defeat of the Axis cannot easily be forced into the classic duality. They best fit in a new category, one I call "War of Legitimacy."

In contrast to the Clausewitzian duality, post-1945 War of Legitimacy stands apart because it is intrastate conflict, usually asymmetrical, and involves outside third parties. Traditional Clausewitzian analysis has concentrated on *inter*state warfare, but Wars of Legitimacy have been *intra*state wars fought to gain control of an existing state, to force its merger with another, or to subdivide it in order to create a new homeland. The fact that there are two, or more, contending parties within a single state means that, usually, only one controls a true government apparatus and the other, or others, are nonstate contenders. This distinguishes Wars of Legitimacy from the classic duality that implies both sides are states or alliances of states. To be sure, this alone does not make this type of war unique or historically novel; any civil war is a War of Legitimacy, and civil wars have raged from time immemorial. I would hazard the guess that Clausewitz overlooked discussing such struggles because they did not pose the most interesting questions of his day, and they did not dominate the attention of military theorists and practitioners for the rest of the nineteenth century or the first half of the twentieth, with the exception of the few, like Mao, who concentrated on guerrilla warfare.

Modern Wars of Legitimacy have generally, but not always, been asymmetrical insurgencies, with only one side bringing to bear the full panoply of conventional warfare. But more important, usually one or more contestants, either an imperial party in a colonial struggle or third-party interveners, have fought outside their homeland, for example, the French and Americans in Vietnam, the Russians in Afghanistan, and NATO peacekeepers in Bosnia. This makes the struggles even more asymmetrical, but in a psychological sense. Indigenous primary contenders fight a life-or-death struggle, while remote interveners see the conflict as more tangential to their interests. Populations engaged directly are subject to the full passion of war and escalate the fighting, but peoples physically remote from the struggle do not push that conflict to extremes because they are not driven by primordial feelings. To the contrary, populations of old colonial states or of third-party interveners have tended to see the war as distant and distasteful and ultimately engage their passions in *resisting* continued violence, forcing the remote contestant to withdraw. Terrorism has played several roles since the Second World War. But its most common and effective has been as an assault against the will of a people, often a third party in contests abroad, as in terrorism against the French during the Algerian War or against the English by the Irish Republican Army (IRA). Fear in the United States today centers on terrorists who view the United States as opponents of Islamic fundamentalism or some other righteous cause and hope to use terrorism to frighten the people of the United States into pressuring their government to disengage. In fact, I would argue that terrorism is best considered as a form of low-intensity conflict, but that is another subject.

The common, almost universal presence of third-party interveners, either as active belligerents or as peacemakers, is in fact both a cause and a reflection of the importance of these wars in the international system. The prevalence of third-party intervention at first followed from the issues of ideology and the bipolar power structure of the Cold War. Sometimes Great Powers intervened themselves; sometimes they engaged in an even more complex form of intervention through surrogates, as did the Soviets by employing Cuban troops in Africa, 1975–1988. With the end of the Cold War, intervention has been more likely to arise from a desire to moderate conflict and reinforce stability for humanitarian and political reasons. Today, major states bound together in an international system that recognizes the importance of collective action are more likely to see their interests in controlling conflicts and imposing peace outside their immediate borders. Thus developments in the international system since 1945 play an important role in defining Wars of Legitimacy.

It may be possible to understand War of Legitimacy as a simultaneous occurrence of both Annihilation and Attrition.[7] The in-country parties are locked in a death grip from which only one will survive, an ultimate War of Annihilation; however, the third parties engage in a match to gain advantage, one that they will walk away from, win or lose, a classic War of Attrition. However, to me this misses the point that it is the interplay between the rival parties and the rival intensities that makes War of Legitimacy unique, a whole that is qualitatively different than the sum of its parts (Figure 8.2). Even as the passions of primary contenders tend to drive violence to extremes, the fact that these conflicts aim at establishing the legitimacy of one side over another encourages certain constraints on violence. The contradictions between unrestrained and restrained violence produce a defining tension in Wars of Legitimacy. Clausewitz argues that war is red in tooth and claw, that attempts

Figure 8.2.
Nature(s) of War Since 1945

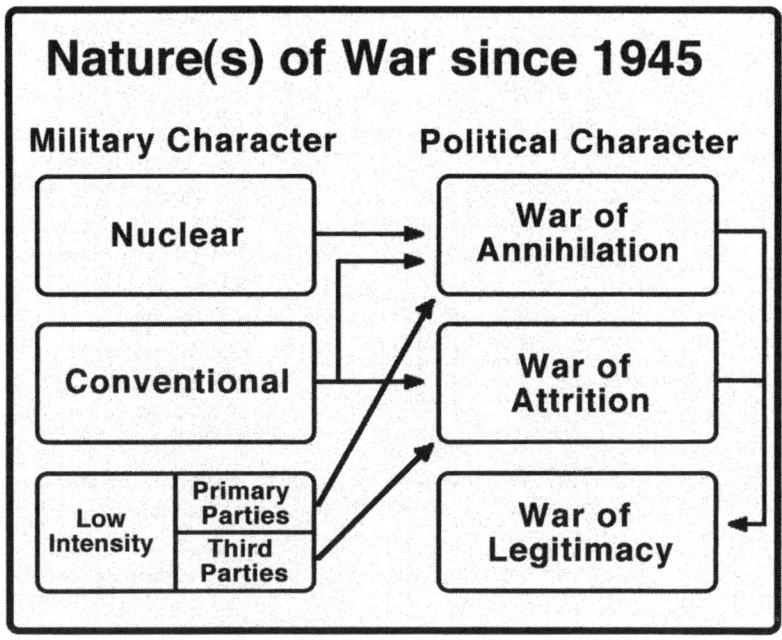

to restrain violence are pointless. At the turn of the century, Europeans read him, perhaps misread him, as emphasizing bloody battle and stressing the need to accept and inflict high casualties, and this contributed to the slaughter of the First World War because it was used to justify the cult of the offense. But if maximum violence makes sense in a strategy of annihilation or attrition, it can be counterproductive in a War of Legitimacy.

In his discussion of guerrilla war, Robert Asprey coined the terms "quantitative violence" and "qualitative violence."[8] Quantitative violence is essentially indiscriminate, and it can be measured in quantitative terms, for example, number of rounds fired, tons of bombs dropped, or body counts of the slain. In contrast, qualitative violence discriminates; it targets only particular victims in such a way as to minimize collateral damage while maximizing political impact. In conventional war, troops taking fire from a village would be likely to call in an air strike against it, but guerrillas facing opposition from a village would be more apt to target village leaders and kill only them, but in such a way as to leave a lasting impression of terror. The images of bodies dismembered and left as examples by Tamil Tiger guerrillas in Sri Lanka burn into the memory. To put it very bluntly, in quantitative violence it matters how many you kill, but in qualitative violence it matters who you kill.

War of Legitimacy has been the primary theater of qualitative violence. So long as primary actors struggle to win power *within* a community, they need to be highly selective about their use of force. Every casualty inflicted can increase hatred against the perpetrator, since kinsmen and friends of victims turn against him. This is why guerrillas often carefully focus the violence they commit while inciting their opponents to commit indiscriminate acts of destruction. Of course, this does not mean that Wars of Legitimacy do not witness horrible acts. Especially if a particular group can be identified as the enemy because of ethnic difference or some other criterion, then they become targets for all the violence their opponents can muster. When the goal is to eliminate ethnic opponents or drive them from their homes, rather than to win over one's own people, techniques in excess of those acceptable in conventional warfare can become the rule. The systematic rape of women in Bosnia as a conscious act of war and of ethnic cleansing stands out as a brutal case in point. Thus Wars of Legitimacy witness a variety of violence, depending on circumstances, but the prevalence of qualitative violence distinguishes them from Wars of Annihilation and Attrition.

Restrictions on the use of violence have been particularly important for third-party interveners for two reasons. In the first place, lack of restraint by a third-party force can undermine the very legitimacy of the side it wishes to aid. Intervention of foreigners in a civil war is likely to be a two-edged sword in any case, and if that sword cuts wildly, it may multiply opposition rather than win it over. Damage inflicted by U.S. troops in Vietnam, for example, turned many South Vietnamese against their own government. In the second place, indiscriminate violence by a third party can erode support for the intervention back home. Scenes of burning villages and injured children, for example, inspired the antiwar movement in the United States.

Some of the most interesting issues of War of Legitimacy have derived from the presence of third-party interveners; in fact, major powers view this issue as central because they have been most likely to intervene. Here the willingness for the home population of a third-party force to back intervention has proven to be vital. This question of tolerance and support sets Clausewitz's notion of the people as the source of "primordial violence, hatred, and enmity" on its ear. Two changes in popular attitudes distinguish War of Legitimacy since 1945 from, for example, the colonial conquests of the nineteenth century. The tolerance for violence directed against "lesser" peoples in the nineteenth century far exceeded tolerance for violence against indigenous "freedom fighters" in the late twentieth. This may be a product of media that now can display the horrors of war during the evening meal, but I think it goes deeper.

The perpetrators of international violence do not want to see themselves as inhumane, and they are more likely to accept their enemies as human beings, instead of seeing them as subhuman obstacles to power and progress. Acts of savagery against native peoples that won approval in nineteenth-century France, England, or the United States would now be condemned.

If tolerance for violence against others has declined, so has willingness to accept casualties in remote conflicts. Pre–First World War analysts built their tactical theories on the need to suffer high levels of casualties in order to defeat a foe, and that has thankfully changed, but the pendulum may have swung so far as to create an expectation of bloodless wars. The great paradox here is that just at a time when Western populations are becoming increasing callous to violence within their borders, they are increasingly sensitive to losses suffered by their armed forces in foreign lands. A second paradox lies in the fact that sensitivity to casualties suffered in far-off fights has grown in the last decade of the twentieth century, just as the need for dangerous peacekeeping and peace-making operations is on the increase. Only the future will tell if fear of casualties will eventually rule out all but the most obviously important armed interventions.

For both these reasons, third-party involvement may act to slow the escalation of violence in a War of Legitimacy, or perhaps there is a threshold at which third parties are likely to bail out of a conflict, leaving the primary contenders to go to extremes. The jury is still out on this question.

THE NATURE OF MILITARY FORCES

Just as the nature of war has altered since 1945, so has the nature of the forces engaged. Such evolution of military forces is something that has engaged me repeatedly in my career because of my study of two renowned watersheds in military history, the Military Revolution of the seventeenth century and the French Revolution at the end of the eighteenth.[9] This has led me before to construct an evolutionary taxonomy of Western army styles from the early Middle Ages through the present. This was done as a historian generating theories about the past rather than as an analyst constructing guidelines for the present or projections for the future. Nonetheless, a backward glance may be useful in orienting ourselves for the journey forward.

A caveat or two about my approach would be prudent before beginning. When most people discuss military evolution, they are interested in technology and tactics; as you have probably gathered by now, that is not my main focus. So when I discuss military evolution of military forces, I am more concerned with institutional development—recruitment, social composition, motivation, command, administration. These matters do have importance when considering not only who fights but how they fight, but my emphasis is on infrastructure more than superstructure. Also, my work is primarily concerned with armies, and I have been accused of not giving navies and, later, air forces their due. To this I must plead guilty, but since I am more interested in proposing issues here than in providing formulas, I will proceed, though imperfectly. Another warning is that I am concerned with the militaries fielded by major states in the West, although I will offer some comments on nonstate and non-Western forces. And I guess it is only honest to also admit in advance that my comments on the second half of the twentieth century are most concerned with the United States, a product of working with or for the armed services and security community in my native land.

With all that said, what watersheds appear to this parachutist? I would argue that we are now in the midst of a key evolutionary transition from one kind of military force to another, a transition yielding the seventh style of military force the West has seen since A.D. 800, long before the last millennial event.[10] The twentieth century inherited a style of army from the nineteenth. That century began with a "popular-conscript" military force that had emerged with the French Revolution and that would remain the European standard until after the German triumph over France in 1871. Obviously, conscription was fundamental to this style, but other traits also defined it. The *levée en masse* mobilized all of French society for war in August 1793 and produced a wartime army over twice as large as any France had ever seen. The *levée* established the principle of universal conscription across Europe and relegated the voluntary principle to the peripheral insular powers, Great Britain and the United States. Conscripts were expected to feel a new national loyalty or patriotism, and while an equivalent sentiment would take time to spread across Europe, spread it did. The popular-conscript army was supposed to be a people's, or popular, force, composed only of the nationals of a given state, as opposed to the substantially mercenary armies of the past.

The popular-conscript army as created by France grew out of political and social revolution. However, its revolutionary origins made it difficult for some powers to copy this style whole. It proved to be a form that was most likely to be imitated only in part, as in Prussia and Russia. Still, this style entailed elements that were or became the Western core standard—more general conscription, patriotic motivation, and technical elements such as organization into army corps.

Unable to copy the French system in its entirely, the Prussians adopted some aspects of it but innovated new elements that would serve as the basis of the next stage in military evolution. Most important, the Prussians ensured the dominance of merit in the officer corps by creating the general staff and multiplied their manpower through an effective system of reserves. The "mass-reserve army" evolved out of these innovations. Prussian victories between 1864 and 1871 made it the new paradigm, which other states copied over the next two decades. This mass-reserve army was very different from the style that proceeded it. Whereas the peacetime standing army had been seen before as the state's primary fighting force, now it was seen as a device to train a large reserve that could be mobilized in time of war. Conscription, which still produced the rank and file, now netted a far larger number of troops for the major armies of France, Germany, Russia, and Austria. Troops served full-time for shorter periods, usually only two or three years, and then passed into the reserves. By turning from expensive full-time professionals to far cheaper part-time reserves, the mass-reserve army eased the budgetary restrictions imposed upon governments. The acceptance of mass-reserve armies also was linked to a belief that the great majority of the people were politically reliable. With the mass-reserve style, the size of mobilized armies rose dramatically, yielding the armed hordes of the First and Second World Wars.

The key to realizing the full potential of these much enlarged armies was rapid mobilization, and it in turn required a product of industrialization—steam power. Before industrial age weapons multiplied the killing power of armies, the extent of war was transformed by the carrying capacity of railroads and steamships. If railroads were to make possible the Napoleonic ideal of assembling forces quickly, extensive planning and skillful coordination were required, so the adoption of a Prussian-style general staff became an absolute necessity in the second half of the nineteenth century. The rough war plans previously drafted by European commanders would not bear comparison with the detailed plans carried out by German forces in the Franco-Prussian War.

Through most of the twentieth century, mass-reserve armies were the perfect instruments for total war, first the real struggles of the two world wars and then the potential clash threatened by the Cold War. After 1945 the new military paradigms were resident in the Soviet Union and the United States, although they served as models to very different constituencies. The superpowers in this unique bipolar competition owed their positions to a set of common factors: great military power born of population and wealth; ideological leadership in the Cold War; ability to supply arms to allies and clients; and capacity to train and advise other armies. Ideological barriers compelled, or at least encouraged, lesser military powers to look only to one or the other of the two superpowers. The Soviets directed one path of military evolution, while the United States guided another. The postcolonial and ideological contexts of the Cold War also turned both superpowers into examples for emerging nations, and thus they carried Western military institutions into the developing world.

The two world wars demonstrated that the mass-reserve army was the style most liable to be transformed by a long war. Based upon short service and large reserves—that is, made up primarily of amateurs—mass-reserve forces were composed of men of limited abilities at the outset of conflicts. Concern with this fact led to the crude tactics and high casualties at the outset of the First World War and also shaped French tactics going into the Second World War, for example. The Germans lessened this problem by more intensive training, but the fact remained that mass-reserve forces tended to evolve from amateur to professional only through the harsh agency of war. During the years of conflict, citizens became soldiers, administration became more competent, and tactics became more sophisticated. However, it also is in the nature of things that mass-reserve armies showed a tendency to return to a lesser level of competence with the return of the routines of peacetime service.

The political costs of imposing conscription and the economic costs of maintaining huge forces, as well as the technological promise of maximizing mobility and power in smaller forces, have led to the key emergence of today's "volunteer-technical" army. The British can claim to have initiated the trend with the phasing out of national service, 1957–1963, but the crucial move came when the United States abandoned the peacetime draft after the Vietnam War. U.S. policymakers saw the elimination of the drafts as one way to heal the self-inflicted political wounds of the Vietnam War. The incentive to downsize military forces expanded throughout Europe and the former Soviet Union with the end of the Cold War, as a declining threat could no longer justify the existence of large forces and governments and populations could think of better things to do with resources previously committed to the military. If a political and economic push drives states toward volunteer technical forces, the promise of technology to multiply effectiveness exerts a pull. Even that original birthplace of universal conscription, France, has ended compulsory service. This trend is not, however, universal. Israel, for example, needs to keep as large an army as possible until reliable peace comes to the Middle East. And although the U.S. Army acts as the paradigm army in the West, it is unlikely to become a paradigm for the entire world, because only the developed countries can match its level of weapons technology.

Quantity, sheer numbers of men and weapons that had seemed the prerequisite of victory in the world wars, gave way to quality. Conventional weapons became more lethal and complex; but their use demanded greater expertise and coordination, which, in turn, demanded improved education, doctrine, and training. Fewer but more able troops could accomplish more on the battlefield than could the mass armies of earlier decades. Smaller forces could be maintained through selective voluntary enlistment, although the state reserves the right to return to conscription. Voluntary enlistment also promised higher levels of education and motivation among the rank and file. As officers and enlisted personnel had to master more sophisticated forms of warfare, longer terms of service returned. Reserves remain substantial, but they have also changed in character, intended to flesh out, not replace, the standing army.

Importantly, volunteer-technical forces promise to be far better suited to a War of Legitimacy than were mass-reserve forces. As long as the threat of a new round of total war encouraged the maintenance of large forces on land, sea, and the air, these were trained and organized for the quantitative warfare of great clashes. This meant that they were less well prepared for the qualitative warfare of intrastate conflict. The immediate post–Second World War period brought an inherent paradox of forces. Militaries had to be constructed to deal with a War of Annihilation that never came, and although this left them able to conduct a War of Attrition, they were far less suited to a War of Legitimacy, which proved to be the most common form of conflict.

Those directing the reconfiguration of U.S. forces are more aware than ever before of the need to tailor forces to meet the new challenges of conflicts short of a War of Annihilation. This may be expressed in the U.S. Army's concept of Force XXI. It aims at creating an army with "doctrinal flexibility, strategic, mobility, tailorability and modularity, joint and multinational connectivity, and the versatility to function in War and OOTW (Operations Other Than War)."[11] From the point of view of someone who has been privileged to work with the Marine Corps, it is gratifying to see the army follow the Marine Corps lead with such good grace—for the Marine Corps has prepared itself along these lines for some time. The implications of OOTW, War of Legitimacy, and volunteer-technical forces are less comfortable for the navy and least comfortable for the air force—because both would have to increase transport and logistic capacities more than new combat technologies. This logically leads to what is anathema to the air force, the need to multiply transports instead of adding new generations of fighter aircraft. In any case, the volunteer-technical military promises greater congruity between force and threat.

CONCLUSION

To wrap this all up and return to earth, let me give you a final report from altitude. I see the twentieth century as a greater inheritor of the nineteenth than do most, for I see key characteristics of war and military institutions continuing through the first half of the century at least— these were the dominance of War of Annihilation with mass-reserve militaries applying unlimited military force. In addition, I see a major watershed in the nature of war after 1945, not simply the apparition of nuclear destruction but the emergence and eventual prevalence of War of Legitimacy. Forces changed, too, after the Second World War, although the continued threat of Great Power war slowed this evolution. Still in the last quarter of the century the paradigm of military forces shifted to smaller, more mobile, and more technologically sophisticated forces. This change came for a number of reasons, only partly because of the complexities of War of Legitimacy, but the end result would seem to be a better match between potential conflict and the military forces of the major powers, particularly the United States, by the close of the century.

With my feet once again firmly on the ground the instincts of the truffle-grubber in me return, so I must end with a modest disclaimer. As a dyed-in-the-wool academic, I intend only to bring matters up for consideration, not to offer final answers. In fact, to me, it is the questions rather than the answers that matter most, particularly when turning from the history to policy.

NOTES

1. Much of what I will say here derives from articles that came out in 1996, so that a few of you, very few I would suppose, might have some sense of déjà vu, although the same clay is molded differently in this chapter. Another saying by the noted scholar of my years also comes to mind: "At this age, we write so little, yet we publish so much." I interpret this to mean that after spending many years writing and teaching, one begins to plagiarize oneself. We are allowed to repackage our published material into new bundles, with new meanings. My two essays mined for material here are, first and foremost, John Lynn, "War of Annihilation, War of Attrition, and War of Legitimacy: A Neo-Clausewitzian Approach to Twentieth-Century Conflicts," *Marine Corps Gazette*, 80.10 (October 1996), 64–71, and second, "The Evolution of Army Style in the Modern West, 800–2000," *International History Review* 18.3 (August 1996), 505–45. I would like to express my thanks to Col. John Greenwood at the *Marine Corps Gazette* and Dr. Edward Ingram at the *International History Review* for granting me permission to import large swatches of those articles into this chapter.

2. Carl von Clausewitz, *On War*, Michael Howard and Peter Paret, trans. (Princeton, NJ: Princeton University Press, 1976), 89.

3. Ibid., 76.

4. Note by Clausewitz in Peter Paret, "Clausewitz," in Peter Paret, ed., *Makers of Modern Strategy* (Princeton, NJ: Princeton University Press, 1986), 196–97.

5. This combination of guerrilla with "conventional" forces goes by the somewhat confusing title of "mobile war" in the military writings of Mao Tse Tung.

6. It is very interesting and important to point out that both of these can be portrayed as Wars of Legitimacy as well, since parties viewed Korea and Viet-

nam as single nations. Also, both the wars in Korea and Vietnam involved third-party interveners at some point.

7. The attending alternative diagram was suggested to me by Dr. Robert Rush, when he was a graduate student at the Ohio State University. He drew the illustration somewhat differently than I have, but the notion of splitting low-intensity conflict by primary and third-party contenders and showing diagrammatically how one fought a War of Annihilation while the other engaged in a War of Attrition was his.

8. Robert Asprey, *War in the Shadows*, 2 vols. (Garden City, NY: Doubleday, 1975).

9. The classic definition of the Military Revolutions is 1560–1660 in the seminal essay Michael Roberts delivered in an inaugural lecture in 1954, later published as "The Military Revolution, 1560–1660" (Belfast: Queen's University, 1956). Geoffrey Parker extends the dates in his *The Military Revolution: Military Innovation and the Rise of the West, 1500–1800* (Cambridge: Cambridge University Press, 1988). For my discussion of the Military Revolution and the Wars of the French Revolution, see John Lynn, *The Wars of Louis XIV, 1667–1714* (London: Longman, Ltd., 1999), *Giant of the Grand Siècle: The French Army, 1610–1715* (NY: Cambridge University Press, 1997), and *The Bayonets of the Republic: Motivation and Tactics in the Army of Revolutionary France, 1791–94*, rev. ed. (Boulder, CO: Westview Press, 1996).

10. In my "Evolution of Army Style in the Modern West, 800–2000," I identified and dated seven army styles that I would now date roughly as follows: Feudal (800–1200), Medieval Stipendiary (1200–1450), Aggregate Contract (1450–1650), State Commission (1650–1790), Popular Conscript (1790–1880), Mass Reserve (1880–1970), Volunteer-Technical (1979–present).

11. U.S. Army Training and Doctrine Command (TRADOC), *Force XXI Operations: A Concept for the Evolution of Full-Dimensional Operations for the Strategic Army of the Early Twenty-first Century* (Washington, DC: Department of the Army, 1994).

Selected Bibliography

Aldcroft, Derek. *The European Economy, 1914–1970*. London: Croom Helm, 1978.
Allan, James. "Reluctant Heroes: Assembling the United Nations Cyprus Force, 1964." *International Journal*, 53.4 (Autumn 1998), 733–52.
Ally, G., Chroust, Peter, and Pross, Christian. *Cleansing the Fatherland: Nazi Medicine and Racial Hygiene*. Baltimore, MD: Johns Hopkins University Press, 1994.
Anderson, Benedict. *Imagined Communities: Reflections on the Origin and Spread of Nationalism*. Rev. ed. London: Verso, 1991.
Aronsen, Lawrence. *American National Security and Economic Relations with Canada, 1945–1953*. Westport, CT: Praeger, 1997.
Asprey, Robert. *War in the Shadows*. 2 vols. Garden City, NY: Doubleday, 1975.
Axworthy, Lloyd, and Taylor, Sarah. "A Ban for All Seasons: The Landmines Convention and Its Implications for Canadian Diplomacy." *International Journal*, 53.2 (Spring 1998), 189–203.
Baker, James A. *The Politics of Diplomacy: Revolution, War, and Peace, 1989–1992*. New York: Putnam's, 1995.
Ball, George W. *Diplomacy for a Crowded World: An American Foreign Policy*. Boston: Little, Brown, 1976.
Barrett, David M. *Uncertain Warriors: Lyndon Johnson and His Vietnam Advisers*. Lawrence: University Press of Kansas, 1993.
Bender, Thomas. "Wholes and Parts: The Need for Synthesis in American History." *Journal of American History*, 73 (June 1986), 120–36.
Berman, Larry. *Planning a Tragedy: The Americanization of the War in Vietnam*. New York: Norton, 1982.

Berube, Allan, and D'Emilio, John. "Archives: The Military and Lesbians during the McCarthy Years." *Signs*, 9 (Summer 1984), 759–75.

Black, Cyril. "The Turkish Straits and the Great Powers." *Foreign Policy Reports*, 23.14 (1947), 174–82.

Blechman, Barry. *The Control of Naval Armaments: Prospects and Possibilities.* Washington, DC: Brookings Institution, 1975.

Blum, John M. *V Was for Victory.* New York: Harcourt Brace Jovanovich, 1976.

Bock, Ernest. "Soviet Economic Expansionism." *Problems of Communism*, 7 (July–August 1958), 32–33.

Bowden, Mark. *Black Hawk Down: A Study of Modern War.* New York: Atlantic Monthly Press, 1998.

Boyer, Paul. *By the Bomb's Early Light: American Thought and Culture at the Dawn of the Atomic Age.* New York: Pantheon, 1989.

Brands, H.W. "The Age of Vulnerability: Eisenhower and the National Insecurity State." *American Historical Review*, 94 (1989), 963–89.

———. *Cold Warriors: Eisenhower's Generation and American Foreign Policy.* New York: Columbia University Press, 1988.

Brandt, Alan M. *No Magic Bullet: A Social History of Venereal Disease in the United States since 1880.* New York: Oxford University Press, 1987.

Brant, S. [Pseud.]. *The East German Rising, 17th June 1953.* London: Thomas and Hudson, 1955.

Brebner, John B. *North Atlantic Triangle: The Interplay of Canada, the United States and Great Britain.* New York: Columbia University Press, 1945.

Brogan, Denis W. "The Illusion of American Omnipotence." *Harper's Magazine*, 205 (December 1952), 21–28.

Bruce, Valerie. "The Empire Strikes Back: The Transformation of the Eastern Bloc from a Soviet Asset to a Soviet Liability." *International Organization*, 39 (Winter 1985), 1–46.

Brzezinski, Zbigniew. *The Soviet Bloc: Unity and Conflict.* Cambridge: Harvard University Press, 1967.

Burke, John H., and Greenstein, Fred I. *How Presidents Test Reality: Decisions on Vietnam 1954 and 1965.* New York: Russell Sage Foundation, 1989.

Burns, Richard, and Chapin, Seymour. "Near Eastern Naval Limitation Pacts, 1930–1931." *East European Quarterly*, 4.1 (1970), 77–87.

Carter, Paul. *Another Part of the Fifties.* New York: Columbia University Press, 1983.

Caute, David. *The Great Fear: The Anti-Communist Purge under Truman and Eisenhower.* New York: Simon & Schuster, 1978.

Chace, James. *Acheson: The Secretary of State Who Created the American World.* New York: Simon & Schuster, 1998.

Chilton, Paul A. *Security Metaphors: Cold War Discourse from Containment to Common House.* New York: Peter Lang, 1996.

Clausewitz, Carl von. *On War.* Michael Howard and Peter Paret, trans. Princeton, NJ: Princeton University Press, 1976.

Cole, Barbara. *The Elite: The Story of the Rhodesian Special Air Service.* London: Three Knights, 1984.

Connolly, William E. *Identity/Difference: Democratic Negotiations of Political Paradox.* Ithaca, NY: Cornell University Press, 1991.

Coontz, Stephanie. *The Way We Never Were: American Families and the Nostalgia Trap*. New York: Basic Books, 1992.
Corber, Robert J. *In the Name of National Security: Hitchcock, Homophobia, and the Political Construction of Gender in Postwar America*. Durham, NC: Duke University Press, 1993.
Costigliola, Frank. " 'Unceasing Pressure for Penetration': Gender, Pathology, and Emotion in George Kennan's Formulation of the Cold War." *Journal of American History*, 83 (March 1997), 1309–39.
Crabb, Cecil V., Jr., and Mulcahy, Kevin. *Presidents and Foreign Policy Making: From FDR to Reagan*. Baton Rouge: Louisiana State University Press, 1986.
Croft, Stuart. *Strategies of Arms Control: A History and Typology*. Manchester: Manchester University Press, 1996.
Daniels, Roger, Taylor, Sandra C. and Kitano, Harry H.L., eds. *Japanese Americans: From Relocation to Redress*. Rev. ed. Seattle: University of Washington Press, 1991.
Dawson, William Harbutt. *Richard Cobden and Foreign Policy*. London: Allen & Unwin, 1926.
Desbarats, Peter. *Somalia Coverup: A Commissioner's Journal*. Toronto: McClelland & Stewart, 1997.
Dewar, Michael. *Brush Fire Wars: Minor Campaigns of the British Army since 1945*. London: Robert Hale, 1984.
Djilas, Milovan. *Conversations with Stalin*. Michael B. Petrovich, trans. New York: Harcourt, Brace, 1962.
Douglas, Mary. *Purity and Danger: An Analysis of the Concepts of Pollution and Taboo*. London: Ark Paperbacks, 1989.
Dyke, Richard Wayne. *Mr. Atomic Energy: Congressman Chet Holifield and Atomic Energy Affairs, 1945–1974*. Westport, CT: Greenwood Press, 1989.
Edmonds, Anthony O. "America in the 1950s: The Roots of Our Discontent." In *Silhouettes on the Shade: A Symposium at the Carmichael Project*. Muncie, IN: Ball State University, 1973.
Eisenberg, Carolyn. "Working Class Politics and the Cold War: American Intervention in the German Labor Movement, 1945–49." *Diplomatic History*, 7 (Fall 1983), 283–306.
English, John. " 'A Fine Romance': Canada and the United Nations, 1943–1957." In Greg Donaghy, ed., *Canada and the Early Cold War, 1943–1957*. Ottawa: Department of Foreign Affairs and International Trade, 1998.
———. *The Worldly Years: The Life of Lester B. Pearson*. Vol. 2: *1949–1972*. Toronto: University of Toronto Press, 1992.
Etzhold, Thomas H., and Gaddis, John Lewis, eds. *Containment: Documents on American Policy and Strategy, 1945–1950*. New York: Columbia University Press, 1978.
Faille, Maxime. "Towards a UN Rapid Reaction Capability: A Canadian Initiative." *Canadian Defence Quarterly* (December 1995), 14–15.
Fitzpatrick, Joan J. *Human Rights in Crisis: The International System for Protecting Human Rights during States of Emergency*. Philadelphia: University of Pennsylvania Press, 1994.
Follain, John. *Jackal: The Complete Story of the Legendary Terrorist, Carlos the Jackal*. New York: Archade Publishers, 1998. Published in the United Kingdom

as *Jackal: The Secret Wars of Carlos the Jackal*. London: Trafalgar Square, 1998.

Ford, Thomas. "The Genesis of the First Hague Peace Conference." *Political Science Quarterly*, 51(1936), 354–82.

Fossedal, Gregory A. *Our Finest Hour: Will Clayton, the Marshall Plan, and the Triumph of Democracy*. Stanford, CA: Hoover Institution, 1993.

Franck, Thomas M. *The Power of Legitimacy among Nations*. New York: Oxford University Press, 1990.

Freedman, Lawrence, and Karsh, Efraim. *The Gulf Conflict 1990–1991: Diplomacy and War in the New World Order*. Princeton, NJ: Princeton University Press, 1993.

Gaddis, John Lewis. *The United States and the Origins of the Cold War, 1941–1947*. New York: Columbia University Press, 1973.

Gardner, Richard N. *Sterling-Dollar Diplomacy: Anglo-American Collaboration in the Reconstruction of Multilateral Trade*. Oxford: Clarendon Press, 1956.

Garrison, Dee. "Our Skirts Gave Them Courage: The Civil Defense Protest Movement in New York City, 1955–1961." In Joanne Meyerowitz, ed., *Not June Cleaver: Women and Gender in Postwar America*. Philadelphia: Temple University Press, 1994.

Gathorne-Hardy, G.M. *A Short History of International Affairs, 1920–1939*. London: Oxford University Press, 1950.

Gati, Charles. *Hungary and the Soviet Bloc*. Durham, NC: Duke University Press, 1986.

Gatzke, Hans. *Stresemann and the Rearmament of Germany*. Baltimore: Johns Hopkins Press, 1954.

George, Alexander L., and George, Juliette L. *Presidential Personality and Performance*. Boulder, CO: Westview Press, 1998.

Gilbert, Martin. *"Never Despair" Winston S. Churchill, 1945–1965*. London: Heinemann, 1988.

Glanz, Susan. "Economic Platforms of the Various Political Parties in the Hungarian Elections of 1945." *Hungarian Studies Review*, 22.1 (Spring 1995), 31–45.

Glynn, Patrick. *Closing Pandora's Box: Arms Races, Arms Control, and the History of the Cold War*. New York: Basic Books, 1992.

Goldhagen, Daniel. *Hitler's Willing Executioners: Ordinary Germans and the Holocaust*. New York: Knopf, 1996.

Goldstein, Erik, and Maurer, John, eds. *The Washington Conference, 1921-22: Naval Rivalry, East Asian Stability, and the Road to Pearl Harbor*. London: Frank Cass, 1993.

Goldstein, R. J. *Political Repression in Modern America from 1870 to the Present*. Cambridge, MA: Schenkman, 1978.

Gollner, Andras B. "Foundations of Soviet Domination and Communist Political Power in Hungary, 1945–1950." *Canadian-American Review of Hungarian Studies*, 3 (Fall 1976), 85–94.

Goodwin-Gill, Guy S. *The Refugee in International Law*. 2nd ed. Oxford: Clarendon Press, 1996.

Gourevitch, Philip. *We Wish to Inform You That Tomorrow We Will Be Killed with Our Families: Stories from Rwanda*. New York: Farrar, Straus & Giroux, 1998.

Graebner, Norman A., ed. *The National Security: Its Theory and Practice, 1945–1960.* New York: Oxford University Press, 1986.
Greenstein, Fred L. *The Hidden-Hand Presidency: Eisenhower as Leader.* New York: Basic Books, 1982.
Hamby, Alonzo L. *Man of the People: A Life of Harry S. Truman.* New York: Oxford University Press, 1995.
Hannum, Hurst. *Guide to International Human Rights Practice.* 2nd ed. Philadelphia: University of Pennsylvania Press, 1992.
Hathaway, Robert. "Economic Diplomacy in Time of Crisis." In William H. Becker and Samuel F. Wells, Jr., eds., *Economics & World Power.* New York: Columbia University Press, 1984.
Haynes, John E. *Red Scare or Red Menace: American Communism and Anticommunism in the Cold War Era.* Chicago: Ivan R. Dee, 1996.
Heale, M. J. *American Anticommunism: Combating the Enemy Within, 1830-1970.* Baltimore, MD: Johns Hopkins University Press, 1990.
Heinrichs, Terry. "Free Speech and the Zundel Trial." *Queen's Quarterly,* 95 (1988), 837–54.
Henkin, Alice, ed. *Honoring Human Rights: From Peace to Justice, Recommendations to the International Community.* Washington, DC: Aspen Institute, 1998.
Henkin, Louis. *The Age of Rights.* New York: Columbia University Press, 1990.
———, ed. *The International Bill of Rights: The Covenant on Civil and Political Rights.* New York: Columbia University Press, 1981.
Herring, George C., and Immerman, Richard H. "Eisenhower, Dulles, and Dienbienphu: 'The Day We Didn't Go to War' Revisited." *Journal of American History,* 71 (1984), 343–63.
Hillmer, Norman. "Canadian Peacekeeping: Old and New." In *Peacekeeping 1815 to Today. Proceedings of the XXIst Colloquium of the International Commission of Military History.* Quebec City, Quebec: Défense nationale, 1995.
———. "Peacekeeping: Canadian Invention, Canadian Myth." In Sune Åkerman and J. L. Granatstein, eds., *Welfare States in Trouble: Historical Perspectives on Canada and Sweden.* Uppsala, Sweden: Swedish Science Press, 1995.
Hillmer, Norman, and Chapnick, Adam. "The Axworthy Human Security Revolution." In Fen Osler Hampson, Norman Hillmer, and Maureen Molot, eds., *Canada among Nations 2001: The Axworthy Legacy.* Don Mills, Ontario: Oxford University Press, 2001.
Hillmer, Norman, and Oliver, Dean. "The NATO–United Nations Link: Canada and the Balkans, 1991–1995." In Gustav Schmidt, ed., *A History of NATO: The First Fifty Years.* New York: Palgrave Macmillan, 2001.
Hinsley, F.H. *Power and the Pursuit of Peace: Theory and Practice in the History of Relations between States.* Cambridge: Cambridge University Press, 1963.
Holloway, David. *Stalin and the Bomb.* New York: Yale University Press, 1994.
Holmes, John. *The Shaping of Peace: Canada and the Search for World Order, 1943–1957.* Vol. 1. Toronto: University of Toronto Press, 1979.
Holsti, K. J. *The State, War and the State of War.* New York: Cambridge University Press, 1996.
Horak, Stephan, ed. *Poland's International Affairs, 1919–1960: A Calendar.* Bloomington: Indiana University, 1964.

Howard, Harry. "The Turkish Straits after World War II: Problems and Prospects." *Balkan Studies*, 11.1 (1970), 35–60.

———. "The Turkish Straits and the Great Powers." *Foreign Affairs*, 13 (October 1936), 199–202.

Immerman, Richard H. "Eisenhower and Dulles: Who Made the Decision?" *Political Psychology*, 1 (1979), 13–20.

Isenberg, Irwin. *The Soviet Satellites of Eastern Europe*. New York: Scholastic Book Services, 1963.

Ivie, Robert L. "Cold War Motives and the Rhetorical Metaphor: A Framework of Criticism." In Martin J. Medhurst, Philip Wander, Robert L. Ivie, and Robert L. Scott, eds., *Cold War Rhetoric: Strategy, Metaphor, and Ideology*, 71–79. Westport, CT: Greenwood Press, 1990.

———. "Literalizing the Metaphor of Soviet Savagery: President Truman's Plain Style." *Southern Speech Communication Journal*, 51 (1986), 91–105.

Jackson, Kenneth. *Crabgrass Frontier: The Suburbanization of the United States*. New York: Oxford University Press, 1985.

James, Alan. "The History of Peacekeeping: An Analytical Perspective." *Canadian Defence Quarterly* (September 1993), 11.

James, D. Clayton, and Wells, Anne Sharp. *Refighting the Last War: Command and Crisis in Korea, 1950–1953*. New York: Free Press, 1993.

Jeansonne, Glen. *Women of the Far Right: The Mothers' Movement and World War II*. Chicago: University of Chicago Press, 1996.

Jeffreys-Jones, Rhodri. *Changing Differences: Women and the Shaping of American Foreign Policy, 1917–1994*. New Brunswick, NJ: Rutgers University Press, 1995.

Kalshoven, Frits. *Constraints on the Waging of War*. Geneva: International Committee of the Red Cross, 1991.

Kant, Immanuel. *Perpetual Peace: A Philosophical Essay*. M. Campbell Smith, trans. and ed. London: Thoemmes Press, 1903.

Kaser, Michael. *Comecon: Integration Problems of the Planned Economies*. London: Oxford University Press, 1967.

Kaser, M., and Zielinski, J.G. *Planning in East Europe*. London: Bodley Head, 1970.

Kennan, George F. *Memoirs, 1925–1950*. Boston: Little, Brown, 1967.

———. *Sketches from a Life*. New York: Pantheon Books, 1989.

Kennedy-Pipe, Caroline. *Stalin's Cold War: Soviet Strategies in Europe, 1943 to 1956*. New York: St. Martin's Press, 1995.

Kimball, Warren. *Swords or Plowshares? The Morgenthau Plan for Defeated Nazi Germany, 1943–1946*. Philadelphia: Lippincott, 1976.

Kiss, Judit. *The Defence Industry in East-Central Europe: Restructuring and Conversion*. Oxford: Oxford University Press, 1997.

Klehr, Harvey, Haynes, John Earl, and Firsov, Fridrikh Igorevich, eds. *The Secret World of American Communism*. New Haven, CT: Yale University Press, 1995.

Kochavi, Arieh J. *Nuremberg; Allied War Crimes Policy and the Question of Punishment*. Chapel Hill: University of North Carolina Press, 1999.

Kohler, Heinz. *Economic Integration in the Soviet Bloc with an East German Case Study*. New York: Praeger, 1965.

Kolko, Joyce, and Kolko Gabriel. *The Limits of Power*. New York: Harper & Row, 1972.

Koppes, Clayton R., and Black, Gregory D. *Hollywood Goes to War: How Politics, Profits, and Propaganda Shaped World War II Movies*. Berkeley: University of California Press, 1990.

Kovel, Joel. *Red Hunting in the Promised Land: Anticommunism and the Making of America*. New York: Basic Books, 1994.

LaFeber, Walter. *America, Russia, and the Cold War, 1945–1990*. New York: McGraw-Hill, 1990.

Lake, David A., and Mastanduno, Michael, eds. *The State and American Foreign Economic Policy*. Ithaca, NY: Cornell University Press, 1988.

Laquer, Walter, and Rubin, Barry, eds. *The Human Rights Reader*. New York: New American Library, 1989.

Leffler, Melvyn P. "New Approaches, Old Interpretations, and Prospective Reconfigurations." In Michael J. Hogan, ed., *America in the World: The Historiography of American Foreign Relations since 1941*. New York: Cambridge University Press, 1995.

———. *A Preponderance of Power: National Security, the Truman Administration, and the Cold War*. Stanford, CA: Stanford University Press, 1992.

Leibman, Nina. *Living Room Lecture: The Fifties Family in Film and Television*. Austin: University of Texas Press, 1995.

Levine, Lawrence W. *Black Culture and Black Consciousness: Afro-American Folk Thought from Slavery to Freedom*. New York: Oxford University Press, 1977.

Link, Arthur. *Wilson the Diplomatist*. Baltimore, MD: Johns Hopkins Press, 1957.

Lippmann, Walter. *U.S. Foreign Policy: Shield of the Republic*. Boston: Little, Brown, 1943.

Lipsitz, George. *Rainbow at Midnight: Labor and Culture in the 1940s*. Urbana: University of Illinois Press, 1994.

Lord, Carnes. *The Presidency and the Management of National Security*. New York: Free Press, 1988.

Lundestad, Geir. *The American "Empire."* New York: Oxford University Press, 1990.

Lynn, John. *The Bayonets of the Republic: Motivation and Tactics in the Army of Revolutionary France, 1791–94*. Rev. ed. Boulder, CO: Westview Press, 1996.

———. "The Evolution of Army Style in the Modern West, 800–2000." *International History Review*, 18.3 (August 1996), 505–45.

———. *Giant of the Grand Siècle: The French Army, 1610–1715*. New York: Cambridge University Press, 1997.

———. "War of Annihilation, War of Attrition, and War of Legitimacy: A Neo-Clausewitzian Approach to Twentieth-Century Conflicts." *Marine Corps Gazette*, 80.10 (October 1996), 64–71.

———. *The Wars of Louis XIV, 1667–1714*. London: Longman, Ltd., 1999.

Malcolmson, Robert W. *Nuclear Fallacies: How We Have Been Misguided since Hiroshima*. Kingston and Montreal: McGill-Queen's University Press, 1985.

Maloney, Sean. *Securing Command of the Sea*. Annapolis, MD: U.S. Naval Institute Press, 1989.

Mastny, Vojtech. *The Cold War and Soviet Insecurity: The Stalin Years*. New York: Oxford University Press, 1996.

——. *Russian's Road to the Cold War*. New York: Columbia University Press, 1979.
Max, Stanley. *The United States, Great Britain and the Sovietization of Hungary, 1945–1948*. Boulder, CO: East European Monographs, Columbia University Press, 1985.
May, Ernest R., ed. *American Cold War Strategy: Interpreting NSC 68*. Boston: Bedford Books, 1993.
McInnes, Colin. *Hot War, Cold War: The British Army's Way in Warfare 1945–95*. London: Brassey's, 1996.
McKercher, B.J.C., and Aronsen, Lawerence, eds. *The North Atlantic Triangle in a Changing World: Anglo-American-Canadian Relations, 1903–1956*. Toronto: University of Toronto Press, 1996.
McNeill, William H. *Plagues and Peoples*. Garden City, NY: Doubleday, 1976.
Melanson, Richard, and Mayers, David, eds. *Reevaluating Eisenhower: American Foreign Policy in the Fifties*. Urbana: University of Illinois Press, 1987.
Metcalf, Lee Kendall. "The Creation of a Socialist Trading System." *East European Quarterly*, 29 (January 1996), 465–85.
Mikesell, Raymond F. "Negotiating at Bretton Woods, 1944." In Raymond Dennett and Joseph E. Johnson, eds., *Negotiation with the Russians*. Boston: World Peace Foundation, 1955.
Miller, Douglas T., and Nowak, Marion. *The Fifties: The Way We Really Were*. New York: Doubleday, 1977.
Mrozek, Donald J. "The Cult and Ritual of Toughness in Cold War America." In Ray B. Browne, ed., *Rituals and Ceremonies in Popular Culture*. Bowling Green, OH: Bowling Green, University Press, 1980.
Musalo, Karen, Moore, Jennifer, and Boswell, Richard. *Refugee Law and Policy*. Durham, NC: Carolina Academic Press, 1997.
Nadel, Alan. *Containment Culture: American Narratives, Postmodernism, and the Atomic Age*. Durham, NC: Duke University Press, 1995.
Naimark, Norman M. *The Russians in Germany: A History of the Soviet Zone of Occupation, 1945–1949*. Cambridge, MA: Belknap Press of Harvard University Press, 1995.
Neier, Aryeh. *War Crimes: Brutality, Genocide, Terror and the Struggle for Justice*. New York: Times Books, 1998.
Nelson, Anna. "The 'Top of Policy Hill': President Eisenhower and the National Security Council." *Diplomatic History*, 7 (1983), 307–26.
Nicolson, Harold. *Peacemaking 1919*. Boston: Houghton Mifflin, 1933.
Palmer, Alan. *Alexander I: Tsar of War and Peace*. London: Weidenfield & Nicholson, 1974.
Paret, Peter, ed. *Makers of Modern Strategy*. Princeton, NJ: Princeton University Press, 1986.
Parker, Geoffrey. *The Military Revolution: Military Innovation and the Rise of the West, 1500–1800*. Cambridge: Cambridge University Press, 1988.
Parmet, Herbert. *George Bush; The Life of a Lone Star Yankee*. New York: Scribner, 1997.
Paterson, Thomas G. *On Every Front: The Making and Unmaking of the Cold War*. New York: W.W. Norton, 1992.

———. *Soviet-American Confrontation: Postwar Reconstruction and the Origins of the Cold War*. Baltimore, MD: Johns Hopkins University Press, 1983.
Paterson, Thomas G., and Adler, Les K. " 'Red Fascism': The Merger of Nazi Germany and Soviet Russia in the American Image of Totalitarianism, 1930's–1950's." *American Historical Review*, 75 (April 1970), 1046–64.
Patton, Cindy. *Sex and Germs: The Politics of AIDS*. Boston: South End Press, 1985.
Peck, Julianne. "The UN and the Laws of War: How Can the World's Peacekeepers Be Held Accountable?" *Syracuse Journal of International Law and Commerce*, 21 (1995), 283.
Pessen, Edward. *Losing Our Souls: The American Experience in the Cold War*. Chicago: Ivan R. Dee, 1993.
Pimlott, John, ed. *British Military Operations 1945–1985*. London: Military Press, 1986.
Plant, Richard. *The Pink Triangle: The Nazi War against Homosexuals*. New York: Henry Holt, 1988.
Pollard, Robert. *Economic Security and the Origins of the Cold War, 1945–1950*. New York: Columbia University Press, 1985.
Powell, Colin. *My American Journey*. New York: Random House, 1995.
Prados, John. *Keepers of the Keys: A History of the National Security Council from Truman to Bush*. New York: Morrow, 1991.
———. *The Soviet Estimate: U.S. Intelligence Analysis and Russian Military Strength*. New York: Dial Press, 1982.
Pritchard, John R., ed. *The Tokyo War Crimes Trials*. New York: Garland, 1981.
Pryor, F.L. *The Communist Foreign Trade System*. Cambridge: MIT Press, 1963.
Radner, Hilary. *Shopping Around: Feminine Culture and the Pursuit of Pleasure*. New York: Routledge, 1995.
Rice, Condoleezza. "Defense Burden-Sharing." In David Holloway and Jane M.O. Sharp, eds., *The Warsaw Pact: Alliance in Transition?* Ithaca, NY: Cornell University Press, 1984.
Rogers, A.P.V. *Law on the Battlefield*. Manchester: Manchester University Press, 1996.
Ross, Andrew. *No Respect: Intellectuals and Popular Culture*. New York: Routledge, 1989.
Rothschild, Joseph. *Return to Diversity: A Political History of East Central Europe since World War II*. New York: Oxford University Press, 1993.
Ruhm von Oppen, Beate, ed. *Documents on Germany under Occupation, 1945–54*. London: Oxford University Press, 1955.
Russell, Edmund P. " 'Speaking of Annihilation': Mobilizing for War against Human and Insect Enemies, 1914–1945." *Journal of American History*, 82 (March 1996), 1505–29.
Savage, William W., Jr. *Comic Books and America, 1945–1954*. Norman: University of Oklahoma Press, 1990.
Sayre, Nora. *Running Time: Films of the Cold War*. New York: Dial Press, 1979.
Sharp, Mitchell. *Which Reminds Me . . . A Memoir*. Toronto: University of Toronto Press, 1994.
Shaw, Arnold. *The Rock Revolution*. New York: Paperback Library, 1971.
Sherry, Michael S. *In the Shadow of War: The United States since the 1930s*. New Haven, CT: Yale University Press, 1995.

Shils, Edward. *The Torment of Secrecy: The Background and Consequences of American Security Policies*. Rev. ed. Chicago: Ivan R. Dee, 1996.

Sidorowicz, Andre. "The British Government, the Hague Peace Conference, and the Armaments Question." In B.J.C. McKercher, ed., *Arms Limitation and Disarmament: Restraints on War, 1899–1939*. Westport, CT: Praeger, 1992.

Skolnick, Arlene. *Embattled Paradise: The American Family in an Age of Uncertainty*. New York: Basic Books, 1991.

Slusser, Robert M., ed. *Soviet Economic Policy*. New York: Research Program on the U.S.S.R., 1953.

Slusser, Robert M., and Triska, Jan F., eds. *A Calendar of Soviet Treaties 1917–1957*. Stanford, CA: Stanford University Press, 1959.

Smith, Bradley F. *Reaching Judgment at Nuremberg*. New York: Basic Books, 1977.

Smith, Geoffrey S. "Beware, the Historian! Hiroshima, the *Enola Gay*, and the Dangers of History." *Diplomatic History*, 22 (Winter 1998), 121–30.

———. "National Security and Personal Isolation: Sex, Gender, and Disease in the Cold-War United States." *International History Review*, 14 (May 1992), 307–37.

Sokolov, V.M. *Soviet Use of German Science and Technology, 1945–1946*. New York: Research Program on the U.S.S.R., 1955.

Sontag, Susan. *AIDS and Its Metaphors*. New York: Farrar, Straus and Giroux, 1989.

———. *Illness as Metaphor*. New York: Farrar, Straus and Giroux, 1978.

Spigel, Lynn. *Make Room for TV: Television and the Family Ideal in Postwar America*. Chicago: University of Chicago Press, 1992.

Staar, Richard F. *Poland 1944–1962: The Sovietization of a Captive People*. New Orleans: Louisiana State University Press, 1962.

Stacey, C.P. "The Myth of the Unguarded Frontier, 1815–1871." *American Historical Review*, 56 (1950), 1–18.

Stairs, Denise. "Canada and the New World Order." In Michael J. Tucker, Raymond B. Blake, and P.E. Bryden, eds., *Canada and the New World Order: Facing the New Millennium*. Toronto: Irwin, 2000.

Steiner, Henry J., and Alston, Philip. *International Human Rights in Context: Law, Politics, Morals*. Oxford: Clarendon Press, 1996.

Stevens, John N. *Czechoslovakia at the Crossroads*. New York: Columbia University Press, 1985.

Stouffer, Samuel A. *Communism, Conformity, and Civil Liberties: A Cross-section of the Nation Speaks Its Mind*. Garden City, NY: Doubleday, 1955.

Swain, Geoffrey, and Swain, Nigel. *Eastern Europe since 1945*. New York: St. Martin's Press, 1993.

Swinarski, Y., Sandoz, C., and Zimmerman, B., eds. *Commentary on the Additional Protocols of 8 June 1977 to the Geneva Conventions of 12 August 1949*. Geneva: International Committee of the Red Cross, 1987.

Taylor, Ella. *Prime-Time Families: Television Culture in Postwar America*. Berkeley: University of California Press, 1989.

Towle, Philip. *Enforced Disarmament from Napoleon to the Gulf War*. Oxford: Clarendon Press, 1997.

Selected Bibliography

U.S. Army Training and Doctrine Command (TRADOC). *Force XXI Operations: A Concept for the Evolution of Full-Dimensional Operations for the Strategic Army of the Early Twenty-first Century*. Washington, DC: Department of the Army, 1994.

Van De Mark, Brian. *Into the Quagmire: Lyndon Johnson and the Escalation of the Vietnam War*. New York: Oxford University Press, 1991.

Watt, D. Cameron. "British Intervention in East Africa: An Essay in Strategic Mobility." *Revue Militaire Générale*, 5 (May 1966), 606–618.

———. *How War Came: The Immediate Origins of the Second World War, 1938–1939*. New York: Pantheon Books, 1989.

———. "1939 Revisited. On Theories of the Origins of Wars." *International Affairs*, 65.4 (Autumn 1989), 685–92.

Weart, Spencer. *Nuclear Fear: A History of Images*. Cambridge: Harvard University Press, 1988.

Webster, C.K. *The Foreign Policy of Castlereagh*. Vol. 2: *1815–1822: Britain and the European Alliance*. London: G. Bell, 1963.

Weigand, Kate. "The Red Menace, the Feminine Mystique, and the Ohio Un-American Activities Commission: Gender and Anti-Communism in Ohio, 1951–1954." *Journal of Women's History*, 3 (Winter 1992), 70–94.

West, Nigel. *The Secret War for the Falklands*. London: Little, Brown, 1997.

Wheeler-Bennet, John W. *The Nemesis of Power: The German Army in Politics, 1918–1945*. London: St. Martin's Press, 1964.

White, Hayden. *Tropics of Discourse: Essays in Cultural Criticism*. Baltimore, MD: Johns Hopkins University Press, 1978.

Whitfield, Stephen J. *The Culture of the Cold War*. Baltimore, MD: Johns Hopkins University Press, 1991.

Winston, Victor. "The Soviet Satellites—Economic Liability?" *Problems of Communism*, 7 (January–February 1958), 14–20.

Wirick, Gregory, and Miller, Robert, eds. *Canada and Missions for Peace: Lessons from Nicaragua, Cambodia and Somalia*. Ottawa: International Development Research Centre, 1998.

Wittner, Lawrence S. *One World or None: A History of the World Nuclear Disarmament Movement through 1953*. Stanford, CA: Stanford University Press, 1993.

Woods, Randall B., and Jones, Howard. *Dawning of the Cold War: The United States' Quest for Order*. Athens: University of Georgia Press, 1991.

Yates, Rachel S.M. "Images of Dissent, Persistence of an Ideal: Gender in Television Sitcoms in the 1950s." Master's thesis. Queen's University, 1997.

Zaloga, Steven J. *Target America: The Soviet Union and the Strategic Arms Race, 1945–1964*. Novato, CA: Presidio, 1993.

Zeiler, Thomas W. *Free Trade Free World: The Advent of GATT*. Chapel Hill: University of North Carolina Press, 1999.

Zimmern, Alfred. *The League of Nations and the Rule of Law, 1918–1935*. 2nd ed. London: Macmillan, 1939.

Zubok, Vladislav, and Pleshakov, Constantine. *Inside the Kemlin's Cold War*. Cambridge: Harvard University Press, 1996.

Zwass, Adam. *The Council for Mutual Economic Assistance*. Armonk, NY: Sharpe, 1989.
Zyzniewski, Stanley J. "The Soviet Economic Impact on Poland." *American Slavic and East European Review*, 18.2 (April 1959), 206–9.

Index

Abyssinian crisis (1935–1936), 9, 10, 23, 46
Acheson, Dean, 81, 90, 131–32, 141–42
Aden, 32, 40
air power, 26, 40–41
aircraft carriers, 199
Afghanistan War (1979–1990), 7, 28, 34, 39
Africa, 3, 20, 34, 39; East Africa, 32; sub-Saharan Africa, 35
Al Qaeda, 8
Albania, 179
Alexander, Field Marshal Lord, 22
Alexander I (Czar), 46, 60
Algeria, 32, 35
Allende, Salvador, 184
Amin, Idi, 39
Amnesty International, 181
Angell, Norman, 52
Angle, Brigadier H.H., 146
Anglo-American naval rivalry (1918–1930), 53–54
Anglo-French Entente (1904), 24

Anglo-German Naval Agreement (1935), 51
Anglo-German naval arms race (1904–1914), 47, 49
Anglo-Russian convention (1907), 24
Arab-Israeli wars: 1956, 31; 1967, 9, 31; 1973, 31
Arbour, Louise, 179
Argentina, 21, 34
arms control, 46–47, 49, 54–55, 56–57, 58, 59, 61; geographic, 60. *See also* disarmament
arms limitation, 52–53
arms production and marketing, 30–31, 33–34; increasing cost of arms, 36
Asprey, Robert, 207. *See also* war in the twentieth century, postmodern wars
asymmetry, as an approach to war, 203, 205–6
atomic weapons, 5, 7, 67, 100, 104, 198; "Atoms for Peace" program and, 101

Attlee, Clement (Prime Minister), 22, 75
Australia, 186
Austria (post-1918), 20, 51, 160
Austria-Hungary (1867–1918), 24, 46
Austrian Empire (1805–1867), 45–46

Baker, James, 139, 140
Baldwin, Stanley, 55
Balkan Wars (1912–1913), 23
Balkans, 10, 179
Ball, George, 136, 138, 139
Bay of Pigs invasion (1961), 39
Belgium, 24; decolonization and, 34, 149
Benes, Edward, 73
Bentham, Jeremy, 47
Berend, Ivan, 78
Beria, Laventri, 70
Bernhardi, General Friedrich von, 2–3, 8, 10
Bierut, Bolesleaw, 71
Bismarck, Prince Otto von, 4, 41
Black Sea, 60
Bloch, I. S., 52
Bohlen, Charles, 102
Borneo "confrontation," 36
Bosnian crisis (1990s), 9, 156, 157, 159, 186, 187
Bouchard, Lucien, 159
Boutros-Ghali, Boutros, 156, 157–58
Bretton Woods Conference (1944), 74–75; its financial systems and, 66, 74
Brezhnev, Leonid, 60, 182
British Army, 31–32, 38
British Empire, 20, 23, 24
British Commonwealth, 24, 146, 151, 155
British Dominions. *See* British Commonwealth
brushfire wars. *See* war in the twentieth century, postmodern wars
Brussels Treaty (1948), 27
Brzezinski, Zbigniew, 72, 82
Bulgaria, 52, 76–77
Bull, Hedley, 53–54
Bullitt, William, 102
Bundy, McGeorge, 135–36, 138

Burma, 174
Burns, General E.L.M., 148
Bush, George W., Sr., 130, 139–41, 142
Byers, Rod, 152, 154

Campaign for Nuclear Disarmament (CND), 49
Cambodia, 59, 147, 179
Canada, 9, 27, 75, 150–51, 155–56, 186; (1994), 158–59; International Control Commissions and, 147, 153; North Atlantic Triangle and, 66, 74–76, 80, 85–87, 88–89, 151–52, 153; peacekeeping and, 145, 146–49, 149–50, 150–51, 153–54, 159–60, 161, 185; peacekeeping criticisms and, 152, 158; Quebec and, 151, 157; UN peacekeeping forces receiving the Nobel Peace Prize and (1988), 154, 159; White Paper on Defence and (1971), 152–53
Caribbean, 30
Carnegie Endowment for International Peace, 48
Casals, Pablo, 111
Castlereagh, Lord, 46, 60
casualties, acceptability of, 209
Central America, 30, 34
Central Intelligence Agency (CIA), 39, 100, 130, 140
Chaco War (1932–1935), 23
Chamberlain, Neville, 4, 56
chemical and biological warfare, 38–39, 54–55, 60; Biological Weapons Convention and (1972), 57; Geneva Protocol and (1925), 54–55, 57
Cheney, Richard, 139–140, 141
Chile, 184
China, 10, 23, 27, 29, 30, 37, 104; Communist China, 139; Nationalist China, 133
Chrétien, Jean, 145, 159–60, 161
Churchill, Winston, 6, 22, 36, 47, 54, 57, 73, 89, 90, 101
civil conflicts. *See* war in the twentieth century, postmodern wars
clandestine warfare. *See* war in the

twentieth century, postmodern wars
Clark, Joe, 155
Clausewitz, Carl von, 2, 197; theories of war, 199–200, 205, 206–7, 208. *See also* War in the 20th Century, Wars of Annihilation, Wars of Attrition
Clay, General Lucius, 74
Clayton, William, 90
Clifford, Clark, 139
Cobden, Richard, 48
CoCom. *See* Coordinating Committee (CoCom)
Cold War, 2, 3, 6–7, 10–11, 27–28, 57–60, 203, 204, 206; alliances and, 66; containment and, 80–81, 100–101; cultural approaches to study of, 98, 104–5
"collective security," 9
COMECON. *See* Council for Mutual Economic Assistance (COMECON)
Cominform. *See* Communist Information Bureau
Committee of Imperial Defence, British, 22
Communist Information Bureau, 76
Communist Party USA (CPUSA), 105–6
Congo, 34, 149–50, 156
conscription, 210–13; abandonment of, 37–38; in Third Reich, 52
Convention on the Prevention and Punishment of the Crime of Genocide (1948), 167
conventional war, 201–3, 207. *See also* World War I (1914–1918); World War II (1939–1945)
Coordinating Committee (CoCom), 67, 74, 81
Coplon, Judith, 107, 108
Corber, Robert, 104
Costa Rica, 58
Council for Mutual Economic Assistance (COMECON), 67, 79–80, 81–82, 90
Cuba, 39
Cutler, Robert, 134, 135

Cvetic, Matt, 106–7
Cyprus, 32, 150–51, 154, 155
Czechoslovakia, 7, 66, 68, 70, 73, 75, 77–78, 81, 82–84, 88

Daladier, Edouard, 4
Dallaire, General Romeo, 155
Dayton Accords (1995), 181–82
decolonization, wars of. *See* War in the 20th Century, postmodern wars
Delbrück, Hans, 200
demilitarized zones, 59
DeMille, Cecil B., 108
Denmark, 160
Derrida, Jacques, 97–98
Diefenbaker, John, 149
Dien Bien Phu, Battle of (1954), 31, 134–35
Dies, Martin, 105
disarmament, 45, 49–52, 57, 58–59, 61; peace movements and, 8–9, 10, 46, 48–49, 52, 56–57; Preparatory Commission, 55, 56; qualitative, 56; roots of, 45–47, 52; utopianism and, 47–49; verification, 50; voluntary, 58; World Disarmament Conference and (1932–1934), 8, 55. *See also* arms control
Djilas, Milovan, 69
Dominican Republic, 159
Douet, Giulio, 26
Dulles, John Foster, 133, 135

Eagleburger, Lawrence, 141
Economic Community of West African States, 185
Egypt, 31, 33, 148, 153
Eisenhower, Dwight, 130, 133–34, 139, 141–142
El Salvador, 159, 179
electronics, impact on warfare, 198
Ethiopia. *See* Abyssinian crisis (1935–1936)
"ethnic cleansing." *See* war in the twentieth century, postmodern wars
Ethniki Organosis Kipriakoú Agónos (EOKA), 8

European Coal and Steel Community (1952), 81
European Recovery Program (1948), 67, 74, 76–77, 80–81, 89, 90, 99

Falklands War (1982), 21, 29, 34, 36, 203, 205
Federal Bureau of Investigation (FBI), 35, 100, 105, 107, 109
Finland, 151
First World War. *See* World War I (1914–1918)
Force XXI, 213
Foucault, Michel, 97–98
France, 9, 26, 27, 30, 35, 45–46, 50, 53, 60, 76; conscription and, 37; decolonization and, 32; Indo-China War and (1946–1954), 31, 134–35; Suez crisis and (1956), 24, 148
Franco-Prussian War (1870–1871), complexity of war plans, 211
Freed, Alan, 113
Freidan, Betty, 109
French Revolution, 200, 210

G-7 Powers, 155
Gardner, Richard, 80
Gates, Robert, 140
General Agreement on Trades and Tariffs (GATT), 67, 74, 80
Geneva Conference (1949), 167, 178–79, 183, 184, 186, Convention IV Relative to the Protection of Civilian Persons in Time of War and, 167, 171–73, 178–79, 182, 186, 187; (1954), 135, 147, 186, 187, International Control Commissions and, 147
Geneva Convention, on treatment of prisoners of war (1929), 21
Geneva Disarmament Conference (1932–1934). *See* Disarmament, World Disarmament Conference
Geneva Protocol, prohibiting poison gas and biological weapons (1925), 54–55, 57
Geneva Protocols, on treatment of prisoners, civilian, identifiable armed forces, objects of survival, medical care, and relief operations (1977), 169–70, 178–79, 182, 183, 186; (1988), 182, 186
genocide, 184
Germany, 57; conscription and, 52; East Germany (1945–1991), 40, 65, 66, 68–69, 70, 78, 88, 90; Holocaust and, 174–75; Third Reich (1933–1945), 4, 5, 8, 10, 20, 24–25, 26, 51–52, 59; Weimar (1918–1933), 49–50, 51; West Germany (1945–1991), 28, 37, 39, 76; Wilhelmine (1871–1918), 2–3, 4, 8, 10, 28–29, 47; united Germany (since 1991), 49
Giap, General, 31
Goldstone, Richard, 182
Gorbachev, Mikhail, 58
Great Britain, 4, 5–6, 9, 28–29, 30, 36, 46, 47–48, 49, 50, 53–54, 56, 60, 75–76, 80–81, 168, 186; conscription and, 37–38; decolonization and, 32–33, 35–36; defence administration and, 40; defence planning and, 22, 26, 37, 40, 46–47; Falklands War and (1982), 21, 34, 36; North Atlantic Triangle and, 66, 74–76, 80–81, 89–90; Sandys reforms and (1958), 40; Suez crisis and (1956), 24, 148
Greece, 150–51, 155
Green Peace, 2
Greenstein, Fred, 133
Gregor, Alexander, 80
Grey, Sir Edward, 49
Grotius, 176
Guatemala, 159
Gubitchev, Valentin, 107
guerrilla warfare. *See* war in the twentieth century, postmodern wars
Gulf War (1990–1991), 3, 9–10, 24, 57, 60, 139–41, 155, 158, 205

Hague conferences (1899–1907), 20, 46–47
Haiti, 59, 159, 179
Hammarskjöld, Dag, 149
Hayes, Helen, 108

Head, Ivan, 152
Healy, Denis, 36
Helsinki Agreements of 1975, 20
Hiss, Alger, 104, 108
Hitler, Adolf, 4, 5, 8, 10, 20, 24–25, 51, 56, 174
Ho Chi Minh, 138
Holland, 23, 160; decolonization and, 32, 33
Honduras, 159
Hoover, J. Edgar, 35, 98, 105, 107, 110
House Committee on Un-American Activities (HUAC), 105, 108, 109; baby Houses on Un-American Activities, 105–6
Human Intelligence (HUMINT), 32
human rights, 167–68, 168–69, 171–73, 176–78, 178–82, 185–87; geopolitical change and, 174; globalization and, 173–74; international criminal law and; 174–75; international legitimacy and, 174
Human Rights Watch, 181
Humphrey, George, 134–35
Hungary, 7, 51, 65, 66, 68, 71, 77–78, 83, 84, 90
Hussein, Saddam, 8, 10, 25, 39, 41, 140
Hyde Park Agreement (1941), 75

Iceland, 58
Imperial Japanese Navy, 29, 54
India, colonial period (pre-1947), 20, 23; independence period (post-1947), 28, 31, 146
Indian Ocean, demilitarization of (1974), 60
Indo-China War (1946–1954). See Southeast Asia
Indonesia, 32, 33
Inter-Allied Control Commissions, 50
intergovernmental organizations (IGOs), 173, 185–86
internal combustion engine, impact on warfare, 198
International Bank for Reconstruction and Development, 74
International Court of Justice, 186

International Covenant on Civil and Political Rights, 181
International Criminal Tribunal for the Former Yugoslavia (ICTFY), 182–83, 185
International Military Control Commission (IMCC), 51
International Monetary Fund, 74
International War Crimes Tribunal, 8, 24, 25, 169, 181; "Nuremberg Principle" and, 169
interstate conflict, 205. See also conventional war
intrastate conflict, 205. See also war in the twentieth century, postmodern wars; terrorism
Iran, 9, 31, 33–34, 39, 174
Iraq, 9–10, 21, 23, 24, 25, 33–34, 57, 59, 60, 139–41, 174
Iraq-Iran War (1980–1988), 33–34
Ireland, 151; Irish Civil War (1916–1921), 23; Northern Ireland, 32
Irish Republican Army, 8
Israel, 148, 153
Italy, 3, 10, 23, 51, 53, 76

Jagger, Dean, 108
Japan, 3, 5–6, 10, 20, 25, 26, 28, 53, 57, 152
Japanese Defence Force, 57
Johnson, Louis B., 132
Johnson, Lyndon Baines, 130, 135–36, 137–39, 142
Jomini, Antoine Henri, 2

Kant, Immanuel, 47
Karadzic, Radovan, 182
Kashmir, 145, 146
Kaufman, Irving, 107–8
Kellogg-Briand Pact (1928), 23–24, 49
Kennan, George, 90, 97, 98, 108, 114, 131; "Long Telegram" and, 101–4
Kennedy, John Fitzgerald, 135, 136, 139
Kenya, 32, 159
Keynes, Lord, 74–75
Khrushchev, Nikita, 25
King, William Lyon, 90, 146–47

Kissinger, Henry, 60
Korean peninsula, 28, 56; North Korea, 29, 61
Korean War (1950–1953), 3, 6, 27–28, 31, 67, 82, 85, 104, 130–31, 132–33, 141, 146, 147, 202, 205
Kosovo, 35, 41, 179, 182, 184, 187
Kutler, Stanley, 106
Kuwait, 9–10, 21, 24, 32, 139–41

land mines, 56
Laos, 147
Lattimore, Owen, 108
Lauent, Saint Louis, 146
Lawyers Committee for Human Rights, 181
League of Nations, 2, 8, 9, 10, 20, 23–24, 48, 50, 145; disarmament and, 50–51, 53, 54–55, 57; Permanent Advisory Committee for Military, Naval, and Air Questions, 50–51, 57
Lebanon, 34, 35
levée en mass, 210
Levitt, William J., 105
Libya, 58, 174
Lichtenstein, 58
Link, Arthur, 48
Lippmann, Walter, 54
Locarno pact (1925), 51
London Naval Treaty, (1930), 53, 54; (1936), 53, 60
Louis XVI (King), 4
low-intensity conflict. *See* war in the twentieth century, postmodern wars
Luftwaffe, 29, 51–52
Lundestad, Geir, 73, 85–87

MacArthur, General Douglas, 57, 133
Macedonia, 179
Mackinder, Sir Halford, 29
Madagasacar, 32
Malaya, 32, 33
Malenkov, Georgi, 68, 70–71, 90
Mansfield, Mike, 137, 139
Maoism, 203
Marshall, General George, 90, 131

Marshall Plan. *See* European Recovery Program
Martin, Paul. Sr., 151
Marxism-Leninism, 204
"mass-reserve army," 211–12
Mastny, Vojtech, 71–72, 76
Maurer, John, 61
McCarey, Leo, 108
McCarthy, Joseph, 104, 105
McDougall, Barbara, 155, 156, 157
McGrath, Howard, 98
McKenzie, General Lewis, 156
McNamara, Robert, 135–36, 137–38, 142
Middle East, 3, 9–10, 28, 37
Middlemiss, Dan, 158
Mikolajcyk, Stanislas, 72
Military Revolution, 219 n.9, 215
Milosevic, Slobodan, 41, 145, 183, 184
Minc, Hilary, 82
Mladic, Ratko, 182
mobilization: during First and Second World War, 201, 211–12; "mass-reserve army" and, 211–12; under French Revolution and Napoleon, 200, 210–11; war plans and, 212
Montreaux Convention (1936), 60
Morel, E.D., 52
Morgenthau Plan (1944), 74
Morocco, 23, 32
Mozambique, 59, 159
Mulroney, Brian, 155, 156
Munich conference (1938), 129
Mussolini, Benito, 4, 5, 10

Nadel, Alan, 106
Napoleon I (Emperor), 3, 45–46
Napoleon III (Emperor), 46
Napoleonic Wars (1798–1815), 32
Nasser, Abdel, 33, 148, 151
Neier, Aryeh, 174
neocolonialist wars. *See* war in the twentieth century, postmodern wars
Netherlands. *See* Holland
Nicaragua, 6
Nicholas II (Czar), 46
Nicholson, Harold, 49

Nixon, Richard, 60, 135, 182
nongovernmental organizations (NGOs), 173, 186
North Atlantic Treaty Organization (NATO), 6, 9, 27–28, 41, 58, 85–86, 99, 145, 147, 150–51, 155, 157, 159, 179, 184, 186, 187, 204, 205–6; Implementation Force and, 159, 182; NATO Stabilization Force and, 182
North Vietnam, 31, 136–37, 139
Norway, 160
NSC-68. *See* United States, National Security Council
nuclear weapons, 7, 21, 22, 38, 39, 58, 61, 100, 198, 200, 201–3; intercontinental ballistic missiles and, 26–27, 29, 38, 69; intermediate ranger ballistic missiles, 70; Nuclear Non-Proliferation Treaty (1968), 57
Nuremburg international tribunals. *See* International War Crimes Tribunal
Nyon Agreement of 1937, 60

Oman, 32, 39
Opération des Nations Unies au Congo (ONUC), 149–50, 151
Operations Other Than War (OOTW), 213
Organization of American States, 204
Organization of European Economic Cooperation (1948), 81
Ottoman Empire. *See* Turkey
Ouellet, André, 160

Pakistan, 146
Palestine, 32
Palmerston, Lord, 46
peacekeeping, 9, 148–49, 149–50, 150–51, 153–54, 154–55, 160–61, 179–81, 185, 204, 205–6, 209; "second generation", 157–58; "traditional," 157; UN peacekeeping forces receiving the Nobel Peace Prize and (1988), 154, 159; Vanguard Concept and, 160
peacemaking, 204, 209
peace movements. *See* disarmament

Pearson, Lester B., 145, 146–47, 148–49, 150, 154, 161
Peel, Sir Robert, 48
Perez de Cuellar, Javier, 168–69
Persian Gulf, 20, 40
Peter I ("the Great"), 3–4
Philbrick, Herbert, 107
Pickering, Thomas, 140
Pinochet, Augusto, 176, 183, 184–85
Poland, 7, 65, 66, 68, 71–72, 73, 75, 77–78, 82–83, 160
Policy Planning Staff, 131
Polish-Soviet Treaty of Friendship (1945), 72
"popular-conscript" armies, 210–11
Ponsonby, Arthur, 52
Potsdam Agreement (1945), 68–69
Powell, General Colin, 139, 140–41
Presley, Elvis, 113–14
Protocol Relating to the Status of Refugees (1967), 177
Prussia, 45
Puerto Rico, 186

qualitative violence, 207–8
quantitative violence, 207–8
Quayle, Dan, 140
Quebec, 151, 157, 186

Radford, Admiral Arthur, 134
Raeder, Admiral Erich, 29
Ramirez Sanchez, Illich ("Carlos the Jackal"), 40
Reagan Ronald, 58
Red Cross, International Committee of the, 178–79, 183, 186
refugees, 66–67, 68, 71, 74, 75, 167, 170, 171–73, 176–78, 178–82, 185–87; geopolitical change and, 174; globalization and, 173–74; international criminal law and; 174–75; international legitimacy and, 174
Reichsmarine, 29
Revolution in Military Affairs (RMA), 198
restrictions on violence in war, 208–9
Reykjavik Summit (1986), 58
Rhodesia, 35–36

Robertson, Norman, 149, 150
Robinson, Mary, 179
Roosevelt, Franklin Delano, 4, 5, 90, 130
Rosenberg, Ethel, 107–8
Rosenberg, Julius, 107–8
Royal Air Force, 26
Royal Navy, 26, 29
Rush-Bagot agreement (1817), 60
Rusk, Dean, 135–36, 137, 138
Russia, alliances and, 66; conscription, 37; czarist period (pre-1917), 23, 24, 46; defence planning and, 38, 68, 69–70, 89–90; Eastern Europe and, 65, 66–67, 67–73, 76–80, 81–84, 87–88, 89–90; new republic (post-1990), 20, 34, 58; Red Air Force, 69–70; Red Army, 68, 69, 70, 90; Red Navy, 58, 90; Soviet period (1917–1990), 6–7, 20, 21, 23, 25, 26, 27, 30, 31, 33, 34, 36, 39–40, 53, 58, 60, 75, 101–4, 106, 115, 139, 153, 168;
Russo-Japanese War (1904–1905), 23
Rwanda, 9, 159, 174, 175, 179–81, 183–84, 187

Sahara, Western, 159
Salinger, J.D., 106
Saudi Arabia, 23, 33, 140–41; Arabian Gulf, 159
Schlesinger, Arthur M., Jr., 99
Schmitt, Helmut, 37
Schwarzkopf, General H. Norman, 141
Scowcroft, General Brent, 139–41
Second World War. *See* World War II (1939–1945)
Secret Intelligence Service (SIS), 39
Serbia: pre-1914, 24, 35; post-1990, 41
Sharp, Mitchell, 153, 154
Simon, John, 56
Sinatra, Frank, 11
Singapore, 33
Sino-Japanese War (1937–1945), 3, 6
Sino-Soviet split, 7
Somalia, 23, 39, 156–57, 159, 185, 186
South Africa, 35–36
South Vietnam, 31

Southeast Asia, (pre-1945), 29; (post-1945), 3, 6, 28, 31, 34, 40; Indo-China War and (1946–1954), 31, 32, 147
Special Air Service (SAS), 21, 39
Spillane, Mickey, 107
Sri Lanka, 34, 35
Stairs, Denis, 157
Stalin, Josef, 25, 27, 65, 67, 69, 72, 76, 81–82, 102; Stalinization and, 65–66, 84, 102–3
Stanhope, Lord, 55
Star Wars. *See* Strategic Defence Initiative
Stassen, Harold, 134
Steed, Henry Wickham, 46
Stevenson, Adlai, 108
Stoddard, George, 109
Strategic Arms Limitation Talks (SALT), 53, 54
Strategic Defence Initiative, 27, 36
Stresemann, Gustav, 51
Sudan, 34
Suez Canal crisis (1956), 21, 24, 145, 147, 148–49, 157
Sukarno, 33
Sullivan, Ed, 114
Sununu, John, 140
Sweden, 151, 160
Syria, 33

tactical weapons, 41
tanks, 198–99
Taiwan, 132
technology, as factor in changing warfare, 198–99. *See also names of specific technologies*
terrorism, 8, 39–40, 206
third-party intervention, 206–7; use of violence and, 208–9
Thompson, Craig, 110
Tito, Marshal Josip Broz, 174
Tokyo international tribunals. *See* International War Crimes Tribunal
Trenchard, Air Marshal Lord, 26
Trudeau, Pierre, 152, 154
Truman, Harry, 73–74, 98–99, 104, 105, 130–31, 132–33, 141

Index

Tunisia, 32
Turkey, 60, 150–51, 155, 159; Ottoman Empire, 35

Uganda, 39
Ukraine, 58
Union for Democratic Control (UDC), 52
United Arab Republic, 33
United Kingdom. *See* Great Britain
United Nations, 2, 8, 9, 33, 41, 42, 59, 132, 140, 141, 146–47, 149–50, 151, 156, 157, 167–68, 175–76, 183, 185–86, 204; Charter, 168–69, 174; Field Service and, 146; Military Staff Committee and, 145–46; peacekeeping and, 9, 42, 145–46, 147–48, 149–50, 150–51, 156–58, 159–60, 179–81, 185; weapons inspection, 57; UN peacekeeping forces receiving the Nobel Peace Prize and (1988), 154
United Nations Emergency Force (1956), 148, 151; (1973), 153
United Nations Force in Cyprus (UNFICYP), 151
United Nations High Commissioner for Refugees (UNHCR), 167, 170–71, 179, 187; Convention Relating to the Status of Refugees and (1951), 167, 170, 171–73, 177
United Nations Human Rights Field Operation, 179–181
United Nations International Criminal Tribunal for the Former Yugoslavia, 179
United Nations Military Observer Group, 146
United Nations Operation in Somalia, 156
United Nations Operations, Brahimi Panel on (2000), 160–61
United Nations Protection Force in the former Yugoslavia, 156, 158
United Nations Relief and Rehabilitation Administration (UNRRA), 66–67, 68, 71, 74, 75
United Nations Social and Economic Council (UNSOC), 80

United Nations Stand-by Forces High Readiness Brigade (SHIRBRIG), 160
United Nations Truce Supervisory Organization (UNTSO), 146, 147, 148
United States, 7, 9–10, 20, 23–24, 30, 33, 36, 39, 47–48, 50, 51, 52–53, 53–54, 56, 58, 60, 66–67, 168, 186; alliances and, 66, 85–87, 88–89; Civil War (1861–1865), 4, 5–7; Cold War culture and, 98–100, 104–6, 108–10, 111–14; conscription and, 37; containment and, 80–81, 98, 101–4; decolonization and, 33; defence planning and, 26–27, 27–28, 38, 39, 80–81, 129–30; former Yugoslavia and, 159; Joint Chiefs of Staff and, 129; National Security Council, 7, 129–31, 132–33, 133–34, 135–39, 139–41, 142; North Atlantic Triangle and, 66, 74–76, 85–87, 88–89, 151–52, 153; NATO and, 27–28, 51; NSC and, 68, 85, 99, 104, 132; peacekeeping in Somalia and, 156–57; State-War-Navy Coordinating Committee and, 129; Vietnam War and, 135–39, 142, 151; Western Europe and, 65–67, 73–76, 80–81, 85–87
United States Arms Control and Disarmament Agency (1961–1999), 58
Universal Declaration of Human Rights (1948), 167, 168, 171–73
Universal Peace Congress (1843), 47–48
University of California Board of Regents, 105
U.S. Air Force, 26–27, 40–41
U.S. Marines, 30, 156
U.S. Navy, 26–27, 29, 30

VENONA documents, 107–8
Versailles, Treaty of (1919). *See* World War I (1914–1918)
Viet Cong, 136–37
Vietnam War (1946–1975), 2, 3, 6, 7, 28, 31, 34, 36, 135–39, 142, 151, 152–3, 202–3, 204, 212; International Control Commissions and, 147

"volunteer-technical" army, definition and benefits of, 212

Walker, Robert, 108
Wallace, Henry, 99
war in the twentieth century: conduct of, 1–2, 5–6, 10; evolution of, 210–13; human rights and, 167, 169–70, 171–73, 173–75; Islamic concepts and, 20–21; laws of and legal definition of war, 6, 19–21, 23–24, 41–42, 167–68, 174–75, 176–78, 178–82; little wars, 10, 23, 41; modern wars, 30–31, 41–42; nature of, 3, 4, 5–6, 10–11, 19, 23–24, 28–29, 41–42; planning, 5–6, 7, 10–11, 21–22, 25–27, 29–30, 41–42; postmodern wars, 30, 31–41, 203–4, 205–6, 208 n.5, 215; principles and theory of, 1–2, 4, 10, 21–22; propaganda and, 3, 5–6, 7–8; public opinion and, 2, 4, 5–6, 7–8, 39, 47–49, 56–57, 66; strategy and doctrine and, 1–2, 4, 5–6, 7, 10–11, 25–27, 29, 30, 40–41; technology and, 2, 5–6, 10, 21–22, 26, 36, 38–39; total war, 2–3, 5–6, 7–8, 10, 21–22, 30, 41; Wars of Annihilation, 197, 200, 201, 205, 206, 208; Wars of Attrition, 200, 205, 206, 208; Wars of Legitimacy, 197–98, 205–9 n.6, 215 n.7. *See also names of specific wars*
Warsaw Pact, 6
Washington Conference (1921–1922), 53–54
Washington Naval Treaty (1922), 53, 54
Webster, William, 140

White, Harry Dexter, 74
William I (German Kaiser, 1887–1918), 23
Wilson, Woodrow, 52–53
Winsor, Hugh, 153–54
Wohlstetter, Albert, 58
Women's International League for Peace and Freedom, 2
Woodward, Sir Llewellyn, 24–25
World Bank. *See* International Bank for Reconstruction and Development
World Court, 8
World Economic Conference (1933), 55
World Peace Foundation, 48
World War I (1914–1918), 2, 3, 4, 10, 19–20, 22, 23, 28–29, 32, 46–47, 48, 49, 52, 198, 199, 201–2, 212; origins, 24–25; Treaty of Versailles and (1919), 20, 23, 49–50, 52, 59
World War II (1939–1945), 3, 5–6, 10, 20, 22, 23, 32, 36, 40, 129, 198, 199, 201, 202, 212; origins, 24–25
Wylie, Philip, 103, 108

Yemen, 33
Yom Kippur War, 153
Yugoslavia, 9, 174; former Yugoslavia, 34, 35, 39, 59, 156, 157, 159, 174, 175–76, 179–81, 182–83

Zaire, 159
Zeiler, Thomas, 89
Zhdanov, Andrei, 69–70
Zhou En-lai, 182
Zimmern, Alfred, 55

About the Contributors

LAWRENCE R. ARONSEN is a Professor of History at the University of Alberta, where he specializes in twentieth century American and Cold War history. Recent publications include *American National Security and Economic Relations with Canada, 1945–1954* (Praeger, 1996).

DONNA E. ARZT, formerly an Assistant Attorney General for the Commonwealth of Massachusetts, is a Professor of Law at the Syracuse University College of Law, where she specializes in human rights law, refugee law, and international criminal law. She is currently writing a book on the Lockerbie bombing and the impact on its victims for Syracuse University Press.

ERIK GOLDSTEIN is chairman of the Department of International Relations at Boston University. The founding editor of the journal *Diplomacy & Statecraft*, his research interests include diplomacy, the formulation of national diplomatic strategies, conflict origins and resolution, and negotiation. Recent titles include *The First World War Peace Settlements: From Versailles to Locarno, 1919–25* (2002), and the multi-edited volume, *Guide to International Relations and Diplomacy* (2003).

MICHAEL A. HENNESSY is head of the History department and an Associate Professor of History and War Studies at the Royal Military College of Canada, where he specializes in military and naval history, the history of technology, low intensity conflict, and intelligence. His most recent book is *Strategy in Vietnam: The Marines and Revolutionary War in I Corps, South Vietnam, 1965–1973* (Praeger, 1997).

GARY R. HESS is a Distinguished Research Professor at Bowling Green State University. His research and teaching focus on U.S. foreign and national security policy. A past President of the Society for Historians of American Foreign Relations, he is also a past recipient of several NEH and Fulbright Awards. His most recent book is *Presidential Decisions for War: Korea, Vietnam, and the Persian Gulf* (2001).

NORMAN HILLMER, Professor of Canadian History at Carleton University, is the former Senior Historian of the Canadian Defence Department. He has a distinguished record of publication on Canadian, Canadian military, and Canadian diplomatic history. Recent contributions include *Empire to Umpire: Canada and the World to the 1990s* (1994), and with M.A. Molot, *Canada Among Nations 2002: A Fading Power* (2003).

JOHN A. LYNN, Professor of History at the University of Illinois at Urbana-Champaign, specializes in the study of war, society, and culture. Most of his work has centered on French military history, 1610–1815, but his most recent book is a broad survey of war, *The Art of Battle: A History of Combat and Culture* (2003).

B.J.C. MCKERCHER, a fellow of the Royal History Society, is the head of the War Studies program at the Royal Military College of Canada, where he is also a Professor of History, specializing in civil military relations, arms control, and British diplomatic history. His recent monographs include *Transition of Power: Britain's Loss of Global Preeminence to the United States, 1930–1945* (1998), and with Michael L. Dockrill, eds., *Diplomacy and World Power: Studies in British Foreign Policy, 1890–1950* (2002).

GEOFFREY S. SMITH, past President of the Peace History Society, is a Professor of History at Queen's University. Interested in social, cultural, and diplomatic history of the United States in the twentieth century, his most recent work addresses employment of gender and disease metaphors as mobilizing concepts during the Cold War.

DONALD CAMERON WATT, after a distinguished career as a diplomatic historian based at the London School of Economics, is now a Professor Emeritus.

U
42
.W379
2003